ACCOUNTING
AN INTERNATIONAL PERSPECTIVE

The Irwin Series in Undergraduate Accounting

ACCOUNTING
AN INTERNATIONAL PERSPECTIVE

Fourth Edition

Gerhard G. Mueller
University of Washington

Helen Gernon
University of Oregon

Gary K. Meek
Oklahoma State University

IRWIN

Chicago • Bogotá • Boston • Buenos Aires • Caracas
London • Madrid • Mexico City • Sydney • Toronto

Irwin Book Team

Publisher: *Michael W. Junior*
Associate editor: *George Werthman*
Marketing manager: *Heather L. Woods*
Project supervisor: *Mary Conzachi*
Production supervisor: *Pat Frederickson*
Cover designer: *Michael Kerner*
Prepress buyer: *Charlene R. Perez*
Compositor: *Weimer Graphics, Inc., Division of Shepard Poorman Communications Corp.*
Typeface: *10/12 Times Roman*
Printer: *Times Mirror Higher Education Group, Inc., Print Group*

Times Mirror
Higher Education Group

Library of Congress Cataloging-in-Publication Data

Mueller, Gerhard G.
  Accounting : an international perspective / Gerhard Mueller, Helen Gernon, Gary Meek. — 4th ed.
    p.   cm.
  Includes index.
  ISBN 0-256-17082-7
  1. International business enterprises—Accounting.   2. Comparative accounting.   3. Accounting—Standards.   I. Gernon, Helen Morsicato, 1946-   . II. Meek, Gary. III. Title.
  HF5686.I56M835   1997
  657'.96—dc20   96–17360

Printed in the United States of America
1 2 3 4 5 6 7 8 9 0 WCB 3 2 1 0 9 8 7 6

To Our Families

We approach the 21st Century knowing that global events will increasingly affect our lives. New nations and new economic powers are emerging. As a result, old alliances are changing, and there are shifts in the well-worn patterns of trade and international commerce. The dismantling of the former Soviet Union, the fast-growing economies of Southeast Asia, the integration of the European Union, and the implementation of the North American Free Trade Agreement all illustrate the dramatic changes that are under way. Advances in computer and communications technology are also having their impact. For example, currency markets are open continuously, 24 hours a day, as they move around the world from New York to Tokyo to London to New York. Foreign exchange trading now stands at $1.3 trillion per day. Information can travel long distances quickly, and it is increasingly easier and cheaper to get. Indeed, new technology makes the internationalization of product and finance markets possible. Corporations, too, are making themselves over to adapt to the global economy. Flexibility is the key as more and more of them reorganize as networks and stress interdependent alliances and strategic partnership with other companies, rather than self-sufficiency in all areas. Information, including accounting information, is a critical resource in these makeovers, supporting the linkages both internally and with the outside world.

This book is dedicated to the proposition that the international dimension of accounting is an integral part of the subject. Students who do not learn about it have not been adequately prepared for the world they will soon enter. Thus, the authors believe that the study of accounting, including the first-year course in accounting, is incomplete without considering its international aspects. *Accounting: An International Perspective* is designed for the introductory accounting course. It supplements existing introductory accounting textbooks. The book provides a general, nontechnical overview of the subject matter of international accounting.

This book is also a testament to the positive influence of research on teaching. At the time of writing, "research bashing" has become popular. According to this line of thinking, academic research has little or nothing to do with what goes on in the classroom. However, this book is largely a synthesis of international accounting research. Nearly everything we say in this book is based on research findings over the past 30 years or so. Thus, as the material is taught in the classroom, research findings are directly transferred to students of accounting.

In June 1992 the Accounting Education Change Commission issued *Position Statement No. 2,* "The First Year Course in Accounting." According to the *Statement,* "the primary objective of the first year course is for students to learn about accounting as an information development and communication function that supports economic decision making." Among its recommendations: students completing the first course should (1) develop a broad view of the role of accounting in satisfying society's need for information, (2) understand that the effectiveness of an accounting system depends on the circumstances and uses to which it is put, and (3) have the ability to confront problems with more than one defensible solution. In general, the first year course should be about the uses of accounting information, in addition to its preparation. In our opinion incorporating the international dimension into the first year course through the use of this book helps to accomplish these objectives.

CONTENTS AND CHANGES IN THE FOURTH EDITION

The book contains 12 chapters, modularized so the teacher can pick and choose among them and use them in a different order than they are presented here. The first six chapters deal with financial accounting issues. Chapter 1 discusses the factors that influence the development of financial accounting practices and which, therefore, explain the similarities and differences in financial accounting around the world. Chapter 2 describes the important areas of difference in worldwide financial accounting practices. Institutional efforts to harmonize accounting diversity are the subject of Chapter 3, while Chapter 4 discusses the ways multinational corporations report to financial statement users in other countries. Chapter 5 focuses on disclosure trends, notably some innovative disclosures coming from Europe. Finally, Chapter 6 deals with consolidations and foreign currency translation. International financial statement analysis is the subject of Chapter 7. It bridges into the next four chapters—Chapters 8 through 11—which deal with managerial accounting issues. Chapter 8 discusses accounting information systems in multinational corporations. Chapter 9 looks at planning and control, while Chapter 10 is about performance evaluation in multinationals. The interrelated topics of multinational transfer pricing and international taxation are covered in Chapter 11. The book ends with Chapter 12 in which we identify and discuss what we believe to be the most important emerging issues in international accounting.

Every chapter starts with the enumeration of five specific learning objectives. At the end of each chapter are study questions, designed to review the chapter material; several short cases that integrate, and sometimes extend, the material; and a list of additional readings for those who wish to delve further into the subjects. Each list has two or three readings that are fairly easy, while the rest are more difficult.

An *Instructor's Manual* accompanies this book. It contains chapter outlines, solutions to the study questions and cases, and an exam bank with answers. We also offer suggestions on how to use this book and recommend where our chapters fit in with topics taught in introductory accounting courses. The *Instructor's Manual* is designed to be user friendly, with the expressed intention of making *Accounting: An International Perspective* as easy to use as possible.

The Fourth Edition adds many new illustrations from MNC annual reports and the professional international accounting literature. Footnote references have been increased to facilitate follow-up. Several sections of each individual chapter were rewritten, adding and deleting to reflect the current state of the art of the field of international accounting. The entire text has been thoroughly updated.

CONCLUSION

As noted in Chapter 12, the forces of internationalization are irreversible. The key drivers that will keep it going are the increasingly multinational structure of business organizations, the globalization of markets, and the political and regulatory development of regionalism. These forces were alluded to in the first paragraph of this Preface. Related accounting issues include information systems design; performance evaluation in complex, multinational organizational structures; optimal forms of reporting to various user groups around the world; and the development of an accounting esperanto. These are but a sampling of the issues discussed in this book. *Your authors welcome you to the study of accounting in a global context!*

ACKNOWLEDGMENTS

The authors gratefully acknowledge the advice of a number of our colleagues in the development of this text. Early drafts of the First Edition received in-depth reviews from Michael A. Diamond (The University of Southern California) and Daniel L. Jensen (The Ohio State University). In preparing this Fourth Edition, we received review comments from Yass Alkafaji (Northeastern Illinois University), Marinus Bouwman (University of Arkansas), Amy Lau (Oklahoma State University), Grace Pownall (Emory University), Shahrokh Saudagaran (Santa Clara University), and William Shenkir (University of Virginia). We are indebted to these individuals for the generous contribution of their time in suggesting improvements to our book. In addition, informal comments from other colleagues have been invaluable to us.

All sins of omission or commission are to be debited to the authors. Comments from users will be credited—gladly and without deferral. We hope to hear from you if you have occasion to use this book.

Gerhard G. Mueller
Helen Gernon
Gary Meek

C O N T E N T S

ACCOUNTING
AN INTERNATIONAL PERSPECTIVE

C H A P T E R

1

AN INTERNATIONAL PERSPECTIVE ON FINANCIAL ACCOUNTING

LEARNING OBJECTIVES

1. Demonstrate how accounting is influenced by its environment and responds to the information needs of those who use it.
2. Understand the link between accounting and the global economy.
3. Explain the major environmental variables that shape accounting development.
4. Show that accounting around the world is different to the extent that business environments are different, and similar, to the extent that they are similar.
5. Identify and explain the four major accounting "models" in the non-Communist world—British-American, Continental, South American, and mixed economy.

From a business perspective, accounting is typically defined as a process providing information about various types of enterprises that is useful for making decisions about resource allocations. *Financial* accounting information is oriented primarily toward those parties external to the business enterprise who provide capital to it. Those who have funds to invest or lend may decide where to place their resources based on the *financial reports* (i.e., financial accounting information) that business enterprises prepare. Exhibit 1–1 illustrates this relationship

---

EXHIBIT 1–1   Financial Accounting Information and Capital Resource Flows

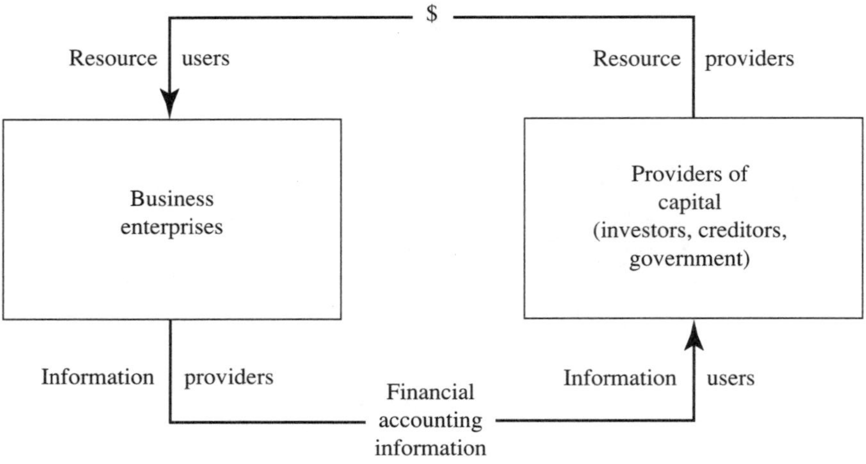

---

between business enterprises and capital providers. Accounting exists because it satisfies a need—in particular, a need for information. And in order to be relevant to the resource providers, accounting information must be responsive to their needs.

ACCOUNTING AND THE ENVIRONMENT

Accounting is shaped by the environment in which it operates. Just as nations have different histories, values, and political systems, they also have different patterns of financial accounting development. Accounting as we know it in the United States is not like accounting in other countries. Indeed, diversity is what we see. This diversity is an outgrowth of the variety of business environments around the world and the fact that accounting is environmentally sensitive. It is interesting to note, too, that when countries' business environments are similar, their financial accounting systems also tend to be similar.

In a number of countries (such as the United States), financial accounting information is directed primarily toward the needs of investors and creditors, and "decision usefulness" is the overriding criterion for judging its quality. However, in other countries, financial accounting has a different focus and performs other roles. For example, in some countries financial accounting is designed primarily to ensure that the proper amount of income tax is collected by the national government. This is the case in most South American countries. In other countries financial accounting is designed to help accomplish macroeconomic policies, such as achieving a predetermined rate of growth in the nation's economy. Whether income tax and economic policy information is also useful to individual investors and creditors is somewhat beside the point. For the moment we are concerned only with the *primary* orientation of a national financial accounting system.

The consequences of national financial accounting differences are all around us. They are reflected in the relative popularity of accounting as a major for university studies, and in the numbers of people with accounting backgrounds becoming senior government officials or top corporate executives. There is a different national emphasis on the use of accounting information in assessing environmental damage liabilities and especially in regulating public securities markets.

GLOBAL CHALLENGES FOR ACCOUNTING

As stated in the Preface, your authors firmly believe that the global economy and its transnational business and investment networks are here to stay. The World Bank underscores this in its prospectus for its *World Development Report 1995:*

> The world is in the midst of two crucial changes: rising global integration—via trade, technology, capital flows, and migration; and the decline in state interventionism—due to the general failure of state-led development to increase jobs, incomes, and living standards.

Called on to perform globally even though anchored nationally puts lots of stress on the accounting environment. Just think of the enormous transaction volumes that accounting must cope with in connection with all the privatizations[1] launched in recent years. A sample of some privatization "Big Deals" is shown on Exhibit 1–2.

By way of yet another illustration, Exhibit 1–3 reports foreign direct investment (FDI) flows to and from the United States between 1973 and 1993 as well as a 1992 breakdown of areas of origin for inbound FDI. This represents another aspect of the global economy where significant accounting resources must be brought to bear.

VARIABLES SHAPING ACCOUNTING DEVELOPMENT

Relationship between Business and the Provider(s) of Capital

The Industrial Revolution in the United States and Britain created a tremendous amount of new wealth in these countries—wealth that spread widely among the general populace. As companies grew, their needs for capital also grew, and

---

[1]Privatization is the sale of government-owned business assets to private persons or enterprises.

EXHIBIT 1–2   Selected Recent Large Privatizations

Company	Business	Year	Sale Price ($mil)	Percent Private	Major Buyer(s)
JAPAN					
NTT	Telecom.	1987	$73,490	35%	Public offering
East Japan Railway	Railroad	1993	10,090	63	Public offering
Japan Tobacco	Tobacco production and sales	1994	5,730	20	Public offering
Japan Airlines	Airline	1987	4,690	100	Public offering
PERU					
ENTEL-CPT	Telecom.	1994	$ 2,000	35%	Telefonica de Espana (Spain)
Empresa Mineral Especial Tintaya SA	Copper mining	1994	218*	100	Magma Copper (U.S.)
Banco Continental	Banking	1995	195	60	Banco Bilbao Vizcaya (Spain)
Empresa Minera del Hierro del Peru	Iron ore mining	1992	120	100	Shougang Group (China)

*Buyer also committed to make substantial future investments in enterprise.

POLAND					
FSM	Auto maker	1994	$ 1,230*	90%	Fiat (Italy)
Bank Slaski	Banking	1993	155	56	ING Bank (Netherlands)
Bank Przemyslowo-Handlowy	Banking	1995	150	59	Public offering
Stalexport	Steel trader	1994	94	62	Public offering
Stocznia Szczecinska	Shipyard	1993	†	59	Group of Polish creditors

*Includes 500 million German marks equity investment and 1.5 billion German marks in debt write-offs.
†Debt-for-equity swap.

UNITED KINGDOM					
British Telecom	Telecom.	1984	$21,990	~100%	Public offering
British Gas	Gas supply	1986	12,930*	~100	Public offering
British Steel	Steelmaker	1988	4,150	~100	Public offering
BAA	Owns and operates airports	1987	2,090	97	Public offering
Rolls-Royce	Jet engines	1987	1,770	100	Public offering
British Airways	Airline	1987	1,400	~100	Public offering
British Coal	Coal	1995	1,280†	~100	RJB Mining (U.K.)

*Includes debt redemption totaling $4.16 billion.
†Price paid for about 80% of assets; remainder sold separately.

SOURCE: *The Wall Street Journal Reports,* "The Big Deals" (World Business), Oct. 2, 1995, pp. R12–13.

EXHIBIT 1–3   Foreign Direct Investment (FDI) in the United States

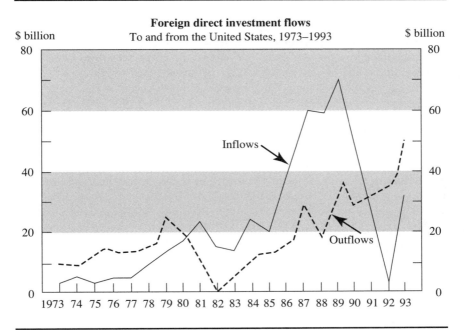

Foreign direct investment flows
To and from the United States, 1973–1993

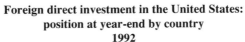

SOURCE: OECD/DAF—Balance of payments data.

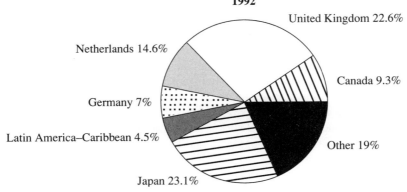

Foreign direct investment in the United States:
position at year-end by country
1992

United Kingdom 22.6%

Netherlands 14.6%

Canada 9.3%

Germany 7%

Latin America–Caribbean 4.5%

Other 19%

Japan 23.1%

SOURCE: OECD. *OECD Reviews of Foreign Direct Investment—United States*. Paris: OECD, 1995, pp. 12, 19.

the rising middle class became a source of much of this needed capital. What emerged from this phenomenon had an important impact on financial accounting in these two countries. First, the investor/creditor group became large and diverse, and companies acquired a widespread ownership (i.e., many shareholders). Second, the owners became divorced from the management of their companies, and the professional, nonowner manager developed. Investors became essentially uninvolved in the day-to-day running of the companies they owned.

In such an environment, financial accounting information becomes an important source of data about how well a company is doing. Since it is impractical for the shareholders to contact the company president or personally inspect the accounting records, the professional managers provide financial reports to investors and creditors in order to communicate their stewardship over the resources entrusted to them. With such a relationship, it is hardly surprising that financial accounting is oriented toward the information needs of investors and creditors. Financial accounting in Britain and the United States has had such an orientation for many years. Moreover, these countries have large and developed stock exchanges and bond markets. As a result, a great deal of information is disclosed in companies' financial reports; and determining profitability (i.e., management performance) is an objective of financial accounting.

In other countries (such as Switzerland, Germany, and Japan), the environment is characterized by a few, very large banks that satisfy most of the capital needs of business. Ownership also tends to be concentrated. The information needs of the resource providers are satisfied in a relatively straightforward way—through personal contacts and direct visits. Since the business enterprises have to deal with only a few creditors—and maybe even just one—direct access is an efficient and practical way to have the company's financial health monitored. The national governments require some public disclosure, and so companies still prepare financial reports. Not surprisingly, though, they tend not to contain as much information as U.S. companies' reports. And since banks are the primary source of capital, financial accounting is oriented toward creditor protection. One sees, for example, such practices as conservatively valuing assets and overvaluing liabilities in order to provide a "cushion" for the bank in the event of default. These practices also reduce the dividend demands of shareholders.

France and Sweden offer still another orientation of financial accounting. National government plays a strong role in managing the country's resources, and business enterprises are expected to accomplish the government's policies and macroeconomic plans. Governments also actively ensure that businesses have adequate capital and will lend or even invest in companies if necessary. Financial accounting is oriented toward decision making by government planners. Firms follow uniform accounting procedures and reporting practices, which facilitate better government decisions.

Of course, the relationship between a business enterprise and providers of business capital changes quite drastically when new capital is secured in international financial markets. Then the information demands of both domestic and international funds sources have to be satisfied, which typically means going beyond national expectations and customs in providing financial reports. This topic is explored in Chapter 4.

In summary, the following have an impact on a country's financial accounting orientation:

1. Who the investors and creditors—the information users—are (individuals, banks, the government).
2. How many investors and creditors there are.
3. How close the relationship is between businesses and the investor/creditor group.
4. How developed the stock exchanges and bond markets are.
5. The extent of use of international financial markets.

Political and Economic Ties with Other Countries

Accounting technology is imported and exported just as political systems and ideologies are, and countries have similar accounting for this reason. The United States has influenced accounting in Canada due to geographic proximity and close economic ties and because a number of Canadian companies routinely sell shares of common stock or borrow money in the United States. The United States is Mexico's principal trading partner; and, also because of proximity, accounting in Mexico is very much like that in the United States.[2] As a former protectorate of the United States, the Philippines has similar accounting requirements. Finally, accounting in Israel is heavily influenced by U.S. accounting practices as a result of the historical and sociological ties between the two nations. It is interesting to see that Japanese accounting is increasingly feeling the influence of U.S. standards. More and more Japanese firms are raising capital and establishing manufacturing facilities in the United States.

Another significant force in worldwide accounting has been the United Kingdom, principally England and Scotland. Almost every former British colony has an accounting profession and financial accounting practices patterned after the U.K. model. These countries include Australia, New Zealand, Malaysia, Pakistan, India, and South Africa. The British not only exported their brand of accounting but also "exported" many accountants. (In fact, Britain is the only major former colonial power to transfer both its accounting ideas and its accountants.) Former colonies of France and Germany have been similarly influenced by their respective "mother countries," though not quite so profoundly as those of the United Kingdom.

---

[2]The North American Free Trade Agreement (NAFTA—further referenced in Chapter 3) will further integrate already existing Canadian, U.S., and Mexican accounting similarities.

Since the early 1970s, the European Union (EU) has been attempting to harmonize the accounting practices of its 15 member states. Recall from our earlier discussion that Britain, Germany, and France have fundamentally different orientations about the role and purpose of financial accounting. However, as European allies and members of the EU, they have a number of similar economic interests, and they are seriously attempting to bring their accounting practices closer together.

Political and economic ties among nations shape their accounting development; thus, one cannot help but wonder whether the world's growing interdependence will force accounting practices to become more similar.

Indeed, this type of thinking has given rise to the international accounting standards movement. As explored more fully in Chapter 3, the International Accounting Standards Committee (IASC) has become the signal force worldwide to develop international financial accounting standards and seek their widest possible acceptance and use. The International Federation of Accountants (IFAC), among many other activities, develops and issues international auditing standards (also see Chapter 3), which were accepted in 1992 for financial reporting in international financial markets. In Europe, accounting *Directives* are issued by the EU and are incorporated into the national corporate legislation of all EU member countries in due course. Many world agencies like the United Nations (UN), the Organization for Economic Cooperation and Development (OECD), the Association of South East Asian Nations (ASEAN), and the International Monetary Fund (IMF) have operating units specifically concerned with international financial standard setting and reporting. The internationalization of our political and economic environments is directly driving the internationalization of accounting.

Legal System

Many dichotomize the accounting world into those countries with a "legalistic" orientation toward accounting and those with a "nonlegalistic" orientation. The legalistic approach to accounting is predominantly represented by so-called code law countries, and the preponderance of countries with a nonlegalistic approach are the so-called common law countries. Laws in code law countries are a series of "thou shalts" that stipulate the minimum standard of behavior expected. Citizens are obligated to comply with the letter of the law. In most code law countries, accounting principles are national laws; that is, accounting practices are codified much as the tax code is in the United States. These accounting practices and rules tend to be highly prescriptive, detailed, and procedural. Also, the primary role of financial accounting in these countries is to determine how much income tax a company owes the government. Argentina, France, and Germany have legalistic approaches to accounting.

The nonlegalistic approach is usually found in common law countries. Laws are a series of "thou shalt nots" that establish the limits beyond which it is illegal to venture. Within these limits, however, latitude and judgment are permitted and encouraged. Accounting practices in common law countries are largely determined by accountants themselves (rather than by national legislators) and thus tend to be more adaptive and innovative. The United Kingdom and the United States are common law countries.

Levels of Inflation

Accounting in many countries (including the United States) is based in part on the *historical cost principle*. This principle is itself based on an assumption that the currency unit used to report financial results is reasonably stable. In other words, the historical cost principle assumes that the dollar (for U.S. companies) does not change in value—that there is little or no inflation. As one might expect, the less realistic this assumption becomes, the greater the strain on the historical cost principle.

Briefly, the historical cost principle means that companies originally record sales, purchases, and other business transactions at transaction prices and make no adjustments to these prices later. Generally speaking, the historical cost principle affects accounting most significantly in the area of asset values, mainly those assets (such as land and buildings) that the company keeps for a long time. Obviously, the reasonableness of the historical cost principle varies inversely with the level of inflation. Germany and Japan, two of the staunchest adherents to the historical cost principle, have experienced very little inflation in recent years. South American countries, ravaged by inflation problems for years, long ago abandoned any attachment to strict historical cost. Companies in many of these countries routinely write up the values of their assets based on changes in general price levels.

The United States experienced very little inflation in the post-World War II era until the 1970s. Most U.S. accountants were happy with historical cost accounting, and interest in adjusting for changes in price levels was mainly confined to a few academicians. However, once inflation became persistent and high (at least by U.S. standards), interest in measuring the effects of price-level changes on business enterprises began to grow. In 1979 the Financial Accounting Standards Board (FASB), the organization that determines acceptable accounting practices for U.S. companies, required the largest U.S. firms to experiment with ways to account for changes in prices. Eventually, these firms had to report the effects of changing prices in their published annual reports and in filings with the Securities and Exchange Commission (SEC). However, this requirement was rescinded in 1984 as inflation levels in the United States returned to more modest levels.

Interest in incorporating the effects of changing prices into a company's accounting records waxes and wanes with the degree that a country is affected by inflation. Countries with a long history of inflation have already done something about it, while those with low inflation do not even consider abandoning historical cost. Some of the most novel ideas dealing with inflation accounting were proposed in Europe during the 1920s and 1930s, when that continent experienced hyperinflation. More recently, accountants in the United Kingdom and the United States have written some provocative essays about how to account for price-level changes.

Size and Complexity of Business Enterprises, Sophistication of Management and the Financial Community, and General Levels of Education

These factors define the limits of a country's accounting sophistication. Larger, more complex business enterprises have more difficult accounting problems. Highly trained accountants are needed to handle these more difficult problems; accounting cannot be highly developed in a country where general education levels are low, unless that country imports accounting talent or sends bright citizens elsewhere for the necessary training. At the same time, the users of a company's financial reports must themselves be sophisticated—or else there will be no demand for sophisticated accounting reports.

Most multinational corporations are headquartered in the wealthy, industrialized nations (e.g., Japan, Germany, Great Britain, and the United States). These countries have sophisticated accounting systems and highly qualified professional accountants. In contrast, education levels in most developing countries are low and businesses are small; as a result, accounting is primitive. From earlier discussions, however, it may occur to you that if accounting responds to information needs, then accounting in developing countries may very well be at an appropriate level of sophistication under the circumstances. While many accountants hold this view, some feel that the lack of sophisticated accounting ability in less developed countries actually impedes their potential for economic progress. It does appear, though, that newly developed countries (such as Taiwan, South Korea, and Brazil) have been able to overcome their rudimentary accounting expertise. Accounting development and economic development clearly go hand in hand. Just as most of the world can be divided between the "haves" and "have nots," there are accounting "have" and "have not" nations.

Culture

The variables just enumerated are in varying degrees part of the culture of individual countries, races, religions, geographic areas, and other delineating features. Sometimes "culture" is defined as the collective programming of the human mind. So all the things we learn, observe, feel, believe, or prioritize have cultural dimensions. Even though culture is variously defined and research on its relationship to accounting sparse and inconclusive, there is increasing attention in the accounting literature to cultural links as components of accounting concepts, standards, and practices. For example, it appears that individualistic cultures tend to have higher levels of accounting disclosure than group-oriented cultures. The latter tend to restrict the "need to know" to those within the group. To quote one researcher: ". . . research has identified that environmental factors, especially cultural factors, exert considerable influence on a country's accounting practice development."[3]

It is imperative to recognize that accounting development is not random or arbitrary. Despite the difficulty of directly tying accounting development to cultural factors, many seasoned observers are convinced that such a link does exist.

ACCOUNTING CLUSTERS

The variables shaping the development of financial accounting overlap to some degree. For example, most code law countries have historically relied on either banks or the government to supply capital to businesses, whereas common law countries have historically relied on their more developed stock and bond markets to satisfy businesses' capital needs. If we accept the idea that accounting is influenced by its environment, then it is logical to expect accounting similarities among countries with similar business environments.

Indeed, nations can be grouped or clustered according to accounting similarities. Before discussing such clusters, however, it is important to emphasize the word *similarities*. No two countries have *identical* financial accounting practices. Each country is a unique mixture of environmental variables that together have influenced the pattern of accounting development in that country. Therefore, in order to cluster countries, one must blur some dissimilarities. However, at a broad level of generalization, four major accounting models can be identified. Countries represented by each model are listed in Exhibit 1–4 and depicted in Exhibit 1–5.

British-American Model

In international accounting circles, one often hears the term *British-American* (or sometimes *Anglo-Saxon*) to describe the accounting approach found in the United Kingdom and the United States. The Dutch approach is quite similar; and, to be more precise, one should really call this model *British-North American-Dutch*. The United Kingdom, the United States, and the Netherlands are the trend-setting countries for this cluster. Their accounting is oriented toward the decision needs of investors and creditors, and they have large, developed common stock and bond markets, where companies raise large amounts of capital. Education levels are very high, and users of financial accounting information tend to be quite sophisticated. These countries also possess many large, multinational corporations. (Philips, a Dutch multinational, manufactures Norelco brand products. Unilever is a British/Dutch company whose U.S. subsidiary,

---

[3]Harry H. E. Fechner and Alan Kilgore, "The Influence of Cultural Factors on Accounting Practice," *International Journal of Accounting 29*, no. 3 (1994), p. 265.

EXHIBIT 1–4   List of Selected Countries Comprised by the Four Major
Accounting Models

British-American Model

Australia	Hong Kong	Panama
Bahamas	India	Papua New Guinea
Barbados	Indonesia	Philippines
Benin	Ireland	Puerto Rico
Bermuda	Israel	Singapore
Botswana	Jamaica	South Africa
Canada	Kenya	Tanzania
Cayman Islands	Liberia	Trinidad & Tobago
Central America	Malawi	Uganda
Colombia	Malaysia	United Kingdom
Costa Rica	Mexico	United States
Cyprus	Netherlands	Venezuela
Dominican Republic	New Zealand	Zambia
Fiji	Nigeria	Zimbabwe
Ghana	Pakistan	

Continental Model

Algeria	France	Norway
Angola	Germany	Portugal
Austria	Greece	Senegal
Belgium	Guinea	Sierra Leone
Burkina	Italy	Spain
Cambodia	Ivory Coast	Sweden
Cameroon	Japan	Switzerland
Denmark	Luxembourg	Togo
Egypt	Mali	Turkey
Finland	Morocco	Zaire

South American Model

Argentina	El Salvador	Paraguay
Bolivia	Guatemala	Peru
Brazil	Guyana	Uruguay
Chile	Honduras	
Ecuador	Nicaragua	

Mixed Economy Model

Albania	Georgia	Russia
Armenia	Hungary	Serbia
Azerbaijan	Kazakhstan	Slovak Republic
Belorussia	Kirgizia	Slovenia
Bosnia-Herzegovina	Latvia	Tadzhikstan
Bulgaria	Lithuania	Turkmenistan
Croatia	Moldavia	Ukraine
Czech Republic	Poland	Uzbekistan
Estonia	Romania	Vietnam

EXHIBIT 1–5   Map of Countries Comprised by the Four Major Accounting Models*

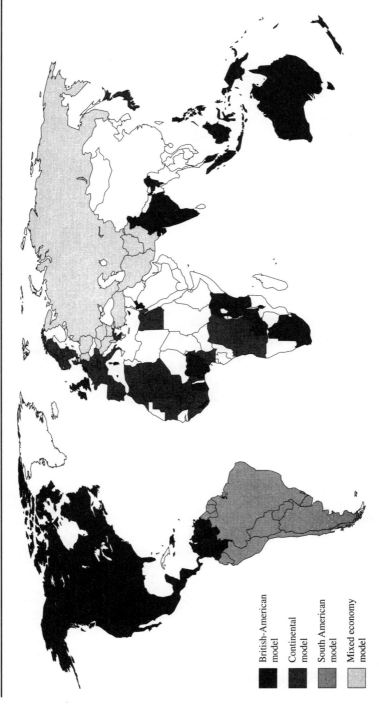

British-American model

Continental model

South American model

Mixed economy model

*As of September 1995, the United Nations had 185 country members (*World Almanac 1996*, pp. 843–44). This map classifies 114 of these members.

Lever Brothers, manufactures and sells such products as *All* detergent.) As can be seen from Exhibit 1–4, these three countries represent a sphere of influence over accounting in many other countries as well.

Continental Model

Countries in this cluster include most of continental Europe and Japan. Businesses here have very close ties to their banks, which supply most capital needs. Financial accounting is legalistic in its orientation, and practices tend to be highly conservative. Accounting is not primarily oriented toward the decision-making needs of the capital providers. Instead, it is usually designed to satisfy such government-imposed requirements as computing income taxes or demonstrating compliance with the national government's macroeconomic plan. French-speaking African countries, by-and-large, follow the Continental financial accounting model.

South American Model

The third model includes most countries in South America. With the exception of Brazil, which speaks Portuguese, these nations share a common language—Spanish. They also share a common heritage. What distinguishes the South American model from the British-American and Continental models is the persistent use of accounting adjustments for inflation. These countries have a great deal of experience coping with inflation, and their accounting reflects this. Generally speaking, accounting is oriented toward the needs of government planners, and uniform practices are imposed on business entities. Tax-basis accounting is often used as well for financial reporting purposes.

Mixed Economy Model

The 1989–1990 political upheavals in Eastern Europe and the former USSR have spawned a very environment-specific accounting model seeking to be responsive to both remnants of tight central economic planning and control as well as market-oriented enterprise activities. Where this model applies, enterprises typically operate dual accounting systems. One track produces information for managers used to the former system oriented toward a command economy and relying heavily on uniform charts of accounts and budgeted rather than actual financial information. (Refer to the discussion at the end of this chapter on accounting in Communist countries.) The other track has a capitalist markets orientation, tries to emulate the British-American accounting model (with special reference to IASC standards), and seeks to provide information primarily for investors, bankers, and corporate financial analysts from capitalist countries. Reconciling these two very different conceptual approaches to financial accounting is difficult if not impossible. Among the big challenges for the mixed economy model are joint venture accounting, establishing values for productive assets for the privatization of economic units, education and organization of effective local and national accounting professions, and regulatory control over needed accounting development. The UN Centre for Transnational Corporations is particularly active in supporting the mixed economy model.

International Standards Model

An emerging model of distinct accounting practices might be called the international standards model. Its roots lie in the international harmonization of financial accounting—especially for multinational corporations and international financial markets participants. Quite a few large corporations already note that their annual financial reports are in conformity with international financial accounting standards. The international standards movement was briefly mentioned earlier in this chapter and is discussed more fully in Chapter 3.

The move toward a free-standing international standards model is gathering momentum in several respects. The European Union (EU) is embarked on a major thrust to align its accounting *Directives* with IASC standards (see Chapter 3). Regulators of securities markets around the world are seeking formal acceptance of the IASC standards for companies listing their securities on foreign capital markets (also see Chapter 3). We already mentioned that accounting developments in countries falling into the mixed economy model aim for consistency with IASC standards. And finally we note that the most recent Chinese accounting regulations are benchmarked to IASC standards as well. Of course, the Chinese effort exists so far on paper only, but it is an indication of the direction that accounting development will take in this still tightly controlled economy.

Accounting in Communist Countries

This chapter focused on the non-Communist world. We end it with a brief description of accounting in Communist countries, such as Cuba and North Korea. Communist governments own all productive resources (no private ownership) and supply all capital needs; therefore, it stands to reason that high uniformity is required and that the primary users are government planners. Uniform accounting is necessary for tight central economic control. Financial statements are not prepared for outsiders but for various agency administrators and government planners. Financial reports normally include budgetary information.

In contrast to capitalist economies, the basic inputs to production in command (i.e., Communist) economies are not purchased (nor are outputs sold) on open markets. The states allocate firms a specified quantity of resources, and firms are expected to produce a predetermined level of output. Success is not measured by the amount of income earned; rather, the emphasis is on achieving production quotas and on determining production costs. Since private ownership of productive resources is absent, valuing fixed assets is not emphasized as much as it is in capitalist economies. Indeed, financial accounting per se does not exist; what we refer to as *managerial accounting* comes closer to illustrating the overall accounting scene in Communist regimes. China, of course, is the present bulwark of the command economy world. Her basic accounting systems are fully consistent with Marxist principles. As market economy concepts and practices are slowly gaining recognition, the command economy accounting model has begun to wither away. It seems fair to observe that China is well on her way to the mixed economy model of accounting.

CONCLUSION

One should not say that the accounting in one country is of better quality than the accounting in another country. Accounting exists because it fulfills a need, and as long as accounting satisfies the needs of its user groups, it is doing what it is supposed to do. Accounting develops in and is nurtured by its environment. That the world is a potpourri of accounting practices reflects the diversity of uses to which it is put.

STUDY QUESTIONS

1. Why is accounting shaped by the environment in which it operates?
2. Why is there diversity in financial accounting practices around the world?
3. List the variables that shape the development of accounting around the world and briefly discuss the influences of each.
4. Japanese investors will soon own most of America, that is, U.S. business assets. Is this assertion warranted? Is NAFTA likely to influence U.S. FDI patterns?
5. The world's key political organizations (e.g., UN, OECD, IMF, EU, ASEAN) have operating units specifically concerned with international financial accounting standard setting and reporting. What is driving this international attention to accounting?
6. What are the four major accounting models? What are the distinguishing characteristics of each?
7. Show how the variables listed in question 3 have affected each of the accounting models identified in question 6.

CASES

Nifty NAFTA

Financial accounting and reporting practices in Canada, Mexico, and the United States have much in common. In all three countries, financial reporting focuses on investors and investor decision needs. However, there are some differences. Perhaps the two most important are (1) Mexico has inflation-adjusted accounting, while Canada and the United States practice historical cost accounting, and (2) there is less emphasis on full disclosure in Mexico than there is in Canada and the United States.

Questions

1. Why does accounting in Canada, Mexico, and the United States have much in common?
2. Explain the differences noted in the case.
3. What is the likely impact of the North American Free Trade Agreement (NAFTA) on financial accounting and reporting practices in Canada, Mexico, and the United States? Explain your reasoning.

Law and Order Accounting

"I'll tell you, Günter. Here's what's wrong with German accounting."

Tim O'Reilly has been on assignment at his accounting firm's office in Cologne, Germany, for two weeks. During this time, he has reviewed the financial statements of a number of German companies in order to learn something about German accounting practices. He's learned enough so far to know that German accounting is a lot different than accounting back home in the United States.

"For one thing, too many German companies prepare their statements in German. Hey, Günter, the language of international business is English. How do these companies expect people who don't understand German to read their financial statements?

"For another, you guys give incredible amounts of detail about a lot of things that most people don't care about and not enough information about stuff that's really important. I saw one statement that listed every blasted subsidiary owned by the company—it was a six-page list. But that same company reported nothing at all about how much profit it earned in various parts of the world or how much was made by product line. And German balance sheets and income statements are so detailed, it's really hard to get the 'big picture.'

"Why companies seem to undervalue assets and overvalue liabilities is beyond me—all that does is understate net income. Why, it's almost as if you're being overly conservative on purpose. The companies always say that their financial statements 'comply with the law,' but what the heck does that mean, Günter?"

Questions

1. What specific differences between German and U.S. accounting practices has Tim observed?
2. What environmental variables help explain the German accounting practices that Tim noted?
3. Do you agree with Tim that there is something "wrong" with German accounting?

By Guess and by Gosh

Terri Parker is a financial analyst for foreign financial statements at a large U.S. pension fund. As a matter of policy and investment diversification, the pension fund invests between 15 and 20 percent of its assets in offshore corporate financial securities.

Terri is frustrated. "We're doing well with these foreign securities, but more often than not we select them and monitor them mostly by guess and by gosh,'" she fumes. "Often, I don't fully understand their financial statements; our executive director doesn't understand them, nor does our board of directors. Why can't big corporations around the world use the same financial accounting and reporting standards? Somebody ought to do something!"

Questions

1. Why do financial accounting standards used by large corporations differ from country to country?
2. What is Terri likely to do about a foreign financial report (written in English) that she cannot understand?
3. Whose responsibility is it "to do something" about this situation?

ADDITIONAL READINGS

Bailey, D. "Accounting in Transition in the Transitional Economy." *European Accounting Review 4,* no. 4 (1995), pp. 595–623. (Entire issue devoted to accounting in Eastern Europe and the former U.S.S.R.)

Barrett, G. R. "Is Accounting Becoming the First Truly International Profession?" *Journal of Accountancy* (October 1992), pp. 110–13.

Davidson, R. A., A. M. G. Gelardi, and F. Li. "Analysis of the Conceptual Framework of China's New Accounting System." *Accounting Horizons* (March 1996), pp. 58–74.

Doupnik, T. S., and S. B. Salter. "An Empirical Test of a Judgmental International Classification of Financial Reporting Practices." *Journal of International Business Studies* (First Quarter 1993), pp. 41–60.

O'Malley, S. F. "Accounting across Borders." *Financial Executive* (March/April 1992), pp. 28–31.

United Nations Centre on Transnational Corporations. *Accounting Development in Africa: Challenge of the 1990s.* New York: UNCTC, 1991, 200 pp.

UN Secretary General. "Identification of Accounting Problems Arising during Privatization and Their Solution." *European Accounting Review* (May 1993), pp. 17–46.

C H A P T E R

2

DIVERSITY IN FINANCIAL ACCOUNTING PRACTICES

LEARNING OBJECTIVES

1. Explain why and how financial accounting practice diversity is reduced within countries.
2. Understand why financial accounting practices differ between countries.
3. Describe several important areas of financial accounting diversity around the world.
4. Identify who wins and who loses as a result of worldwide accounting diversity.
5. Assess the likely consequences of worldwide accounting diversity.

In Chapter 1 we discussed the principal environmental variables that shape the development of national financial accounting systems. We identified:

1. Relationship between business and the provider(s) of capital.
2. Political and economic ties with other countries.
3. Legal system.
4. Levels of inflation.
5. Size and complexity of business enterprises, sophistication of management and the financial community, and general levels of education.
6. Culture.

Chapter 3 is devoted to the idea of worldwide harmonization of the existing country-by-country financial accounting diversity. What is this diversity, and is it really problematic? Why is the enforcement of accounting rules and regulations a national activity? Who wins and who loses from national diversity in financial accounting practices? Questions such as these are explored in this chapter.

REDUCING DIVERSITY WITHIN COUNTRIES

Until the Great Depression of 1929 through 1930, companies everywhere could freely choose the accounting methods and rules they thought appropriate for their individual situations. In a 1927 book entitled *Main Street and Wall Street,* William Z. Ripley, then Harvard professor of political economy, described his review of U.S. corporate annual reports in these terms:

> Confronted with a great pile of recent corporate pamphlets on my table, the first impression is of their extraordinary diversity, in appearance, size, content, and intent. One premier concern, the Royal Baking Powder Company, fails to register any fiscal information at all, in as much as it has never issued a balance sheet or financial statement of any kind whatsoever for more than a quarter of a century. . . . Akin to it is the Singer Manufacturing Company, which handles 80 percent of the world's output of sewing machines. Neither hide nor hair of financial data for this firm is discoverable in the usual sources of information. The dance-card, bald balance-sheet, or picture-book variety of corporation report follows hard upon these examples of complete reticence. . . . Yet colored pictures of factories, brightly lighted at night,—as some of these must well have been in view of their extraordinary success,—tell no tales.[1]

Companies in the United States were incorporated under state law statutes, which generally contained only superficial accounting and financial reporting requirements. Code law countries had more elaborate corporate law provisions, but also literally nothing on accounting and financial reporting. This was a world of terrible misinformation and noncomparable financial statements. Essentially, corporate managements picked accounting and reporting rules that often pictured their companies financially better than they were in fact (this is called *window dressing* in accounting).

Remedies began to surface soon after the Great Depression. Countries subscribing to the British-American model of financial accounting created committees or boards of professional practicing accountants (certified public accountants [CPAs] in the United States; chartered accountants [CAs] in Canada and the United Kingdom) to recommend *generally accepted accounting principles* (GAAP) to be used within each country. In the United States, enforcement was assigned to the Securities and Exchange Commission (SEC), which is a federal

---

[1]William Z. Ripley, *Main Street and Wall Street* (Houston, Tex.: Scholars Book Co., reprinted 1972), pp. 162–64.

EXHIBIT 2–1 Financial Accounting Standard Setting in Five Countries

---

Germany relies very heavily on legislation, particularly company law, and on taxation; accounting standards tend to be especially conservative and have very detailed provisions with respect to presentation and valuation.

France also depends on legal and tax decrees, although to a lesser degree than Germany; the concept of "substance over form" has little impact since it is assumed that following the rules will produce a "true and fair view."

Japan is a third country that draws heavily on legal and tax directives, so much so that the private sector has little direct involvement in setting accounting standards; in many ways, Japan's legal and tax systems follow those in Continental Europe.

In the **United Kingdom,** private-sector influence is very strong; standards tend to set out broad principles, with some latitude as to the details.

In the **United States,** the private sector is also the primary source of accounting standards, but with input and influence from the SEC; standard setting is a particularly lengthy process and, in addition to basic pronouncements, there is much detailed guidance.

SOURCE: International Capital Markets Group, *Harmonization of International Accounting Standards.* A paper prepared by the International Federation of Accountants with the assistance of Federation Internationale des Bourses de Valeurs and the International Bar Association Section on Business Law, 1992, p. vii.

government agency created to regulate all domestic markets for financial securities. Enforcement in the United Kingdom is more indirect in that it occurs mainly through litigation and other court processes.

Countries subject to code laws (i.e., those following the Continental and South American models) revised their respective companies' laws to require compliance with various accounting provisions and the orderly publication of financial statements.

Developing accounting and financial reporting methods and rules is called financial accounting *standard setting* (see Chapter 3). As mentioned in Chapter 3, the Financial Accounting Standards Board (FASB) sets financial accounting standards in the United States. There were over 120 FASB standards at the end of 1995. Together with standards set before the FASB was established in 1973, these pronouncements constitute GAAP in the United States.

Other countries have different approaches to producing accounting standards. Exhibit 2–1 provides a comparative summary for five countries.

Most industrialized countries and a few developing countries have their own accounting standard setting boards or committees. By and large, these organizations have been successful. They have greatly reduced accounting and financial reporting diversity within countries and have forged clearly recognizable and nationally acknowledged country-by-country GAAP. The big concern now is that the GAAP of no two countries are the same. This means that financial information does not travel well internationally.

WHY FINANCIAL ACCOUNTING PRACTICES
DIFFER BETWEEN COUNTRIES

Accounting and financial reporting are not the same everywhere. The three trigger factors described and explained so far in this book are

1. Major environmental variables that impact accounting development in any one national setting.
2. Adherence to a particular financial accounting model (by choice, affinity, or historical accident).
3. Approach to and process of national financial accounting standard setting.

There is a fourth critical factor that has to do with the very nature of accounting. This factor, conservatism, relates to all the uncertainties modern business must cope with. Here is how a group of experts describes what is going on:

> Financial statements, which are designed to portray the financial position and results of operations, are prepared at least annually. Businesses nowadays are involved in transactions which extend over significant time periods, and which have inherent uncertainties associated with them. As a result, at any accounting date there are often significant transactions which have not been completed, and where the final outcome is uncertain. This means that preparers of financial statements must make estimates about future events in order to apportion costs and revenues to the appropriate financial periods. Thus estimates have to be made about future costs and revenues on long-term contracts, on future pension costs, asset lives, and on many other matters. These are inherently difficult problems. There are not necessarily 'right' answers, and it is therefore not surprising that countries deal with them in different ways.[2]

Conservatism, one of the cornerstones of financial accounting around the world, is one way to cope with these uncertainties. However, the extent to which conservatism affects accounting practices varies. As noted in Exhibit 2–1, for example, German accounting is especially conservative. U.K. accounting, on the other hand, is much less conservative.

Thus, we have diversity from one set of GAAP to another among different countries. This diversity may well be justified in terms of one or a combination of the four trigger factors mentioned, but the same diversity creates barriers for international financial information flows. It is one of the primary issues in international accounting.

---

[2]International Capital Markets Group, *Harmonization of International Accounting Standards.* A paper prepared by the International Federation of Accountants with the assistance of Federation Internationale des Bourses de Valeurs and the International Bar Association Section on Business Law, 1992, p. 3.

SOME EXISTING PRACTICE DIFFERENCES

When dealing with international accounting at a basic level, it is inappropriate to illustrate existing practice differences with elaborate examples. Therefore, *general* discussions of three topics follow the overview, which is presented first.

The subject matter of financial accounting divides itself into two dimensions—*measurement* and *disclosure.* Measurement concerns economic events and transactions whose effects are reflected directly on the three basic financial statements (i.e., the balance sheet, income statement, and cash flow statement). If an accounting entity borrows money from a bank, the amount of the debt is measured, and both the cash received and the debt payable are reflected on the next balance sheet and cash flow statement. Similarly, when a payroll comes due, all employee pay obligations are measured and social security/unemployment insurance/private pension contributions and other indirect employment costs are added to arrive at an appropriate amount for employment expenses on the next income statement. Measurement activities like these drive all formal accounting systems.

Aside from measurements themselves, readers of financial statements want to know which measurement methods were used and if there are items of interest that somehow could not be measured directly. Difficult-to-measure things include future effects of strikes, mergers, and product development. Also included are environmental protection effects, charitable commitments, or comparisons with another country's GAAP. These are often reported in supplemental disclosures, apart from the basic financial statements. Chapter 5 discusses disclosure issues. Accounting measurements are addressed in the rest of this chapter.

Assets and liabilities are subject to often significant measurement differences around the world. Take something as simple as cash. Most corporate balance sheets have a caption like "cash and cash equivalents." What does this cover? In the United States, demand deposits and highly liquid investments are included. In other countries, bank overdrafts and short-term borrowings are subtracted instead of being reported separately as liabilities.

Of course, there is the additional problem translating national currencies (see Chapter 6). Multinational corporations (MNCs) do business in many different countries and therefore have various bank accounts in as many countries. Companies like Kodak, Nestlé, or Procter & Gamble sell their products in more than 100 different countries and therefore have bank accounts in as many national currencies. To bring them all together into a single balance sheet requires *measuring* them in terms of a single currency. In other words, for Kodak all forms of cash equivalents must somehow be translated (i.e., remeasured) to U.S. dollars. What foreign exchange rate is appropriate for this purpose? Should one represent the resulting total as a U.S. dollar amount when, in fact, the majority of the funds involved is denominated in other national currencies?

If we have so much difficulty with a straightforward item like cash and cash equivalents, it is little wonder that even more substantive issues are encountered in relation to inventories, depreciable assets, intellectual properties, software, research and development, capitalized borrowing costs, leased properties, intercorporate investments, and other assets.

The liabilities side of the accounting equation is equally complex. For decades, accountants have debated how to measure income tax accounting effects when financial accounting differs from tax accounting (i.e., within the British-American model only, since financial and tax accounting are highly similar in all of the other models). If a company takes relatively larger expense deductions for income tax purposes in connection with depreciation or some long-term contracts (and therefore postpones taxable income), should a *deferred income tax* effect be measured and put on the balance sheet? If the answer is yes, is this item a liability like accounts or notes payable?

International liabilities measurement differences exist with respect to leasing contracts and contingencies like the eventual outcome of pending lawsuits. There is little international agreement on how to account for future contracts in the commodities markets, interest rate swaps and similar arrangements in the financial markets, and hedging operations in the foreign exchange markets. Joint venture obligations are also a real measurement problem.

When it comes to measuring business net income or loss, things are still more complicated. The main sources of diversity in this area are

1. Avoidance of the income statement altogether: for example, taking unusual gains and losses, merger premium payouts, or certain financing transactions directly to owners' equity on the balance sheet.

2. Creation of secret reserves in the name of prudence and conservatism in order to "manage" periodic business income reported to outsiders.

3. Impact of legal requirements that may necessitate setting up legal reserves to protect some tax advantages, treating executive bonuses and stock options on or off income statements, or dictating accruals by legal formula rather than economic effect.

In the preceding paragraphs, we have identified a number of accounting topics for which country-by-country measurement differences exist. International accounting textbooks treat these differences in some detail. Many articles and monographs present overviews of selected accounting issues where there is diversity in practice.

We now turn to three specific cases.

Goodwill

When a company buys another company, a business division, or some other business enterprise, it typically anticipates greater benefits than the fair market values of the net assets acquired. Maybe an added team of executives will bring about major synergy, maybe certain patents or processes lend themselves to

EXHIBIT 2-2   Accounting for Goodwill in Selected Countries

	Capitalization and Amortization	Maximum Period of Amortization	Immediate Write-Off against Reserves	Tax Deductible
Australia	Required	20	No	No
Canada	Required	40	No	Yes (75% of amount at the rate of 7% per year)
France	Required	Not specified	No	No
Germany	Permitted	Not specified	Permitted	Yes (over 15 years)
Japan	Required	5	No	Yes (over 5 years)
New Zealand	Required	20	No	No
United Kingdom	Permitted	Not specified	Permitted*	No
United States	Required	40	No	Yes (over 15 years)
International— Revised IAS 22	Required	20	No	Not applicable

*SSAP 22 indicates a preference for this treatment, which is the prevalent practice.

Source: M. C. Miller, "Goodwill Discontent: The Making of Australian and International Accounting Policy," *Australian Accounting Review*, June 1995, p. 8.

higher profit potential, or maybe market access is at stake. Whatever the antici-pated benefit, to the extent that purchase price exceeds total fair market value, something called *goodwill* is created (*negative goodwill* may occur in bargain purchases).

Considerable diversity exists among countries on whether purchased good-will should be carried on balance sheets, and if so, whether it should be amortized and how it should be amortized.

The goodwill accounting diversity is aggravated by a taxation effect. For instance, goodwill amortization is not tax deductible in the United Kingdom or the Netherlands, but it is deductible in Canada, Japan, Germany (post-1986), and the United States (post-1993). Obviously, the diversity involved affects business practices and therefore global competitiveness. If a company can permanently shield its income statements from goodwill amortization, it will report com-paratively higher net earnings and thereby may gain a competitive advantage. Exhibit 2–2 summarizes goodwill accounting in selected countries.

Income Smoothing

Managers of most companies like to present a smooth income pattern from one year to the next, preferably a pattern with steady, predictable annual in-creases. A volatile income pattern normally suggests a company with higher risk of operations, which often leads to lower investor confidence and higher costs of obtaining financing. Smooth income normally means the opposite: less risk, greater investor confidence, and lower financing costs.

The opportunities allowed by GAAP to smooth income vary greatly around the world. The GAAP of some countries, for example the United States, allow little flexibility for income smoothing. By contrast the practice is a notable feature of German and Swiss accounting. Here, GAAP has built-in flexibility which managers routinely take advantage of. The GAAP of still other countries actually encourages income smoothing by companies as a way to stimulate a long-term view of companies' operations and to encourage overall confidence in the nation's economy. Sweden is an example of such a country.

Of course, income smoothing can occur quite apart from anything permitted by a country's GAAP. This is because managers have discretion over the timing of some revenue and expense transactions. For example, advertising costs can easily be shifted from one fiscal year to the next by merely accelerating or delaying expenditures by a week. Additional expenditures can be made just before year-end to reduce income; alternatively, they can be postponed to the first of the next year to increase income in the current year. In the overall scheme of things, such judicious timing of advertising transactions probably has little impact on the company, even in the short run. However, it obviously changes the amount of income reported in each of the two years, and correspondingly alters the year-to-year pattern.

The focus of this section, however, is on the quite legitimate use of accounting principles to shift income from one year to the next. In particular, this section discusses the use of *provisions* and *reserves* as income smoothing devices. While these two terms have other meanings in other accounting contexts, as used here, *provisions* refers to charges against income. They are a type of expense (or sometimes, loss) which normally requires judgment as to the amount. Obviously, there are many items like this, so there are potentially a number of provisions that a company may be dealing with. Examples include risks and uncertainties for product obsolescence and potential foreign exchange losses. Because judgment is involved, the amount of a provision is imprecise, and there is an inherent flexibility in its determination. In other words, a range of amounts is typically involved, and reasonable arguments can be made for any of the amounts within this range. This means that managers have discretion in choosing the amount of the provision that actually reduces income in any given year.

Reserves, as used here, refers to special equity accounts on the balance sheet used to accumulate the provisions taken over the years. When a provision is charged in the accounts, a corresponding amount is added to a reserve account. In other words, reducing income on the income statement by a provision amount means increasing a reserve account on the balance sheet by the same amount.

So how are provisions and reserves used to smooth income? One way is to judiciously choose the amounts of provisions that achieve the desired net income for the year. Or, one might even omit a provision if "necessary" in some year. However, reserves can also be "drawn down" in particularly bad years to increase income. In other words, a reserve is decreased and a *negative* provision recorded in order to *increase* income.

A company may or may not disclose the activity in its provision and reserve accounts. If the amounts of provisions are combined with other expenses and if the amounts of reserves are combined with other stockholders' equity accounts, then a financial statement reader will not be able to tell the extent of their use or the impact on income. Sometimes people refer to this as using *secret* reserves. Alternatively, the effects of income smoothing may be fully revealed, allowing a financial statement reader to understand how income was affected by the use of provisions and reserves.

A dramatic example of the use of reserves to smooth income was revealed by Daimler-Benz, the German automobile manufacturer of Mercedes-Benz, for its 1993 fiscal year. Daimler-Benz had recently listed its common stock shares on the New York Stock Exchange. One of the requirements imposed on non-U.S. companies listing their shares in the United States is that they reconcile their net income according to their home country's GAAP to net income according to U.S. GAAP. (This is a requirement imposed by the U.S. Securities and Exchange Commission, discussed in Chapter 3.) In this way, non-U.S. companies reveal how the major GAAP differences between their home country and the United States affect reported income. Under German GAAP, the 1993 net income of Daimler-Benz was DM615 million (DM = deutsche marks); however, under U.S. GAAP Daimler-Benz reported a net *loss* of DM1,839 million. The most important reason that the company went from a net income position under German GAAP to a net loss position under U.S. GAAP was the use of reserves. Daimler-Benz had drawn down its reserves accounts in 1993 to boost its German GAAP income. Using provisions and reserves to smooth income is not allowed under U.S. GAAP.

Some observers argue that the use of provisions and reserves deceives financial statement readers. While this is arguably possible, it is important to bear in mind that, as discussed here, the practice is a legitimate application of a nation's GAAP, allowed or even encouraged in certain countries. Whether things are kept secret will also depend on what the country's GAAP requires companies to reveal. In addition, income smoothing opportunities are often tied to a nation's income tax laws. In general, income smoothing is more often practiced in code law countries where financial and tax accounting are strongly linked. (See Chapter 1.) Finally, it was noted earlier in this chapter that there is diversity in how conservatism is interpreted and practiced around the world. All things being equal, there will be a tendency to "overprovide" in countries where conservatism is particularly strong, compared to countries where conservatism is not so strong.

Recognition of Inflation and Other Price Changes

Financial accounting in most countries is based in part on the *historical cost principle*. This principle is based on the assumption that the currency unit used to report financial results is reasonably stable—that is, there is little or no inflation.

As a result, strict historical cost accounting does not recognize the effects of inflation or other price changes. Keeping assets valued at their original transaction prices avoids having to make subjective determinations about how much more or less they are worth now compared to some earlier time. Accountants have traditionally believed that objective accounting information is more reliable than subjective information and, therefore, more useful.

However, as discussed in Chapter 1, severe inflation is a potent force that can strain the historical cost principle. Dramatic price changes make historical cost accounting information less believable and, therefore, less useful. The reasonableness of the historical cost principle varies inversely with the severity of price changes.

There are two basic approaches to accounting for changing prices. *General price level (GPL) accounting* (also known as constant dollar accounting) uniformly changes the values of assets and liabilities to reflect the general change in the currency unit's purchasing power. While transactions are initially recorded at their historical costs, they are later notched up or down by changes in the currency's general purchasing power. As a result, the items on the balance sheet and income statement are reported in units of the same purchasing power. *Current value accounting,* on the other hand, changes the historical costs of assets to their current values and recognizes corresponding expenses at the current cost of obtaining the services represented by those expenses. Current value accounting has several variations, of which *current cost accounting* (CCA) is the most widely accepted.

Only a very few countries *require* that the effects of changing prices be incorporated directly into the accounting records and financial statements. This points out that while inflation can put a severe strain on the historical cost model of accounting, historical cost nevertheless has a strong hold on accounting practices. Historical cost is still the predominant basis for preparing financial statements. The GAAP of some countries, though, allow companies to reflect the effects of changing prices if they choose to do so. And the GAAP of still other countries suggest that the impacts of fluctuating prices be disclosed supplementally—apart from the main financial statements.

The International Accounting Standards Committee (IASC) recommends in *Standard 29,* "Financial Reporting in Hyperinflationary Economies," that when a company is reporting in the currency of a country experiencing very high levels of inflation, the financial statements should be restated to reflect the purchasing power of that currency unit at year-end. In other words, *Standard 29* requires comprehensive GPL accounting for a company reporting in the currency of a "hyperinflationary" economy.

Latin America.   Many Latin American countries base their approach on general price level accounting. They have contended with high inflation rates for a long time and, as a result, accounting for changing prices is an issue too serious for their accountants to ignore.

Argentina, Bolivia, Brazil, Chile, and Mexico require companies to comprehensively restate their financial statements on the basis of changes in general price levels. Several others require that fixed assets be revalued at certain intervals for changes in the price level. (Since fixed assets are not replaced as often as current assets, their historical costs are more likely to be out of date with persistently high price changes.) Depreciation expense is calculated on the restated values of fixed assets. A few other Latin American countries also accept such restatements. Interestingly, in Bolivia and Brazil, a company's *taxable* income is also computed after making inflation adjustments—something most tax authorities would never allow. The income statement of the Mexican company, Cemex, shown in Exhibit 4–3 is prepared using general price level accounting.

The Netherlands.   Accounting in the Netherlands is heavily influenced by business economics (or *microeconomics,* the study of the behavior of individual economic agents, such as business firms, and the markets in which they operate). A fundamental notion in business economics is that the input values of a company's goods and services must be less than their selling prices in order to maintain long-run profitability and, hence, ensure survival. The Dutch professor Theodore Limperg (1879–1961) is often called the father of replacement value theory, from which current cost accounting is derived.

CCA is not required in the Netherlands but is strongly encouraged by the Netherlands Institute of Register Accountants either as supplemental information or by incorporation into the primary financial statements. While most Dutch companies continue to use historical cost accounting, some prepare comprehensive current cost financial statements. Those that use historical cost often disclose current cost information supplementally.

United States and the United Kingdom.   The history of accounting for price changes is similar for the United States and the United Kingdom. Both countries experienced what were for them unusually high levels of inflation during the 1970s. By 1980, both had standards in effect to provide information in financial statements about the effects of changing prices. In the United States, the FASB published *Statement 33,* "Financial Reporting and Changing Prices." It required large publicly held companies (approximately 1,300 in all) to supplementally disclose selected financial statement items on both current cost and general price level bases. *Statement of Standard Accounting Practice (SSAP) 16,* "Current Cost Accounting," was issued in the United Kingdom in 1980. It was a comprehensive current cost approach and applied to all public and nationalized companies, plus private companies above a certain size—altogether, 5,000 to 6,000 companies.

Both standards proved to be highly controversial. Many companies preparing the required information protested that it was too costly to produce and that it was unreliable. Compliance with *SSAP 16* by U.K. companies quickly deteriorated. There were also a number of studies that assessed the usefulness of the required disclosures. Most of these studies concluded that the disclosures provided little if any benefit to users beyond the primary historical cost financial statements. By the mid-1980s, requirements in both countries were made nonmandatory.

CONSEQUENCES OF WORLDWIDE ACCOUNTING DIVERSITY

Enough evidence is available to conclude resolutely that GAAP differ (at times substantially) from country to country. Whether this is good or bad depends on the points of view of a variety of interest groups.

Corporate Management

Managers of companies with strictly domestic operations care little. As long as national GAAP are relatively clear, useful, and broadly applied, most medium-sized and small companies feel well served by the accounting rules they have to contend with. In this regard, there are no problems.

MNCs see it differently. They find that working with many different national GAAP requirements is a costly proposition, especially when they list their common stock shares on multiple stock exchanges. They also face global competition every day and sense that accounting diversity affects competitiveness. If a European corporation can bid for a U.S. acquisition target company and immediately write off all premium payouts to owners' equity (bypassing the income statement), it might outbid an equally interested U.S. corporation that must amortize the same premium payouts as goodwill through subsequent income statements. MNCs like "level playing fields" for their global operations. Distorting factors cause barriers and retaliation.

MNCs also worry about accounting for similar events and transactions in a similar manner. If a given set of business activities allows reporting higher net income under one set of GAAP in comparison with another set of GAAP, management immediately seeks to compensate for such accounting effects so that corporate borrowing costs and prices for the corporation's shares and bonds remain unaffected. Given a choice, some MNC managements will attempt to use another country's GAAP if they think the other GAAP are better known and understood than their own. As discussed in Chapter 4, MNCs want to be understood by their customers, bankers, labor unions, suppliers, government regulators, and other interested parties.

Investors

Portfolio investors and their agents, financial analysts, probably dislike international accounting diversity the most. Instant global communications and overall cheap and quick access to global financial markets have made cross-border investing very attractive. Since national business cycles are not synchronized around the world, advantages are available from judicious diversification of investments involving different national securities markets. Financial misinformation short-circuits this process.

Investors experience frustrations when they do not understand whether financial statements merely look similar or are in fact similarly prepared. Underwriters consistently report that worldwide accounting diversity causes some underwriting (i.e., pricing of new securities issues) difficulties. If investors, analysts, and underwriters indeed experience difficulties with GAAP diversity, financial markets are not as efficient as they could be and therefore returns to investors are less than they ought to be. This is a powerful indictment of GAAP diversity.

Stock Markets and Regulators

Accounting and disclosure requirements for listing shares on the world's stock markets vary extensively. Research shows that MNCs consider these requirements to be an important cost when they choose where to list their common stock shares. Indeed, MNCs are less likely to choose stock exchanges that require them to make extensive new disclosures over and above those that they are already making at home.

The United States has the most extensive accounting and disclosure requirements in the world. The U.S. Securities and Exchange Commission (SEC) is the regulatory agency responsible for these requirements. In general, the SEC believes that investors are better protected when there is a "level playing field," that is, when comparable accounting information is provided by U.S. and non-U.S. companies alike. Nevertheless, non-U.S. companies allege that they avoid listing in the United States because they find U.S. requirements too onerous. If this is true, then U.S. citizens are deprived easy access to buying shares in these companies, and the U.S. capital market may become less competitive globally. The situation represents a vexing problem for the SEC which it has yet to resolve.

Accounting Professionals and Standard Setters

Some have suggested that accounting professionals, especially those in the Big Six professional firms, like diversity because it generates fees for them all the way from assisting in setting up new business units for their clients in different GAAP territories to restating financial reports from one set of GAAP to another (see Chapter 4). GAAP diversity also makes cross-border auditing more costly and therefore raises auditing fees. Even though not demonstrated by reliable research, it stands to reason that at least some accounting professionals gain from the GAAP diversity factor.

Accounting standard setters, as guardians of the public interest, would like to have full authority over all GAAP and financial reporting of companies whose securities are publicly held or whose size is so large that the public interest is affected. But regulations are primarily enforced through national laws and national legal systems. Therefore, a national focus is inevitable for accounting regulation—at least for the time being. Moreover, national regulators want discretion over national GAAP. International or any other GAAP are beyond their reach of influence and hence unacceptable. Nationalism is an issue here. Do you want others (i.e., non-nationals) to have determining influence over the GAAP you are required to use? Many countervailing forces come to bear on this point.

CONCLUSION

Worldwide diversity in financial accounting and reporting exists. Four specific reasons explain this diversity. In some instances, the diversity among national GAAP is significant; in others it is not. There are some winners and some losers as a result of the diversity condition. When diversity reaches the point of misinformation, it becomes dysfunctional. National environmental factors together with national laws and national accounting standard setting systems will make some degree of GAAP diversity inevitable. However, in domestic terms, national GAAP have reduced practice diversity. A similar degree of diversity reduction may be desirable on the international level. Harmonization of accounting practices is aimed at such reduction and is explored in Chapter 3.

STUDY QUESTIONS

1. Who wins and who loses from worldwide diversity in financial accounting and reporting practices? Present reasoned answers in no more than four short paragraphs.
2. Are within-country accounting practices more or less diverse than cross-country practices? If there is a difference, please explain.
3. Explain the effect(s) of national financial accounting standard setting on international practice diversity.
4. List the four trigger factors attributed to international accounting practice diversity. Which one do you consider most important? Why?
5. Why is accounting for purchased goodwill a controversial international accounting issue?
6. Explain how companies from certain countries use provisions and reserves to smooth income. Is income smoothing good or bad? Why?
7. National accounting and financial reporting diversity is an established fact. Good or bad? Present three short paragraphs defending the status quo or advocating major change.

CASES

Whose Money?

The world's portfolio investors are heteromonetary when it comes to earning the highest possible returns on their investments.

Sigwan Fund is composed entirely of U.S. investors. It is incorporated in Delaware and pays dividends strictly in U.S. dollars. However, all of its assets are invested in the common stocks of Sigwan companies listed on the SWSE—the Sigwan Stock Exchange. The Sigwan national currency is the Sigi, which is fully convertible and internationally quite stable.

"All of our record-keeping and accounting practices ought to be in U.S. dollars and U.S. GAAP," snorts Shawn Christopher, the fund's general manager. "After all, the United States is our cradle, and that's where we are ultimately accountable. Forget all this Sigi nonsense."

"Wrong, wrong, and wrong again," retorts Alana Tesero, the fund's CFO. "Everything we have is fully invested in Sigwan securities denominated in Sigis. This is what determines our future viability! We must report using Sigwan GAAP and Sigi currency units. Economic reality absolutely dictates this."

Questions

1. Do you agree with Mr. Christopher or Ms. Tesero? Defend your response adequately.
2. Why is the choice of national GAAP and/or national currency an issue in these circumstances? Is the issue contrived?
3. From the perspective of the fund, an identity question bears on the GAAP choice. Does this choice push the fund toward a U.S. or a Sigwan identity? As a fund investor, would you have any preferences?
4. Should Sigwan or U.S. regulators be able to determine appropriate GAAP choices for the Sigwan Fund? Please explain your answer adequately.

Home Country Accounting Isn't Always Good Enough

National stock market regulatory agencies around the world share similar goals, including the following: (1) protecting investors by ensuring adequate financial and other information disclosures, (2) keeping the nation's stock market(s) competitive on a global basis, (3) promoting the availability of investment opportunities for the nation's citizens, and (4) safeguarding the fairness, efficiency, and stability of the nation's stock market(s). The U.S. Securities and Exchange Commission (SEC) is the agency responsible for regulating stock markets in the United States.

U.S. companies face the most extensive accounting and disclosure requirements of any companies in the world. In general, the SEC requires non-U.S. companies wishing to have their shares traded on U.S. stock exchanges to present equivalent information to that by U.S. companies. International accounting diversity presents a particular problem for the SEC. "Leveling the playing field" by requiring additional information from non-U.S. companies treats all MNCs alike and provides investors with comparable information for their decision making. Yet many observers allege that non-U.S. companies are avoiding U.S. capital markets because SEC requirements are so much more extensive than those elsewhere around the world.

Questions

1. What conflicts are inherent in the goals, identified above, of national stock market regulatory agencies?
2. Should the SEC "level the playing field" by requiring non-U.S. companies to provide information equivalent to that provided by U.S. companies? Who wins and who loses in this scenario?
3. Should the SEC allow an "unlevel playing field" by accepting less financial accounting information from non-U.S. companies than it requires from U.S. companies? Who wins and who loses in this scenario?
4. How would elimination of existing international accounting diversity simplify the lives of SEC commissioners?

National Agendas for Accounting

"As a national accounting regulator, I owe allegiance only to my country and its citizens. I will work long hours and expend all the personal energy I have to assure that the best possible accounting information reaches everyone in the economic marketplace in my country. I have some empathy for what other governments and their accounting regulators want to achieve, but this is at best a secondary concern. International efforts always end up watered down and catering to the lowest common denominator. The only way to stay on top is to show the flag and rally around it."

Questions

1. What benefits, if any, have been achieved from following the perspective advocated by the person quoted?
2. Given only the information you presently have, would you support the creation of additional national accounting standard setting authorities in countries that now don't have such agencies?

3. Does cross-country accounting diversity really influence global business competition? Defend your answer in two or three brief paragraphs.

4. If you were master/mistress of the universe, how would you go about reducing the present level of accounting practice diversity around the world?

ADDITIONAL READINGS

Andersen, Arthur & Co., Coopers & Lybrand, Deloitte & Touche, Ernst & Young, KPMG Peat Marwick, and Price Waterhouse. *Survey of International Accounting Practices.* New York: Authors, 1991, 56 pp.

Brown, P. R., and C. P. Stickney. "Instructional Case: Tanaguchi Corporation." *Issues in Accounting Education* (Spring 1992), pp. 57–79.

Clinch, G. "Capital Markets Research and the Goodwill Debate." *Australian Accounting Review* (June 1995), pp. 22–30.

Coopers & Lybrand. *International Accounting Summaries: A Guide for Interpretation and Comparison.* New York: John Wiley & Sons, 1993, 2nd ed., paginated by section. Annual update supplements available.

Doupnik, T. S., E. Martins, and G. Barbieri. "Innovations in Brazilian Inflation Accounting." *International Journal of Accounting 30,* no. 4, 1995), pp. 302–17.

Harris, T. S. *International Accounting Standards versus U.S. GAAP Reporting: Empirical Evidence Based on Case Studies.* Cincinnati: Southwestern College Publishing, 1995, 147 pp.

International Capital Markets Group. *Harmonization of International Accounting Standards.* London, England: International Bar Association, 1992, 67 pp.

C H A P T E R

3

HARMONIZATION OF FINANCIAL ACCOUNTING DIVERSITY

LEARNING OBJECTIVES

1. Understand the rationale for financial accounting and auditing standard setting and the standard setting process in the United States.
2. Become familiar with some pros and cons of setting and applying international accounting and auditing standards.
3. Learn the various processes of international and regional standard setting presently ongoing.
4. Gain ability to compare international accounting standard setting by governmental agencies with such standard setting by private professional bodies.
5. Examine different scenarios for greater international harmonization of accounting, auditing, and financial reporting.

Chapter 1 explains how certain environmental variables shape the development of accounting in a particular country. It also provides a rationale for the worldwide diversity of accounting practices—since accounting reflects the environment in which it operates and since environments differ around the world, it follows that accounting will also be different around the world. The worldwide diversity in financial accounting practices is addressed in Chapter 2.

One way to reduce diversity (i.e., bring harmony) is to set and then enforce common standards for all concerned. Standards we all know about include speed limits on streets and highways, appropriate labeling of consumer products, and grades awarded to college and university students. Accounting and auditing standards play key roles in financial reporting (see Chapter 4).

ACCOUNTING AND AUDITING STANDARDS

Accounting standards are the rules for preparing financial statements: that is, the "generally accepted accounting principles" (GAAP) that specify the type of information that financial statements ought to contain and how that information ought to be prepared. Accounting standards define what are acceptable and unacceptable financial accounting practices.

Auditing standards are the rules governing how an *audit* is performed. An audit of financial statements is the technical process by which an independent person (the auditor) gathers evidence to form an opinion about how well a set of financial statements conforms to GAAP. In most countries, a particular group of accountants is legally sanctioned to conduct financial statement audits. In the United States, for example, it is the certified public accountant (CPA). In the United Kingdom, it is the chartered accountant; in the Netherlands, the register accountant; and in Germany, the Wirtschaftsprüfer. Financial statements conforming to GAAP are said to be "reliable," and reliable information is an important ingredient in good decision making.

Accounting standards and auditing standards are interrelated. Accounting standards presumably define what is *useful* financial information. Auditing standards guide an auditor in determining whether it is also *reliable*. Useful and reliable financial information puts investors, creditors, and others in a position to make better decisions.

Accounting has been called the language of business. That analogy is accurate, since accounting is a form of communication. As with all types of communication, though, misunderstandings can arise unless meanings are reasonably clear.

To counteract the possibility of misunderstood financial communications, approximately 50 countries have created their own national financial accounting standard setting mechanisms. This has harmonized financial accounting diversity *within* countries. Unfortunately, international diversity continues to exist. This diversity results in a general lack of comparability in financial reports from one country to the next. As a result, there is a risk of misunderstanding when financial statements are communicated transnationally. The ensuing problems for users and preparers of financial reports are outlined in Chapter 4.

The problem of different auditing standards is more subtle. Fundamentally, an audit assures users that they can trust the information communicated by the financial statements. However, if auditors around the world are not comparably trained or if they do not observe comparable standards, then their work varies in quality. As a result, the inherent reliability of financial statements also varies.

The existence of different accounting and auditing standards affects the decisions of resource providers to the extent that they fail to either understand or trust the messages communicated by financial statements. A number of international and regional organizations recognize this problem and are endeavoring to harmonize accounting and auditing standards to the extent possible. This chapter discusses the work of these organizations. First, however, we quickly review the three major bodies involved directly in accounting and auditing standard setting in the United States. These organizations indirectly influence accounting in other countries as well, due to the United States' leading position in the accounting world.

U.S. ORGANIZATIONS

The U.S. *Securities and Exchange Commission* (SEC) is a U.S. government agency charged with ensuring adequate accounting and reporting standards for companies whose securities are publicly traded in the United States. The SEC's primary concern is to protect investors from potential losses resulting from insufficient or incorrect financial information. The SEC is empowered to write accounting standards for so-called publicly held companies, although it has typically deferred this task to the Financial Accounting Standards Board. Any corporation whose securities are publicly traded in the United States (even a non-U.S. firm) must abide by the rules of the SEC. The SEC's reporting requirements for non-U.S. firms are similar, though not identical, to the reporting requirements for U.S. companies. In this way, it also exerts influence over the financial reporting of some companies from other countries.

The *Financial Accounting Standards Board* (FASB) is the principal body that writes the generally accepted accounting principles by which the financial statements of U.S. companies must be prepared. The official pronouncements that establish GAAP are known as *Statements of Financial Accounting Standards* (SFAS), and those issued so far concern such diverse topics as accounting for leases (*Statement 13*), foreign currency translation (*Statement 52*), employers' accounting for postretirement benefits other than pensions (*Statement 106*), and accounting for stock-based compensation (*Statement 123*). The FASB has also produced a conceptual framework that deals with theoretical and conceptual issues and is intended to provide an underlying structure for future accounting standards. The conceptual framework pronouncements are called *Statements of Financial Accounting Concepts*. Moreover, in various policy statements, the FASB has committed itself to full consideration of international perspectives in all of its work.

The FASB is a private-sector body (i.e., not a government agency) supported financially by several professional, business, and accounting groups. The board is composed of seven full-time members, who are aided by a staff of some 50 technical specialists plus administrative and other support personnel.

The *American Institute of Certified Public Accountants* (AICPA) is an organization of about 300,000 CPAs. CPAs engage in a number of accounting activities including preparing tax returns, giving tax advice, and conducting audits of financial statements. The AICPA publishes standards to aid auditors in their examinations. *Statements on Auditing Standards* cover such issues as how to plan an audit and supervise assistants, how to report audit findings, the use of statistical sampling on an audit, and what to do when the auditor discovers fraud. Like the FASB, it is a private-sector body.

PROS AND CONS OF INTERNATIONAL ACCOUNTING AND AUDITING STANDARDS

Every international accounting textbook and most international accounting research studies contain long lists of benefits and costs arising from international accounting and auditing standard setting. Among the alleged benefits, these sources mention greater international comparability of financial reports most often. Financial executives think that a more level playing field will result if international accounting standards are widely used—with reference to items such as cross-border mergers and acquisitions, and securing financing outside the home country. Some economists believe that such standards would improve global business competition, and some international agencies (e.g., UN) advocate international standards as a form of assistance to developing countries. In a more operational sense, international standards may reduce bookkeeping costs and allow more efficient preparation of financial statements.

Researchers have identified still other benefits: for example, reconciliation of sometimes adversarial interests between preparers and users of financial statements. Standardization is thought to bring more efficiency to analysis and use of financial reports and, pointedly, increase the credibility of the entire financial reporting system.

Of course, there are also those who object to the very idea of international accounting and auditing standards. In the early 1970s, critics condemned international standard setting as a solution too simple for a problem too complex. Other challenges point to inherent differences in national backgrounds and traditions, the potential breach of national sovereignty, politicalization of the entire field of accounting, plus standards overload if both national and international standards have to be applied concurrently.

A senior U.S. corporate officer gives this perspective:

> I have argued that Global GAAP is unlikely to be achieved due to the institutional impediments in the standards setting process and because there is no demonstrated need in order to fuel the growth of robust international capital markets.[1]

---

[1]R. K. Goeltz, "International Accounting Harmonization: The Impossible (and Unnecessary?) Dream," *Accounting Horizons,* March 1991, pp. 85–88.

Nevertheless, the movement toward international standards for accounting and auditing is growing.

INTERNATIONAL ORGANIZATIONS

We now turn to the international and regional organizations involved in harmonizing accounting and auditing standards within their respective spheres of influence. The organizations discussed can be categorized according to several key variables, and you may want to keep them in mind as you read.

1. Is the organization concerned with accounting standards, auditing standards, or both? Some organizations are trying to harmonize the form and content of financial statements, while others are concerned with professional accountants themselves and the way they do their work.

2. Are the organization's members governments of countries or professional accounting groups from different countries? This sometimes affects the political pressures bearing on the organization's deliberations and the types of interests that the organization represents.

3. Is the organization's effort regional or international in scope? Regional efforts may stand a greater chance of success, since the participants are likely to have more in common than those of a broader based, international effort.

International Accounting Standards Committee

The *International Accounting Standards Committee* (IASC) was formed to develop worldwide accounting standards. Many differences in financial reporting practices among the world's corporations do arise legitimately from differences in business environments. However, not all differences can be thus explained.

Accounting evolves rather slowly, and larger multinationals have literally transcended the environments of their native countries to reflect a global business environment. (Toyota, for example, probably has more in common with General Motors than it does with small Japanese companies.) Yet most multinational corporations still retain the accounting practices of their native countries.

In essence, the IASC is trying to harmonize the world's accounting standards and eliminate those differences that cannot be explained by environmental variables. Even though international standards are meant for all companies, they are especially relevant for multinational corporations.

To date, the IASC has issued 32 *International Accounting Standards* (IASs). Those mentioned elsewhere in this text are

Standard 14, "Reporting Financial Information by Segments."

Standard 15, "Information for Reflecting the Effects of Changing Prices."

Standard 21, "The Effects of Changes in Foreign Exchange Rates."

EXHIBIT 3–1   Professional Accountancy Bodies in the Following Countries Are Members of IASC

Australia	Iceland	Paraguay
Austria	India	Peru
Bahamas	Indonesia	Philippines
Bahrain	Iraq	Poland
Bangladesh	Ireland	Portugal
Barbados	Israel	Saudi Arabia
Belgium	Italy	Singapore
Bolivia	Jamaica	South Africa
Botswana	Japan	Spain
Brazil	Jordan	Sri Lanka
Canada	Kenya	Sudan
Chile	Korea	Swaziland
Colombia	Kuwait	Sweden
Croatia	Lebanon	Switzerland
Cyprus	Lesotho	Syria
Czech Republic	Liberia	Taiwan
Denmark	Libya	Tanzania
Dominican Republic	Luxembourg	Thailand
Ecuador	Malawi	Trinidad and Tobago
Egypt	Malaysia	Tunisia
Fiji	Malta	Turkey
Finland	Mexico	United Kingdom
France	Netherlands	United States of America
Germany	New Zealand	Uruguay
Ghana	Nigeria	Zambia
Greece	Norway	Zimbabwe
Hong Kong	Pakistan	
Hungary	Panama	

SOURCE: IASC, *Annual Review 1994.*

Standard 27, "Consolidated Financial Statements and Accounting for Investments in Subsidiaries."

Standard 29, "Financial Reporting in Hyperinflationary Economies."

The IASC was formed in 1973 by an agreement of the leading professional bodies in Australia, Canada, France, Germany, Japan, Mexico, the Netherlands, the United Kingdom, Ireland, and the United States. It now represents more than 100 accountancy bodies from 82 countries, which are listed in Exhibit 3–1.

Unlike some of the organizations discussed later, governments do not belong to the IASC—it is a private-sector body with representatives from professional accounting organizations. In one sense the IASC is an international counterpart to the U.S.'s FASB.

The International Accounting Standards Committee is governed by a board consisting of representatives from 13 countries, including the founding member countries listed earlier. Before approving a *Standard,* the board exposes it for public comment for six months and seeks input from all IASC member bodies. The board meets several times a year in a different city in order to secure a variety of viewpoints. For example, meetings have been held in Sydney, Seoul, Budapest, and Madrid.

Compliance with IASC *Standards* is voluntary, since the IASC has no power to enforce them. Nevertheless, support for the IASC and recognition of its *Standards* are growing around the world. The IASC is increasingly viewed as an effective voice for defining acceptable "world class" accounting principles. For example, Japan began requiring financial statements prepared on a "consolidated" basis after the IASC issued its initial pronouncement on the topic (see Chapter 6 for more details on consolidation of financial statements). The SEC, in the United States, allows foreign companies with shares traded in the United States to present cash flow statements in conformity with IAS 7 *(Cash Flow Statements)*. It accepts IASC treatment of goodwill amortization, business acquisitions, and translation of the financial statements of subsidiaries operating in hyperinflationary economies—all for registrants who are foreign companies.

The IASC's most ambitious project to date is its comparability project. Announced in 1989 as *Exposure Draft 32,* this undertaking is aimed at eliminating most of the choices between various alternative accounting methods allowed under former IASs. Broad support exists for this project. Financial analysts, attorneys, bankers, labor unions, and other business groups have expressed approval of the process involved. IOSCO (defined in the following section), a key international agency, has voted to support IASC and the comparability project. All changes contemplated by the comparability project will have been finalized by the end of 1996. Implementation of these changes involved selected revisions of existing IASs.

The list of MNCs presently preparing consolidated financial statements in conformity with IASs exceeds the 100 mark and is steadily growing. The new IASC Secretary-General, Sir Bryan Carsberg, aims to have full IOSCO acceptance of a core set of IASC standards by 1999. The two agencies are working together closely toward this goal.[2]

Regarding cooperation with national standard setters, the IASC has launched a joint project with the Canadians (on financial instruments), a concurrent project with the United States (earnings per share), and a Canada/U.S./IASC coordinated effort (segment reporting). It is also of interest that beginning in 1995, several

---

[2]"An Interview with Sir Bryan Carsberg, Secretary-General of the International Accounting Standards Committee," *Accounting Horizons* (March 1996), pp. 110–17.

EXHIBIT 3–2   IFAC's Mission Statement

The International Federation of Accountants (IFAC) is the worldwide organization for the accountancy profession. The mission of IFAC is the development and enhancement of the profession to enable it to provide the public interest with services of consistently high quality.

To achieve this goal, IFAC will pursue the following objectives:

- Enhance the standards and development of the profession by issuing technical and professional guidance and by promoting the adoption of IFAC and IASC pronouncements.
- Promote the profession's role, responsibilities, and achievements in advancing the interests of member bodies and in serving the public interest.
- Foster a strong and cohesive profession by providing leadership on emerging issues, coordinating with regional organizations and member bodies and assisting them to achieve strategic objectives.
- Assist with the formation and development of national and regional organizations that serve the interests of accountants in public practice, commerce, industry, public sector, and education.
- Liaise with international organizations to influence the development of efficient capital markets and international trade in services.

SOURCE: IFAC, *Annual Report 1993.*

discussion memoranda (i.e., *Special Reports*) have been published as joint efforts between the Australian, Canadian, United Kingdom, and U.S. Standards Boards and the IASC. This bodes well for closer coordination among national accounting standard setters and between standard setters and the IASC.

International Federation of Accountants

The *International Federation of Accountants* (IFAC) was formed in 1977 to develop a worldwide accountancy profession. Its purpose is similar to that of the AICPA except on a global basis; that is, it is mainly concerned with professional accountants rather than accounting principles. Its members are drawn from professional accounting bodies in nearly 80 countries. Exhibit 3–2 shows IFAC's mission statement and the related action goals.

IFAC's International Auditing Practices Committee issues *International Standards on Auditing* (ISAs), designed to harmonize the way audits are conducted worldwide. ISAs issued to date include *Standard No. 1* on the objective and scope of an audit, *No. 8* on audit evidence, and *No. 25* on materiality and audit risk. Thirty-one existing ISAs were codified into a single publication in 1994. Its Education Committee works toward harmonizing the qualifications for becoming a professional accountant, while its Ethics Committee tries to make the codes of professional ethics in various countries more compatible with each other. For example, the Education Committee has published a comprehensive *Guideline (No. 9)* dealing with the education and training needed to become an accountant. This *Guideline* was under revision in 1995. The Ethics Committee has developed the *Code of Ethics for Professional Accountants,* which covers, among other items, accountants' integrity, objectivity, and independence, as well as the confidentiality of information obtained during the course of an audit.

Every five years IFAC organizes a World Congress of Accountants, the 14th of which was held in 1992 in Washington, D.C., and the 15th will be held in Paris, France, in 1997. Eighteen countries are represented on IFAC's governing council, and general assemblies of the organization are conducted every two and a half years. Council terms are also two and a half years.

Acceptance of IFAC pronouncements received a major boost when the International Organization of Securities Commissions (IOSCO) voted in 1992 to accept ISAs for purposes of multinational registrations and filings with securities commissions. The strength and influence of IOSCO derives from the fact that the organization is comprised of senior securities administrators from about 50 countries. The SEC is a member of IOSCO.

Also in 1992 IFAC forged a strong linkage with the International Organization of Supreme Audit Institutes (INTOSAI). This organization brings together top public-sector auditors from most of the world's independent nations. Nearly all UN member countries are also INTOSAI members. The organization has just begun to issue public-sector auditing standards—which is the linkage to IFAC.

United Nations

The interest of the United Nations (UN) in accounting and reporting reflects its wider interest in the effects of multinational corporations on the world economy. In 1982 an advisory group reaffirmed a set of *Guidelines* issued in 1977 listing financial and nonfinancial disclosures that multinational corporations ought to provide. Among the suggested financial disclosures are an income statement and balance sheet, expenditures on research and development, and the amounts of new investments in fixed assets. Recommended nonfinancial disclosures include information about employment and transfer pricing policies. While these *Guidelines* have yet to be adopted by the UN itself, they will likely serve as a checklist for countries to use in requiring information of multinationals located within their borders.

One should recognize that the United Nations is a political forum to which nearly every nation belongs. It is heavily represented by developing countries, which are not very industrialized and are often suspicious of the heavily industrialized countries (such as the United States) and their large, multinational corporations. Developing countries are particularly concerned about being exploited. Thus, an implicit objective of the UN disclosure *Guidelines* is to get multinational corporations to provide sufficient information so governments of developing nations can better judge their social performance.

Current financial accounting and reporting endeavors at the UN are carried out by its Intergovernmental Working Group of Experts on International Standards of Accounting and Reporting. This Working Group holds annual working sessions in March of each year. The proceedings of each such session are published as *International Accounting and Reporting Issues: 19xx Review.* For example, the *1993 Review* numbers 245 pages and contains a wealth of information on the theme for the session covered, namely "Global Review of the State of Accounting and Auditing Education and Training." Aside from summaries and conclusions, the *1993 Review* contains 66 individual country reports plus coverage of topics like "Accountants as Contributors to Economic Development and Efficiency" (the latter appearing on p. 28 of the *1993 Review*).

Organization for Economic Cooperation and Development

The *Organization for Economic Cooperation and Development* (OECD) is an organization of 24 governments of nearly all industrialized countries: Australia, Austria, Belgium, Canada, Denmark, Finland, France, Germany, Greece, Iceland, Ireland, Italy, Japan, Luxembourg, the Netherlands, New Zealand, Norway, Portugal, Spain, Sweden, Switzerland, Turkey, the United Kingdom, and the United States. Its purpose is to foster economic growth and development in member countries, and it principally acts as a vehicle whereby member countries consult with each other about general economic matters that concern them all, such as balance of payments or exchange rate problems.

In 1976 the OECD issued a code of conduct for multinational corporations that includes guidelines for voluntary disclosures of financial information. More recently, the OECD began looking at the accounting principles in member countries with a view toward encouraging greater harmonization and comparability of accounting and financial reporting. The OECD intends to act only as a catalyst, however. It has neither the resources nor the desire to actually write generally accepted accounting principles. OECD conferences and seminars are high quality international accounting events. Among its various publications is the *Accounting Standards Harmonization* series (e.g., *No. 6,* "New Financial Instruments," 1991).

REGIONAL ORGANIZATIONS

European Union (EU)

The EU, formerly known as the European Community (EC) and at its start as the European Common Market, was formed in 1957 by the Treaty of Rome and now has 15 members: Austria, Belgium, Denmark, Finland, France, Germany, Greece, Ireland, Italy, Luxembourg, the Netherlands, the United Kingdom, Spain, Sweden, and Portugal. The EU's major aims are the free flow of goods, persons, and capital; a customs union; and harmonization of laws. To encourage capital movement and capital formation, the EU is harmonizing the generally accepted accounting principles of member countries. In order to achieve this objective, the EU has issued various *Directives,* which are EU laws that member states are obligated to incorporate into their own national laws. Since the EU harmonization efforts have the full weight of law behind them, the provisions are mandatory for any company doing business there. Anyone with business dealings in Europe (accountants included) should monitor EU developments as they unfold.

Recall from Chapter 1 that there are some fundamental dissimilarities among the EU countries. A very important one is the distinction between a legalistic/ nonlegalistic accounting orientation. The legalistic orientation produces highly prescriptive, detailed, and procedural accounting, while nonlegalistic accounting is more innovative and adaptive to business situations. Another fundamental dissimilarity is the role accounting plays in society. Accounting in the Netherlands, United Kingdom, and Ireland is oriented toward the decision needs of investors and creditors. Determining profitability in order to judge how well management has run a company is the significant purpose of accounting. Accounting practices in Germany, Luxembourg, and Belgium are overly conservative and designed mainly to protect the interests of banks. France has uniform accounting designed to facilitate the decision making of government planners.

Four EU *Directives* have been issued that have major financial reporting consequences. They are

Fourth Directive, issued July 26, 1978, basically addressing format and content of financial statements ((i.e., constituting EU GAAP).

Directive to Publish Interim Financial Statements, issued February 15, 1982, calling for the publication of six months' interim financial reports within four months of the end of an accounting period.

Seventh Directive, issued June 13, 1983, comprehensively addressing the issue of consolidated financial statements (see Chapter 6).

Eighth Directive, issued April 10, 1984, covering various aspects of the qualifications of professionals authorized to carry out legally required (statutory) audits.

Both the *Fourth* and *Seventh Directives* contain provisions at variance with U.S. generally accepted accounting principles. The *Fourth Directive,* for instance, allows capitalization (and maximum five-year amortization periods) of research and development expenditures, and does not require cash flow statements. In the United States R&D costs are expensed outright, and cash flow statements are mandatory. Thus, for U.S. companies operating in the EU, new and different financial statements may be necessary to comply with these *Directives.*

Given the significantly different business environments and cultures among the EU member countries, it should not be surprising to find that the EU is experiencing some implementation problems with its accounting and financial reporting harmonization efforts. Italy finally adopted the *Fourth Directive* in

1992. This was 14 years after ratification! Also, all EU *Directives* allow various alternative choices to each adopting member country. For example, abridged financial reporting is allowed in some EU jurisdictions but not in others. Segment disclosures (*SFAS No. 14* in the United States) are optional in all member countries. Therefore the implementation status of each *Directive* in each EU country is as important as the *Directive* itself. The EU Commission established an *Accounting Advisory Forum* in 1991 to offer (so far nonbinding) advice on issues not covered by the *Directives*.

Nevertheless, developments in the EU bear watching. For reasons mentioned above, there is some question of how well the EU accounting harmonization effort has worked out. One consequence of this questioning is perceptibly closer working relations between the EU and IASC.

Other Regional Organizations

The *African Accounting Council* was formed in 1979 with the aims of harmonizing accounting practices, upgrading accounting education, and exchanging ideas among member nations. Its members are the *governments* of 27 African countries. National *professional* accounting institutes in 14 African countries have joined to form the *Eastern, Central and Southern African Federation of Accountants* (ECSAFA). The *Asociación Interamericana de Contabilidad* is comprised of accountancy bodies from 21 nations in North and South America, though it is primarily concerned with Latin American accounting issues. Technical accounting papers are presented at group conferences every two or three years. The *ASEAN Federation of Accountants* is an accounting organization of the seven members of the *Association of Southeast Asian Nations* (ASEAN)—Brunei, Indonesia, Malaysia, Philippines, Singapore, Thailand, and Vietnam. Its purpose is to advance the status of the accounting profession in these nations, but it eventually expects to reconcile divergent accounting principles among its members.

The *Confederation of Asian and Pacific Accountants* has representatives from the accounting bodies of some 20 Pacific Rim nations. Its purpose is to develop a coordinated regional accounting profession, and one day it expects to tackle harmonizing accounting standards. The major professional accounting association in Europe is now the *Fédération des Experts Comptables Européens* (FEE—Federation of European Accountants). FEE was established in 1986 as the successor organization of two groups, one with EU ties and the other Europewide. There is a tradition of extensive study groups, conferencing, and publishing activities for the European associations. For example, in 1995 FEE published its *FEE 1994 Investigation of Emerging Accounting Areas*. The database for this study is 10 trend-setting quoted companies from each of 10 EU and 5 other European countries. It is reasonable to expect significant FEE involvement in international accounting matters.

These six organizations are regional in scope and primarily concerned with the accounting profession rather than accounting practices. However, some eventually expect to harmonize accounting practices at a regional level. The activities of the regional accounting organizations have as their main thrust the exchange of information and discussion of common problems at conferences.

HARMONIZATION SCENARIOS[3]

Harmonization of accounting, auditing, and financial reporting has many dimensions—regional versus global, voluntary versus mandated, piecemeal versus comprehensive, political versus professional, and so forth. What will emerge as the most likely development path for the near future? There are three possibilities.

One scenario is the use of *bilateral agreements*. Under this approach, two or more countries agree to recognize each other's national standards on a reciprocal basis. This would have to be done politically and is likely to be difficult to achieve where national standards differ greatly (e.g., between Japan and the United States).

Mutual recognition on a regional level is a second possibility, for instance, between the EU and NAFTA. Here the clout of regional economies would come to bear—again mainly through political channels. This approach also places accounting professionals and their professional organizations in secondary roles.

A third scenario places harmonization at the doorsteps of *private, professional groups* such as IASC and IFAC. They hammer out internal agreements on key issues and then negotiate acceptance with regulators and other political bodies.

The accounting world of the 1990s contains actual examples of each of these three scenarios. At the time of this writing, it appears that the third alternative enjoys a slight edge. But all harmonization efforts require much time and energy, and all are fraught with pitfalls. Moreover, harmonization is a continuous process. Former IASC Chairman Arthur Wyatt observed:

> We all must understand that harmonization is not an effort to remake the accounting and auditing world in the image of any one culture. While it is clear that emerging standards in both accounting and auditing reflect the needs of those economies that rely on a diverse source of capital providers, those standards will hopefully emerge as a blending of the best standards found in practice and a rejection of notions tried and found wanting. The fact that the standards that are emerging will require some adjustments to practices found in all societies should be of some comfort to those who fear the process is dominated by a single culture.[4]

---

[3]This section is adapted from the newsletter *IASC Insight,* December 1991, p. 5.
[4]*Ibid.*

CONCLUSION

The fact that so many groups are involved in accounting harmonization efforts indicates sizable support for the effort. The question of whether harmonization of either accounting principles or auditing practices is necessary may seem silly. The basic rationale for harmonization was expressed earlier. Differences in accounting principles mean that the financial statements of companies from different countries not only look different but impart different information. This basic lack of comparability may cause investors and creditors to make poor decisions. Similarly, if accountants of different nations do not perform audits the same way, then the assurances they give about the reliability of financial information cannot be regarded equally by financial statement users.

Nevertheless, some accountants question the desirability of an organized accounting harmonization effort. They argue that artificially imposing international harmonization on disparate business environments will strip accounting of its basic utility. So, is the work of the IASC, IFAC, EU, and others useless and wasteful? The answer to that depends on whether one believes that accounting principles and auditing practices can be harmonized on their own by the "invisible hand" of free market forces.

Harmonization efforts will be successful to the extent that they reflect environmental similarities among countries. Harmonization cannot be artificially imposed from above; there must be support from below. The regional and international harmonization efforts will continue. It seems reasonable that the combined wisdom of several nations' accountants can produce better accounting and auditing practices than can a single nation alone.

STUDY QUESTIONS

1. What is the difference between accounting standards and auditing standards? How are they interrelated?

2. Which of the organizations described in Chapter 3 are concerned with harmonizing accounting standards? Which with harmonizing auditing standards?

3. What is the basic rationale for harmonizing accounting and auditing standards internationally?

4. Chapter 3 describes IASC and IFAC. How are these two international accounting organizations different from one another? In what respects are they very similar?

5. Identify three accounting topics for which U.S. GAAP differ from corresponding EU *Directives* requirements.

6. Why do some accountants question the necessity of an organized accounting harmonization effort?

7. The text describes three different harmonization scenarios. Identify and describe briefly one other such scenario.

CASES

Accounting Diplomacy

Jonathan Dykes is an accounting analyst working as a member of the strategic planning group of Beltor, Inc., a Fortune 200 U.S. MNC. At a typical weekly planning meeting of the group, Claire Salter, the group's manager, is unhappy about a new assignment from senior management. They just received a draft proposal from the Advisory Council on NAFTA of the U.S. Department of Commerce urging that NAFTA enter into a mutual recognition agreement with the EU regarding GAAP. Senior management wants an analysis brief on this proposal—ASAP!

"One would think these NAFTA experts have more important things to do than worry about accounting rules," fumes Claire. "I can't understand why accounting requirements are all of a sudden so important internationally."

Jon takes issue with her view. "Maybe GAAP rules can be negotiated more easily than a lot of other things that impact governmental budgets," he says. "And an accounting agreement might serve as a model for other 'sticky' negotiating points." "Remember, Claire," Jon grins broadly, "Beltor does support IASs and says so in its annual report." Given his comments, Jon is assigned to draft an outline of the needed analysis brief.

Questions

1. What does "mutual recognition" mean in terms of international harmonization of accounting?

2. Given the predominantly legalistic accounting environment in the EU and the nonlegalistic accounting environment in the NAFTA countries, is "mutual recognition" the best way to achieve accounting harmonization between the EU and NAFTA?

3. "Mutual recognition" is relatively less costly for preparers of financial information and more costly for information users. Why?

4. Is "mutual recognition" consistent with Beltor's support of IASs? Explain why or why not.

Going International

Bud Reynolds is at a business luncheon with Lisa Avila. He is the chief financial officer (CFO) of Cytex, Inc., and she is a Big Six partner in charge of Cytex's independent audit. They are discussing the makeup of this year's Cytex annual report.

"Our company is becoming more and more internationally oriented," observes Bud. "About 40 percent of our sales are outside the country. We have listed our stock on six different foreign stock exchanges, and we borrow a lot of money from international banks. Maybe the time has come to refer to international accounting standards in our annual report."

Lisa cautions by urging careful consideration. She explains, "In the United States, we have no control over IASs. What happens if they come up with a standard simply unacceptable to Cytex? Will you then drop the reference to international standards? That would really be a red flag to financial analysts all over."

"We understand that," Bud counters. "But our research indicates that CPC International, Exxon, FMC Corporation, IBM, and General Electric, for example, refer to IASs in their respective annual reports. Here is FMC's 1993 annual report version (p. 62):

Management Report on Financial Statements

The statements have been prepared in conformity with accounting principles generally accepted in the United States and are generally consistent with standards issued by the International Accounting Standards Committee.

"I know. I know," says Lisa. "It's your annual report for sure. But I don't really see any benefits from referencing IASs—I see mainly risks. Please think carefully before you jump."

Questions

1. Do you support Bud or Lisa on this issue? Defend your answer briefly.
2. What are the likely benefits to Cytex from publicly referring to IASC pronouncements?
3. How do two other U.S. companies reference IASs in their annual reports? (Hint: You may wish to use a computerized database in your business administration library to answer this question.)
4. Should the SEC require all publicly traded U.S. companies to refer to IASs in their respective annual reports? Why or why not?

International Harmonization: Pro or Con?

You are provided the following arguments for and against establishing a harmonized set of international accounting standards:

Pro:

Harmonizing accounting standards internationally will improve the comparability of accounting information around the world and thereby eliminate one source of misunderstanding in transnational financial reporting. More comparability will better the analysis of financial statements; this will, in turn, lower interest rates and improve resource allocation. A single set of financial accounting standards will also save corporations time and money, since they will no longer have to prepare multiple sets of financial statements. Finally, establishing international standards will raise the quality of accounting in many countries.

Con:

Harmonized international accounting standards are unnecessary, since the worldwide competition for investment funds is propelling harmonization to the extent that investors desire it. Corporations in need of funds are compelled to provide financial statement users—the resource providers—with what they want or else pay a penalty in the form of higher interest rates or lower common stock prices. If user needs are similar internationally, then harmonization will result as a matter of course, without an organized effort. If they are not, then requiring a single set of accounting practices may actually worsen the situation. Accounting is relevant only when it is responsive to the environment in which it operates. Imposing harmonization could very well strip accounting of its usefulness in many situations.

Question

Write two paragraphs stating your position on the desirability of establishing a harmonized set of international accounting standards.

ADDITIONAL READINGS

de Reyna, R. "UNCTAD's Activities in Accountancy Development." *IFAC Newsletter* (June 1995), pp. 5–6. (Note: UNCTAD is the United Nations Conference on Trade and Development.)

Gould, J. D. "A Second Opinion on International Accounting Standards." *CPA Journal* (January 1995), pp. 50–52.

"International Access to U.S. Capital Markets—An AAA Forum on Accounting Policy." *Accounting Horizons* (March 1996), pp. 75–94.

International Capital Markets Group. *Harmonization of International Accounting Standards.* London, U.K.: International Bar Association, 1992, 67 pp. (Note: IFAC cooperates closely with the Group.)

Van Hulle, K., and K. U. Leuven. "Harmonization of Accounting Standards: A View from the European Community." *European Accounting Review* (May 1992), pp. 161–72.

Wyatt, A. R. "An Era of Harmonization." *Journal of International Financial Management and Accounting* (Spring 1992), pp. 63–68.

Wyatt, A. R., and J. F. Yospe." Wake-Up Call to American Business: International Accounting Standards Are on the Way." *Journal of Accountancy* (July 1993), pp. 80–82, 84–85.

4

FINANCIAL REPORTING IN THE INTERNATIONAL ENVIRONMENT

LEARNING OBJECTIVES

1. Define transnational financial reporting and explain what has caused the phenomenon.

2. Understand the difficulties involved when accounting information is transmitted internationally.

3. Identify actions that investors can take when they receive financial reports prepared using an unfamiliar language, monetary unit, or set of accounting standards.

4. Distinguish five approaches that multinational corporations take to accommodate foreign readers of their financial reports and evaluate the advantages and disadvantages of each approach.

5. Appreciate why financial statement users must be careful when comparing accounting information of companies from different countries.

Financial accounting practices in a country are determined by a number of environmental variables that interact in a complex way. As discussed in Chapter 1, these variables include the following:

1. Relationship between business and the provider(s) of capital.

2. Political and economic ties with other countries.

3. Legal system.
4. Level of inflation.
5. Size and complexity of business enterprises, sophistication of management and the financial community, and general levels of education.
6. Culture.

Companies prepare the financial statements in their annual report directed toward the needs of their primary users. Financial statements not only look different but report different information, depending on whether the primary user group is, for example, the investor, the creditor, or the government. Moreover, even if companies in different nations orient their financial statements toward similar user groups, there are still likely to be differences in accounting practices and in the way that the annual reports appear. For example, companies from the United States and Great Britain orient their annual reports to the decision needs of investors, but there are still a number of differences in the two countries' accounting and reporting practices.

Transnational financial reporting refers to reporting across national boundaries or, more specifically, to reporting financial results to user groups located in a country other than the one where the company is headquartered. A U.S. company is engaged in transnational financial reporting whenever it sends an annual report to a citizen of another country. If you write to a German company and receive its annual report, transnational financial reporting has occurred.

Transnational financial reporting has been encouraged by two phenomena. The first may be termed the *global financing strategies* of multinational corporations. Global financing includes (1) listing a company's capital stock on stock exchanges outside the home country, (2) selling bonds in various countries, and (3) arranging for loans with foreign banks. Multinational corporations no longer look exclusively to the stock markets, bond markets, and banks of their respective home countries to raise capital. They go wherever the money is most available and cheapest. The second phenomenon is *transnational investing;* those with funds to invest buy the stocks and bonds of foreign companies in addition to those in their own nation. Thus, the multinational corporation (as the resource user) and the investor/creditor (as the resource provider) are responsible for these twin phenomena.

A truly global financial market began to emerge in the 1980s, and it has continued to grow ever since. The increase in international financial transactions is rather startling. For example, consider the following: (1) Cross-border sales and purchases of U.S. Treasury bonds rose from $30 billion to $500 billion between 1983 and 1993. (2) In 1973 daily currency exchange trading worldwide averaged only $10 to $20 billion. In 1983 it was around $60 billion. By 1992 it had grown to $900 billion a day and is estimated to be $1.3 trillion now. (3) The total value of the world's publicly held companies doubled in just four years, growing from $10 trillion at year-end 1990 to $20 trillion at the end of 1994. (4) It is estimated that the *total* stock of financial assets traded in the global capital market increased from $5 trillion in 1980 to $35 trillion in 1992, and it is forecast that the amount will rise to $83 trillion by the year 2000.[1] Transnational financial reporting presents a unique problem to both the multinational corporation (as the information provider) and the investor/creditor (as the information user). When a company prepares a financial report for users in its own country, it can reasonably assume that the users understand (1) the general orientation of financial accounting in that country, (2) the particular accounting practices that the company employs, (3) the language in which the annual report is written, and (4) the currency unit used to present the financial statements. However, any or all of these four items may be different when a company sends a financial report to users in another country. More and more corporations and investors are facing transnational financial reporting problems as both financing and investing are increasingly globalized.

RESPONSES BY USERS

Exhibit 4–1 is the 1994 income statement for the German retailer, Douglas Holding. Suppose that a friend of yours suggests that Douglas would be a good company to invest in, and so you write Douglas, ask for, and receive its annual report. What would immediately strike you after opening the annual report is that it is written entirely in German. In looking at the financial statements, you also notice that all of the amounts are expressed in deutsche marks (DM). The report looks different from U.S. companies' reports (compare Exhibit 4–1 to Exhibit 4–2, the 1994 income statement of Coca-Cola Company), so you may also suspect that Douglas uses German accounting practices. Unless you can read German, know German accounting practices, and are familiar with the mark, you will probably have a difficult time understanding Douglas's annual report. As a result, you may decide not to invest in Douglas since it would be "too much trouble" to extract the information you need from the annual report. You may very well pass up a good investment opportunity, although you will never know it.

Of course, you may also take other courses of action. One would be to get someone to translate the report into English, while you learn all you can about German accounting practices. (Several large CPA firms publish such information, and books are also available on the subject.) At a minimum, this choice would be time-consuming and could even cost you money if, for example, you had to pay someone for the translation. And having done this, the accounting information would still not be directly comparable to that of a U.S. company. In most cases, it is impossible for a *user* to restate financial accounting information so that it conforms to the accounting practices of another country. Another course of action

---

[1]"Who's in the Driver's Seat? A Survey of the World Economy," *The Economist,* October 7, 1995, pp. 9, 10; and "NYSE: The Global Exchange," *The Exchange,* January 1995, p. 1.

EXHIBIT 4–1 Douglas Holding Income Statement

Konzern-Gewinn- und Verlustrechnung

	Anhang	1994 DM	Vorjahr TDM
1. Umsatzerlöse			
a) Bruttoumsatzerlöse	18	3.511.901.590,59	3.451.917
b) in den Umsatzerlösen enthaltene Umsatzsteuer		− 431.711.260,62	− 424.240
		3.080.190.329,97	**3.027.677**
2. Sonstige betriebliche Erträge	19	202.059.698,88	185.335
3. Aufwendungen für Roh-, Hilfs- und Betriebsstoffe und für bezogene Waren		−1.733.919.254,06	−1.697.704
4. Personalaufwand	20	− 638.332.941,76	− 613.348
5. Abschreibungen auf immaterielle Vermögensgegenstände des Anlagevermögens und Sachanlagen	21	− 120.232.864,58	− 135.663
6. Sonstige betriebliche Aufwendungen	22	− 584.984.305,27	− 531.955
7. Beteiligungsergebnis	23	738.308,66	507
8. Abschreibungen auf Finanzanlagen und auf Wertpapiere des Umlaufvermögens		− 18.666,37	− 9
9. Zinsergebnis	24	− 5.236.179,46	− 7.494
10. Ergebnis der gewöhnlichen Geschäftstätigkeit		**200.264.126,01**	**227.346**
11. Steuern vom Einkommen und vom Ertrag	25	− 83.094.032,68	− 128.096
12. Sonstige Steuern	26	− 10.656.823,69	− 10.281
13. Jahresüberschuß		**106.513.269,64**	**88.969**
14. Gewinnvortrag aus dem Vorjahr		142.974,00	199
15. Einstellung in die Gewinnrücklagen		− 53.306.110,72	− 32.632
16. Gewinnanteile anderer Gesellschafter		− 12.983.198,85	− 16.330
17. Verlustanteile anderer Gesellschafter		33.065,93	94
18. Konzerngewinn		**40.400.000,00**	**40.300**

---

is to forgo trying to understand the Douglas annual report and instead rely on the advice of an expert, such as a stockbroker. In fact, investment firms employ people to analyze foreign companies' annual reports and to make recommendations about which companies seem to be good ones to invest in. Such analysis involves a high level of sophistication.

Many accountants are concerned about the effects that an unfamiliar language, monetary unit, and accounting practices may have on investors and creditors. They fear that resource allocation decisions may be based on misunderstanding and, as a result, that these decisions may not be optimal. This is one reason why accountants are trying to harmonize accounting practices around the world. (This effort is discussed in Chapter 3.)

EXHIBIT 4–2   Coca-Cola Company Income Statement

The Coca-Cola Company and Subsidiaries

CONSOLIDATED STATEMENTS OF INCOME

Year Ended December 31,	*1994*	*1993*	*1992*
(In millions except per share data)			
Net Operating Revenues	**$16,172**	$13,957	$13,074
Cost of goods sold	**6,167**	5,160	5,055
Gross Profit	**10,005**	8,797	8,019
Selling, administrative and general expenses	**6,297**	5,695	5,249
Operating Income	**3,708**	3,102	2,770
Interest income	**181**	144	164
Interest expense	**199**	168	171
Equity income	**134**	91	65
Other income (deductions)-net	**(96)**	4	(82)
Gain on issuance of stock by Coca-Cola Amatil	**—**	12	—
Income before Income Taxes and Changes in Accounting Principles	**3,728**	3,185	2,746
Income taxes	**1,174**	997	863
Income before Changes in Accounting Principles	**2,554**	2,188	1,883
Transition effects of changes in accounting principles			
Postemployment benefits	**—**	(12)	—
Postretirement benefits other than pensions			
Consolidated operations	**—**	—	(146)
Equity investments	**—**	—	(73)
Net Income	**$ 2,554**	$ 2,176	$ 1,664
Income per Share			
Before changes in accounting principles	**$ 1.98**	$ 1.68	$ 1.43
Transition effects of changes in accounting principles			
Postemployment benefits	**—**	(.01)	—
Postretirement benefits other than pensions			
Consolidated operations	**—**	—	(.11)
Equity investments	**—**	—	(.06)
Net Income per Share	**$ 1.98**	$ 1.67	$ 1.26
Average Shares Outstanding	**1,290**	1,302	1,317

See Notes to Consolidated Financial Statements.

RESPONSES BY MULTINATIONAL CORPORATIONS

What about multinational corporations? Don't they have a role to play in trying to minimize misunderstandings? Indeed they do. Just as the users of financial reports may take various courses of action to overcome the problems associated with transnational financial reporting, so too do companies approach the problems in various ways. We can classify five approaches that multinational corporations take to accommodate foreign readers of their financial reports:

1. Do nothing.
2. Prepare convenience translations.
3. Prepare convenience statements.
4. Restate on a limited basis.
5. Prepare secondary financial statements.

Do Nothing

A corporation that sends the same financial statements to the foreign user as it does to the domestic user has done nothing to accommodate the foreign user. The financial statements are written in the native language and use the native currency unit and accounting principles. This approach puts the entire burden of understanding the financial report on the user, and it more or less assumes that the report for readers at home is useful to readers in other countries as well. The income statements for both Douglas Holding and Coca-Cola illustrate the do-nothing approach.

This is the most common approach of multinational corporations. Why would a corporation choose to seemingly ignore the information needs of its foreign readers? First of all, if the company raises very little capital outside the borders of its home country, the added expense of taking one of the other four approaches may not be worthwhile. While global financing is becoming more commonplace, many corporations that manufacture and sell products multinationally still raise most of their capital in a single nation—the home country. These companies perceive little benefit in preparing financial statements for readers other than those at home.

Second, some multinationals are able to entice international investment in their securities even though they leave their financial statements in their original form. One way they accomplish this is by selling large blocks of their securities directly to sophisticated overseas investors, such as pension funds. (Such sales are called *private placements*.) Or they may meet directly with investment firms, referred to earlier, to encourage the firms to recommend investments in their securities. Large investment firms, especially, employ analysts who are skilled at interpreting financial statements in their original form. Either way, these multinationals attempt to attract foreign investors without incurring the extra costs associated with the other forms of transnational financial reporting.

A third reason why a multinational corporation may choose to do nothing is that the language, currency unit, and accounting principles of its home country are well known and understood around the world. This is true, for example, of U.S. and U.K. companies, which almost always take this approach. U.S. and U.K. accounting standards are highly regarded and generally understood in other parts of the world. Both the U.S. dollar and the British pound are international currencies, and the English language is referred to as the "language of business." Thus, financial reports useful to native readers may very well be useful to foreign readers.

Prepare Convenience Translations

Convenience translations are financial statements translated into the foreign reader's language. They retain the home country's accounting principles and currency unit, however. Exhibit 4–3 (p. 62) is an example of this approach. It is the income statement of Cemex, a Mexican producer of cement, ready-mix concrete, and aggregate. Note that while the income statement is in English, it still uses Mexican accounting principles and the Mexican peso.

This approach is a relatively inexpensive accommodation to the foreign readership. Companies taking this approach typically prepare English, French, German, and, perhaps, Spanish language versions (as appropriate) of their annual reports. Presumably, any interested reader will understand one of these languages. The user is saved the bother of dealing with an unfamiliar language but must still understand another country's accounting practices and monetary unit. Companies usually prepare convenience translations in order to enlarge the scope of investor/creditor interest beyond the borders of their home country, and they are a low-cost alternative to the do-nothing approach. For this reason, convenience translations are also commonly used with private placements or to attract the attention of foreign investment firms, as discussed above.

Prepare Convenience Statements

This approach takes convenience translations one step further. Not only are the financial statements translated into the language of the foreign reader, but the monetary amounts are also expressed in the reader's currency. However, the accounting principles of the home country are still used to prepare the financial reports. Exhibit 4–4 (p. 63) is an example of a convenience statement for the Japanese electric wire and cable manufacturer, Sumitomo Electric Industries. (Notice that yen amounts are translated into dollars at the year-end exchange rate. An exchange rate is simply how much of one currency it takes to buy so much of another currency. At Sumitomo's year-end, the exchange rate was Yen 103.15 = U.S. $1.00, and so all amounts initially expressed in yen are simply divided by 103.15 to arrive at the dollar figures.)

Convenience statements often lose much of their foreign appearance, and unless users realize that another country's accounting principles are used, they will be misled into thinking that the financial statements can be directly compared to those of companies of their home country. Naturally, readers can comprehend their own language and currency better than those of another country, but they must still be able to understand the accounting practices used in the *company's home country* in order to derive actual meaning from the annual report.

EXHIBIT 4–3   Cemex Income Statement

Cemex, S.A. de C.V. and Subsidiaries

CONSOLIDATED STATEMENTS OF INCOME

(Thousands of constant new pesos of Mexico as of December 31, 1994)

	Years ended on December 31	
	1994	*1993*
Net sales	N$ 10,644,632	9,892,227
Cost of sales	(6,138,951)	(5,964,154)
Gross profit	4,505,681	3,928,073
Operating expenses:		
Administrative	(927,948)	(891,992)
Selling	(720,138)	(626,019)
Total operating expenses	(1,648,086)	(1,518,011)
Operating income	2,857,595	2,410,062
Comprehensive financing income (cost):		
Financial expenses	(1,820,512)	(1,673,696)
Financial income	1,771,794	1,101,249
Foreign exchange loss, net	(727,464)	(159,140)
Monetary position gain	694,733	816,677
Net comprehensive financing (cost) income	(81,449)	85,090
Other expenses, net	(674,652)	(343,518)
Income before income tax, business assets tax, employees' statutory profit sharing, extraordinary item and equity in income of affiliates	2,101,494	2,151,634
Income tax and business assets tax, net (note 16)	(49,790)	(80,701)
Employees' statutory profit sharing (note 16)	(42,984)	(44,463)
Total income tax, business assets tax and employees' statutory profit sharing	(92,774)	(125,164)
Income before extraordinary item and equity in income of affiliates	2,008,720	2,026,470
Extraordinary item:		
Benefit of tax loss carryforwards	—	62,855
Income before equity in income of affiliates	2,008,720	2,089,325
Equity in income of affiliates	123,130	25,060
Consolidated net income	2,131,850	2,114,385
Minority interest net income	228,110	330,912
Majority interest net income	N$ **1,903,740**	**1,783,473**

EXHIBIT 4–4   Sumitomo Electric Industries Income Statement

Sumitomo Electric Industries, Ltd.

CONSOLIDATED STATEMENTS OF INCOME

(For the years ended March 31, 1994 and 1993)

	Millions of yen		Thousands of U.S. dollars (Note 1)
	1994	*1993*	**1994**
Net Sales (Note 7)	**¥1,101,533**	¥1,136,711	**$10,678,943**
Cost of Sales (Note 7)	**902,300**	946,718	**8,747,455**
Gross profit	**199,233**	189,993	**1,931,488**
Selling, General and Administrative Expenses	**143,277**	133,375	**1,389,016**
Operating income	**55,956**	56,618	**542,472**
Other Income (Expenses):			
Interest and dividend income:			
Unconsolidated subsidiaries and affiliates	**2,722**	3,219	**26,389**
Other	**7,213**	9,535	**69,927**
Interest expense	**(16,245)**	(18,843)	**(157,489)**
Gain on sale of securities, net	**1,689**	3,135	**16,374**
Gain on sale of minority interest in joint venture	**1,779**	—	**17,247**
Gain on sale of land	**1,105**	687	**10,713**
Other, net (Note 10)	**1,202**	(1,282)	**11,653**
	(535)	(3,549)	**(5,186)**
Income before Income Taxes	55,421	53,069	537,286
Provision for income taxes (Note 8):			
Current	**(25,016)**	(25,492)	**(242,521)**
Deferred	**(692)**	(42)	**(6,709)**
Minority interest in net income of consolidated subsidiaries	**(4,071)**	(4,075)	**(39,467)**
Amortization of consolidation difference	**269**	319	**2,608**
Equity in undistributed net income of unconsolidated subsidiaries and affiliates	**3,621**	5,281	**35,104**
Net Income	**¥ 29,532**	¥ 29,060	**$ 286,301**

	Yen		U.S. dollars (Note 1)
Per Share of Common Stock			
Net income—Primary	**¥ 41.72**	¥ 41.06	**$ 0.404**
—Fully diluted	**39.83**	39.20	**0.386**

See accompanying Notes to Consolidated Financial Statements.

Restate on a Limited Basis

Compared to the first three, this approach represents a significant step toward accommodating the information needs of foreign readers. The disclosure is in the footnotes section of the company's financial statements. Normally, a company reconciles the net income amount shown on its income statement (prepared using its home-country accounting principles) to a net income amount based on the accounting principles of the reader's country, and often the company restates the balance sheet figures as well. However, sometimes a company restates only selected financial statement items. The annual report is typically written in the reader's language, but the currency is still that of the company's country.

Companies adopting this approach feel a clear need to communicate with their foreign annual report users. If a significant number of investors or creditors are located in other countries and if the company's accounting practices diverge significantly from those found in the reader's country, then the need is real. Companies following this approach must keep more than one set of accounting records. Fortunately computerized accounting systems can significantly reduce the cost and inconvenience of this approach!

A number of companies adopt this approach. The disclosure of the Swedish company Electrolux in Exhibit 4–5 (pp. 65–66) is illustrative. Notice that Electrolux reconciles both net income and shareholders' equity from Swedish to U.S. accounting principles. In addition, balance sheet amounts expressed using Swedish and U.S. accounting principles are shown side by side, on a comparative basis.

Prepare Secondary Financial Statements

This represents a further accommodation to the users of a company's financial statements. Companies continue to prepare their primary financial statements for the home user with the home country's language, currency, and accounting principles. For foreign readers, however, the company completely restates its financial report to conform to another set of accounting standards.

In practice, the other set of accounting standards used most often is either the generally accepted accounting principles (GAAP) of the United States or the standards of the International Accounting Standards Committee (IASC). U.S. GAAP are the most detailed and extensive in the world, and they are generally regarded as "world class" in quality. As a result, many multinationals choose U.S. GAAP when they prepare their secondary financial statements. However, as discussed in Chapter 3, the IASC is increasingly accepted as the voice for acceptable worldwide accounting standards. (As a practical matter, there are few instances where U.S. GAAP conflict with IASC Standards.) Japanese multinationals preparing secondary financial statements tend to use U.S. GAAP, whereas European multinationals that prepare secondary financial statements tend to adopt IASC Standards.

Secondary financial statements are meant for sophisticated, worldwide users. What makes a company go to so much trouble to accommodate the foreign reader? As with the previous approaches, it all comes down to whether the perceived benefits exceed the costs. Multinationals preparing secondary financial statements are normally from countries where accounting is legalistic in its orientation. For them, the British-American model of accounting, with its emphasis on

EXHIBIT 4–5 Electrolux Limited Restatement (from Swedish to U.S. Accounting Principles; Amounts in Millions of Swedish Krona)

18. Consolidated financial statements according to US GAAP

The consolidated accounts have been prepared in accordance with Swedish accounting standards, which differ in certain significant respects from US accounting principles (US GAAP). The most important differences are described below:

Write-ups on assets

In certain situations, Swedish standards permit write-ups of fixed assets in excess of acquisition cost. This does not normally accord with US GAAP.

Adjustment for acquisitions

In accordance with Swedish standards, the tax benefit arising from application of tax-loss carry-forwards in acquired companies is deducted by the Group from the current year's tax costs. According to US GAAP, this tax benefit should be booked as a retroactive adjustment of the value of acquired assets.

Pensions

According to the American recommendations for pensions known as FAS 87 (Employers' Accounting for Pensions), future salary increases, inflation and other factors must be taken into account for computation of the projected benefit obligation. The computed Swedish provision for PRI pensions is not adjusted for future salary increases, but this is offset by the lower discounting rate applied for computation of the provisions for PRI pensions in comparison with FAS 87. The initial difference arising from the first application of FAS 87 (January 1, 1989) is amortized over the future average employment period, so that the effect on net income is insignificant. Other important differences have been adjusted in accordance with US GAAP.

Other benefits

In addition to pensions, some of the Group's subsidiaries, principally in the US, provide employees with benefits in the form of health care and life insurance subsequent to retirement. Recommendation No. 106 of the US Financial Accounting Standards Board (Employers' Accounting for Postretirement Benefits Other Than Pensions), issued in 1990, requires that the estimated future commitment for these benefits be reported as a liability. The Electrolux Group has applied these recommendations as of 1993.

Securities

According to Swedish standards, holdings of debt and equity securities should be reported according to the lowest-value principle. According to FAS 115 (Accounting for Certain Investments in Debt and Equity Securities), these holdings should be classified with respect to intention, i.e. if they are intended to be traded, if they are to be retained until maturity, or if they are in an intermediate category. Valuation and reporting of income differ according to the classification of the securities. For Electrolux, this means that certain securities must be reported at market value in the balance sheet, while the difference between market and acquisition value must be

taken directly to equity, according to US GAAP. In connection with the sale of these securities, the change in value previously reported directly against equity will be reported in the income statement.

Deferred taxes

Taxation and financial reporting are affected during different periods by certain items. Electrolux reports deferred taxes on the most important timing differences, which refer mainly to untaxed reserves, with due consideration in certain cases for the future fiscal effects of tax-loss carry-forwards. US GAAP requires reporting of fiscal effects for all significant differences and tax-loss carry-forwards, with the proviso that deferred tax assets may be reported only if it is probable that the tax benefit will be utilized.

As indicated below, new accounting principles have been applied for taxes as of January 1, 1993. The new recommendation FAS 109 (Accounting for Income Taxes) differs from previously applied principles mainly in that fiscal effects are reported on the basis of the tax rate that will apply at the future date when taxation occurs. The principles applied previously involved reporting fiscal effects on the basis of the tax rates applicable on the date when the difference arose.

Timing differences

According to Swedish accounting principles, provisions for costs referring to a shutdown are booked when the decision is made to shut down the plant. In 1994, a statement by FASB's Emerging Issues Task Force led to a revision of US GAAP with reference to recognition of such costs as liabilities. The new US GAAP rules require meeting additional criteria before making provisions for severance pay and other costs related to shutdowns. Therefore, compliance with US GAAP requires eliminating certain provisions that have been made in accordance with Swedish accounting standards.

Changes in accounting principles

In the Electrolux consolidated accounts according to US GAAP, accounting principles were changed as of January 1, 1993 with regard to income taxes, pension benefits and employee benefits other than pensions. The accumulated post-tax non-recurring effect of these changes was reported in a separate item in the income statement for 1993 as "Effects of changes in accounting principles". In accordance with Swedish accounting principles, the accumulated effect of the changes was reported directly against the Group's opening equity. None of the changes in accounting principles had any effect on liquidity.

The accumulated effect of the changes in accounting principles that was reported in the income statement according to US GAAP amounted in 1993 to SEK −150m and comprised SEK 694m referring to income taxes, SEK −881m referring to employee benefits other than pensions, and SEK 37m referring to pensions.

continued

presenting useful information to investors and creditors, is more likely to attract widespread international investment than is their home country's legalistic model of accounting. (IASC Standards and, of course, U.S. GAAP reflect the British-American model of accounting discussed in Chapter 1.)

Exhibit 4–6 (p. 67) is the 1995 consolidated income statement of Komatsu Ltd., the Japanese heavy equipment manufacturer. Notice that three years' worth of data are presented in Japanese yen, while the 1995 amounts are translated into U.S. dollars using the year-end exchange rate. Exhibit 4–6 also reproduces

EXHIBIT 4–5 *(concluded)*

Application of US GAAP would have the following approximate effects on consolidated net income, shareholders' equity and the balance sheet:

A. *Consolidated net income*

	1994 SEKm	1993 SEKm
Net income as reported in the consolidated income statement	**4,830**	584
Adjustments before taxes:		
Acquisitions	**131**	84
Timing differences	**430**	—
Other	**46**	−21
Taxes	**218**	−123
Approximate net income according to US GAAP, before changes in accounting principles	**5,655**	524
Effect of changes in accounting principles	**—**	−150
Approximate net income according to US GAAP, after changes in accounting principles	**5,655***	374
Approximate net income per share according to US GAAP, before changes in accounting principles, SEK	**77.20**	7.20
Approximate net income per share according to US GAAP, after changes in accounting principles, SEK (no. of shares in 1994 and 1993: 73,233,916)	**77.20***	5.10

*) Net income includes a capital gain of approximately SEK 2,665m (SEK 36.40 per share).
The corresponding amount according to Swedish accounting principles is SEK 2,635m (SEK 36.00 per share).

B. *Shareholders' equity*

	1994 SEKm	1993 SEKm
Shareholders' equity as reported in the consolidated balance sheet	**20,465**	16,853
Adjustments:		
Revaluation of fixed assets	**−164**	−173
Acquisitions	**−1,084**	−1,211
Pensions	**−327**	−358
Securities	**165**	235
Timing differences	**430**	—
Taxes	**1**	−357
Approximate shareholders' equity according to US GAAP	**19,486**	14,989

C. *Balance sheet*
The table below summarizes the consolidated balance sheets prepared in accordance with Swedish accounting principles and US GAAP.

	According to Swedish principles		According to US GAAP	
	1994 SEKm	1993 SEKm	1994 SEKm	1993 SEKm
Current assets	**55,700**	47,670	**57,273**	50,738
Real estate, machinery and equipment	**23,257**	22,354	**23,023**	22,016
Shares and participations	**627**	1,120	**792**	1,355
Deferred taxes	**—**	455	**—**	140
Long-term receivables	**628**	530	**2,329**	810
Goodwill	**3,651**	5,108	**2,637**	4,020
Other assets	**320**	410	**604**	621
Total assets	**84,183**	77,647	**86,658**	79,700
Current liabilities	**35,963**	33,944	**37,058**	36,970
Long-term liabilities	**27,081**	26,460	**29,441**	27,351
Deferred taxes	**144**	—	**143**	—
Minority interests	**530**	390	**530**	390
Shareholders' equity	**20,465**	16,853	**19,486**	14,989
Total liabilities and shareholders' equity	**84,183**	77,647	**86,658**	79,700

Komatsu's footnote indicating that U.S. GAAP are used. Exhibit 4–7 (p. 68) is the 1994 consolidated income statement of the Swiss pharmaceutical company Roche. Two years' worth of data are presented in Swiss francs. The footnote describing the use of IASC Standards is also reproduced in Exhibit 4–7.

WHOSE ACCOUNTING PRINCIPLES?

Restating financial statements to another set of accounting standards, as in limited restatements and secondary financial statements, has its critics. Some believe that financial statements are meaningful only if they are consistent with the underlying environmental variables from which accounting in a company's home country is derived. (The variables affecting accounting development are discussed in Chapter 1.) According to this view, the first three forms of transnational financial reporting make more sense, since they retain the accounting principles of the company's home country. In essence, the argument is that the effects of business decisions, as reflected in financial statements, cannot be

EXHIBIT 4–6   Komatsu Income Statement

Komatsu Ltd. and Consolidated Subsidiaries

CONSOLIDATED STATEMENTS OF INCOME

(Years ended March 31, 1995, 1994, and 1993)

	Millions of yen			Translation into thousands of U.S. dollars (Note 1)
	1995	1994	1993	**1995**
Revenues				
Net sales	**¥918,910**	¥845,853	¥869,928	**$10,562,184**
Interest and other income	**35,911**	29,141	43,133	**412,770**
Total	**954,821**	874,994	913,061	**10,974,954**
Costs and expenses				
Cost of sales	**702,416**	649,512	662,408	**8,073,747**
Selling, general, and administrative	**200,232**	182,843	183,604	**2,301,517**
Interest	**24,174**	24,381	33,791	**277,862**
Other	**3,517**	4,325	2,501	**40,426**
Total	**930,339**	861,061	882,304	**10,693,552**
Income before income taxes, minority interests, equity in earnings, and cumulative effect of accounting changes	**24,482**	13,933	30,757	**281,402**
Income taxes (Notes 1 and 12):				
Current	**12,322**	17,209	19,788	**141,632**
Deferred	**2,192**	(4,309)	2,178	**25,195**
Total	**14,514**	12,900	21,966	**166,827**
Income before minority interests, equity in earnings, and cumulative effect of accounting changes	**9,968**	1,033	8,791	**114,575**
Minority interests in (income) losses of consolidated subsidiaries—net	**(23)**	1,219	648	**(264)**
Equity in earnings (losses) of affiliated companies—net	**280**	221	(6,402)	**3,218**
Income before cumulative effect of accounting changes	**10,225**	2,473	3,037	**117,529**
Cumulative effect of accounting changes (Note 1)				
Postretirement benefits other than pensions	**—**	(1,289)	—	**—**
Income taxes	**—**	119	—	**—**
Net income	**¥ 10,225**	¥ 1,303	¥ 3,037	**$ 117,529**

	Yen			Cents
Earnings per share (Note 1)				
Income before cumulative effect of accounting changes	**¥ 10.19**	¥ 2.47	¥ 3.03	**11.71¢**
Cumulative effect of accounting changes	**—**	(1.17)	—	
Net income	**¥ 10.19**	¥ 1.30	¥ 3.03	**11.71¢**

The accompanying notes to consolidated financial statements are an integral part of these statements.

Note 1: Basis of Financial Statements . . . [T]he accompanying consolidated financial statements have reflected certain adjustments, not recorded in the companies' books, to present them in conformity with accounting principles generally accepted in the United States of America. The major adjustments include those relating to deferred income taxes, accounting for foreign currency translation, postretirement benefits, investments in debt and equity securities, and accruals of certain expenses.

EXHIBIT 4–7   Roche Income Statement

CONSOLIDATED STATEMENTS OF INCOME

(in millions of Swiss francs)

	1994	*1993*
Sales	**14,748**	14,315
Cost of goods sold	**(4,870)**	(5,178)
Gross profit	**9,878**	9,137
Marketing and distribution	**(3,764)**	(3,527)
Research and development[15]	**(2,332)**	(2,269)
Administrative	**(863)**	(821)
Other operating income (expense), net[16]	**(263)**	(172)
Operating profit	**2,656**	2,348
Non-operating income (expense), net[17]	**936**	786
Income before taxes	**3,592**	3,134
Taxes[18]	**(674)**	(622)
Income before minority interests	**2,918**	2,512
Income applicable to minority interest[10]	**(58)**	(34)
Net income	**2,860**	2,478

Note: **Basis of preparation of financial statements.** The financial statements of the Roche Group are based on the separate financial information of the Group companies prepared for the year ending 31 December using the accounting policies summarized below, which are in accordance with the principles formulated by the *International Accounting Standards Committee.* Certain amounts in the 1993 financial statements have been reclassified to be comparable with the 1994 presentation.

---

separated from the accounting principles used to measure and originally record these decisions. The alternative view is that comparability improves investor decision making, and so one of the last two forms of transnational financial reporting is more appropriate. This conceptual conflict presents a dilemma for both users and multinational corporations involved in international financial reporting.

BEWARE THE FOREIGN FINANCIAL STATEMENT

So far, we have discussed the problems confronted by financial statement users when they are provided information that is not in their native language, their native currency, or prepared according to accustomed accounting principles. We have also discussed what corporations do to help financial statement users overcome these problems. Even if readers get financial statements in a language, currency unit, and based on accounting principles that they can understand, they must still consider that the inherent reliability of financial statements can vary because of different auditing standards worldwide. (This issue was discussed in Chapter 3.)

Finally, it should be noted that financial practices (as opposed to accounting practices) and business decision making differ around the world, and readers of foreign financial statements must understand how the business environment in a corporation's home country affects the firm's financial reports. This is especially critical if the user is comparing the accounting numbers of companies from different cultures.

One device used to analyze financial reports is *ratio analysis*. Ratios of key items on the financial statements are calculated to determine such things as riskiness, ability to pay off debts, and profitability. For example, a commonly employed ratio is the debt/asset ratio (total liabilities divided by total assets). Since liabilities must be paid off with company assets, the lower this ratio is, the greater is the company's ability to pay off its debts and, therefore, the safer the company is perceived to be. Generally speaking, creditors should be more willing to lend money to, and investors should be more willing to invest money in, companies with lower debt/asset ratios.

However, applying ratio analysis internationally can be deceptive. For example, Japanese companies tend to have significantly higher debt/asset ratios than comparable U.S. companies, even after Japanese financial statements are restated to conform to U.S. accounting principles. In Japan, the debt/asset ratio is an indication of how much confidence the banks have in a company. Companies have low debt/asset ratios because they are unable to get any more credit from the banks. Rather than demonstrating a risky company, in Japan the reverse is true—companies with high debt/asset ratios are generally safer![2]

What this tells us is that comparability still may not exist even if financial statements are prepared on the basis of comparable accounting standards. Because many business practices are culturally based, they are bound to have an impact on companies' financial statements. One must know something about the business environment of a company's home country in order to fully understand the company's financial statements.

International financial statement analysis is explained more fully in Chapter 7.

---

[2]Frederick D. S. Choi et al., "Analyzing Foreign Financial Statements: The Use and Misuse of International Ratio Analysis," *Journal of International Business Studies,* Spring/Summer 1983, pp. 113–31.

CONCLUSION

Transnational financial reporting arises when a corporation sends its financial statements to users residing and working in other countries. When this happens, one issue that the corporation faces is that the financial statements it prepares for users in its own country may not serve the needs of users in another part of the world. Financial statements are a communications device, and when a company does not communicate effectively with its audience, it pays a penalty. The penalty arises because failure to fully understand a multinational corporation's financial statements (in whole or in part) increases the risk associated with providing capital to that multinational. When the communications breakdown is severe, the resource providers simply refuse to provide funds to the multinational. However, less extreme penalties that the corporation may pay are higher interest costs or lower common stock prices. The multinational will accommodate its foreign audience if it believes that it can reduce the penalties of nonaccommodation. How the company responds to information needs depends on how it views its own cost/benefit equation—the company will try to balance the increased cost of additional accommodation to its financial statement users against the potentially lower penalties that the users may impose.

STUDY QUESTIONS

1. What is transnational financial reporting and why has it become an issue for many multinational corporations?
2. Why does transnational financial reporting present problems to both users and providers of financial accounting information?
3. What can users do to overcome the problems identified in question 2?
4. What happens when a multinational corporation fails to effectively communicate financial information to its foreign readers?
5. Describe the five approaches that multinational corporations take to accommodate their foreign readers. What are the advantages and disadvantages of each approach?
6. Which approaches to transnational financial reporting retain the accounting standards of the company's home country and which approaches restate financial statement information to another set of accounting principles? What is the main argument for retaining home country accounting standards in transnational financial reporting? What is the main argument favoring restatement?
7. Why must a financial statement user be careful when comparing financial ratios of companies from different countries?

CASES

The Mexican Investment

"Holy cow," thought Harlan. "What do I do now?"

For some time Harlan Davis had been considering investing in a few shares of a foreign company. Because he had heard so much about the positive effects of the North American Free Trade Agreement, he thought he would get in on the ground floor by buying some shares of Mexican companies likely to benefit from the agreement.

Harlan mailed letters to a number of Mexican firms, asking for a copy of their most recent annual reports. He figured that after analyzing the financial statements he would be able to choose the best one.

He anxiously awaited the responses, but the first one he received was nothing like what he expected. "It's all in Spanish," he thought with dismay. (Harlan's knowledge of Spanish ended with ordering beer and locating the public facilities.) "I can't even tell the balance sheet from the income statement. Let's see—pesos . . . Oh yeah, that's the Mexican currency, but I can't remember how many pesos it takes to get a dollar. Analyzing this company is going to be tougher than I realized."

Questions

1. Which example of transnational financial reporting is Harlan confronting here? Why might this Mexican company take this approach?
2. What must Harlan do to make the financial statements more understandable?
3. Where can he go to learn about Mexican accounting principles?

How Best to Report?

A Swiss multinational corporation has decided to list its common stock shares internationally, for the first time. Brian Curtis, who works for a large, international accounting firm, has been hired to advise the corporation on how to adapt its annual report so that it effectively serves the information needs of the prospective investors. "I can have a report ready by the end of the week," Brian confidently exclaimed.

Before developing his report, Brian prepared the following background information:

> Swiss financial reporting is legalistic in its orientation. It is highly conservative in that the law specifically permits the undervaluation of assets or the creation of secret reserves. Within reason, these practices are generally accepted in tax law. Banks are the primary source of finance and because they are able to obtain information from companies firsthand, disclosure levels are low and Swiss financial statements have a pervasive air of secrecy surrounding them. German is the dominant language spoken in Switzerland and the Swiss franc is the currency unit.

Help Brian write his report by answering the following questions.

Questions

1. What are the advantages and disadvantages of each of the five approaches to transnational financial reporting?
2. What criteria should a multinational corporation consider in choosing which approach to take in reporting to its foreign readers?
3. As described above, how suitable is Swiss accounting for reporting to investors on a worldwide basis?
4. Which approach to transnational financial reporting should this corporation take? Why?

Chartwell Ltd.

Chartwell Ltd. is a British multinational corporation that has its common stock shares listed on several of the world's major stock exchanges, including London and New York. As an accommodation to its U.S. shareholders, Chartwell includes a limited restatement of net income and shareholders' equity from U.K. to U.S. generally accepted accounting principles (GAAP):

Income statement data	£ million
Net income per U.K. GAAP	813
Goodwill amortisation (1)	(122)
Deferred taxation (2)	(57)
Depreciation (3)	18
Net income per U.S. GAAP	652
Balance sheet data	
Shareholders' equity per U.K. GAAP	1,245
Goodwill adjustment (1)	2,456
Deferred taxation (2)	(484)
Revaluations of fixed assets (3)	(396)
Shareholders' equity per U.S. GAAP	2,821

(1) Goodwill, the excess of the purchase price of acquired businesses over the fair market values of their assets, is written off to shareholders' equity at the time the businesses are acquired. Under U.S. GAAP, goodwill is shown as an intangible asset and amortised against income over 40 years.

(2) While both U.K. and U.S. GAAP calculate deferred income taxes when financial accounting income differs from taxable income, the amount is calculated differently under U.K. and U.S. GAAP. (This affects both the income tax expense on the income statement and deferred tax liability on the balance sheet.)

(3) Certain fixed assets are revalued to their current cost with correspondingly higher depreciation expense. U.S. GAAP does not allow such revaluations, requiring instead that they be valued at historical cost.

Questions

1. What are the benefits and costs to Chartwell providing a limited restatement in its annual report to shareholders?

2. If Chartwell's total assets under U.K. GAAP are £7,477 million, what are total liabilities under U.K. GAAP? What are assets, liabilities, and shareholders' equity under U.S. GAAP?

3. Which GAAP makes Chartwell appear more financially healthy? Which set best reflects economic reality? Why?

4. Is a limited restatement from U.K. to U.S. GAAP more important for financial statement users to have than one from German to U.S. GAAP? Why or why not?

ADDITIONAL READINGS

Bhushan, R., and D. R. Lessard. "Coping with International Accounting Diversity: Fund Managers' Views of Disclosure, Reconciliation and Harmonization." *Journal of International Financial Management & Accounting* (Summer 1992), pp. 149–64.

Biddle, G. C., and S. M. Saudagaran. "Foreign Stock Listings: Benefits, Costs, and the Accounting Policy Dilemma." *Accounting Horizons* (September 1991), pp. 69–80.

Breeden, R. C. "Foreign Companies and U.S. Securities Markets in a Time of Economic Transformation." *Fordham International Law Journal 17,* 1994), pp. S77–S96.

Choi, F. D. S., and R. M. Levich. "Behavioral Effects of International Accounting Diversity." *Accounting Horizons* (June 1991), pp. 1–13.

Frost, C. A., and G. Pownall. "Interdependencies in the Global Markets for Capital and Information: The Case of SmithKline Beecham plc." *Accounting Horizons* (March 1996), pp. 38–57.

Gray, S. J., G. K. Meek, and C. B. Roberts. "International Capital Market Pressures and Voluntary Annual Report Disclosures by U.S. and U.K. Multinationals." *Journal of International Financial Management & Accounting* (Spring 1995), pp. 43–68.

Hellman, N. "A Comparative Analysis of the Impact of Accounting Differences on Profits and Return on Equity: Differences between Swedish Practice and U.S. GAAP." *European Accounting Review* (December 1993), pp. 495–530.

5

DISCLOSURE PRACTICES AROUND THE WORLD

LEARNING OBJECTIVES

1. Distinguish financial and nonfinancial disclosures.
2. Understand the incentives for voluntarily disclosing additional information beyond that required by generally accepted accounting principles.
3. Compare geographic area and product line disclosures of U.S. and non-U.S. multinational corporations.
4. Introduce certain disclosure innovations from Europe.
5. Assess the trends in disclosure practices by multinational corporations and examine the reasons for them.

The term *disclosure,* in its broadest sense, encompasses the release of any piece of information about a particular company. It includes everything contained in the company's annual report, press releases, newspaper and magazine stories, and so on. However, this chapter is more narrowly focused. It is about disclosures contained in annual reports or, more specifically, annual report information besides that in the main financial statements—the balance sheet, income statement, and statement of cash flows. (While the latter is becoming increasingly common worldwide, it is still not required in all countries.)

Measurement issues are concerned with how financial statements should be prepared, which generally accepted accounting principles (GAAP) to employ, and how assets and liabilities are to be valued. Several substantive international accounting measurement issues are discussed in Chapter 2. *Disclosure* issues, on the other hand, relate to the information in an annual report that supplements the financial statements.

If you obtain the annual report of a U.S. company, you typically find a number of supplemental disclosures:

1. A letter from the company president or chairman of the board explaining the major events affecting the firm, significant operating and financing activities, and perhaps, prospects for the future.

2. A description of the major products or services of the company, what markets are served, where facilities are located, and a list of major subsidiary companies.

3. A narrative review of the operations for the past year. This may be broken down by product line or geographic area. This review is much more in-depth than the president's letter and is designed to help the annual report user more easily interpret the financial statements by expanding on the information they contain.

4. A statement of accounting policies. There are often several alternative ways to measure assets, liabilities, revenues, and expenses; and companies may choose the particular GAAP they wish to use. The description of accounting policies can be useful for a user of financial statements, especially if financial statements of several companies using different principles are being compared. This is especially important in an international context, since the differences in accounting worldwide are even more extensive than they are domestically.

5. Notes (or footnotes) to the financial statements. These elaborate on the amounts in the financial statements. Most companies like to keep their financial statements as lean and uncluttered as possible. Extra details and disclosures that do not fit conveniently in the financial statements are then placed in the footnotes.

FINANCIAL AND NONFINANCIAL DISCLOSURE

Disclosures in financial reports are often classified as either financial or nonfinancial. *Financial* disclosures consist of those items of information quantifiable in monetary amounts (dollars, for U.S. companies). For example, companies often report one figure for inventory on the balance sheet but show in a footnote how much of that is finished goods, how much is raw materials, and so on. A company may show one amount for property in the balance sheet and reveal in a footnote how much is located in the United States, how much in Europe, and so forth. When a company signs a long-term contract obligating it to rent property for a number of years, that obligation does not fit the definition of a liability and therefore will not appear on the balance sheet. However, because cash has been committed for future years, much like the commitments that are considered liabilities, companies generally show lease obligations in footnotes. Similarly, if a company is a defendant in a lawsuit, it wants shareholders to know the amounts of potential damages it may be liable for. The case may not have progressed far enough in the courts for the defendant to know whether it will actually have to pay damages. And so, in the meantime, it reveals in a footnote the general circumstances surrounding the lawsuit. These are all types of financial disclosures seen in financial statements. For various reasons, the related monetary amounts do not appear in the financial statements themselves. They are disclosed in footnotes (or elsewhere in the annual report) to more fully inform the reader about the company's financial well-being.

Nonfinancial disclosures are either (1) narrative descriptions, facts, or opinions that do not readily lend themselves to quantification in monetary terms or (2) items of information quantified in something other than money. An example of the former is a company's mission statement. An example of the latter is data about the number of employees located in each country. (Labor *costs* per country are a financial disclosure, but *number* of employees is nonfinancial.) Nonfinancial disclosures may be just another way to express things that are already expressed monetarily in the financial statements. Most of the information that accountants provide is financial— financial statements and financial disclosures. However, not everything can be expressed monetarily, and nonfinancial disclosures can be very important, too.

SOME OBSERVATIONS ABOUT DISCLOSURE

Disclosures can also be distinguished based on whether they are required or suggested, or whether they are voluntary. While most countries *require* certain disclosures to be made by companies operating within their borders, the amount of disclosure required varies by country. Often the GAAP of a particular country will also *suggest* items to be disclosed in companies' annual reports. Many companies, though, disclose information that is neither required nor suggested; that is, some disclosures are completely *voluntary.* Disclosures that are required or suggested in one country may be voluntary in another, and vice versa.

The fact that companies sometimes disclose more than they have to suggests that they perceive some advantages in doing so. In particular, it appears that the worldwide competition for investment funds is the most important force propelling increased levels of disclosure by multinational corporations. MNCs significantly increase disclosure whenever they seek major amounts of new funds.

Disclosure can also enlarge the scope of interest in a company by expanding the annual report's audience. After all, the annual report is the major vehicle for getting people interested in what the company is doing. Chapter 1 explained how companies orient their annual reports to a primary audience group—investors, creditors, the government, and so on. Disclosure enables the firm to maintain the primary orientation of its financial statements and provide information of interest to other parties as well. Continental European companies are especially effective and innovative in doing this.

Disclosure can overcome differences in generally accepted accounting principles. The problems associated with transnational financial reporting for financial statement users and multinational corporations are discussed in Chapters 3 and 4. Until a worldwide harmonization of accounting practices is achieved, disclosure can be an effective mechanism for overcoming these problems.

Deciding what and what not to disclose is not always an easy decision for corporate managements to make. If they decide not to disclose an item of information, in a very real sense, they have chosen to keep something secret from financial statement users. Many things, of course, are simply irrelevant to users of financial statements—the size of the company president's waistline, for example. But for many items of information, managements must use judgment to decide on their usefulness to financial statement readers. If too much information is disclosed, a reader can easily get lost in all of the clutter (i.e., suffer from "information overload"). So managements need a way to pare down the amount of information revealed in financial statements.

Disclosure is a substantive issue, since information *revealed* can potentially affect people's decisions and actions. Unrevealed information does not have that potential. When GAAP require a disclosure, this is tantamount to saying that the information is potentially significant enough to affect decisions and, therefore, ought to be revealed. A suggested disclosure or a voluntary disclosure should be made whenever knowledge of that information has the potential to influence the decisions of financial statement users.

EXAMPLES OF DISCLOSURE

This chapter examines disclosure from an international perspective. It also illustrates certain disclosures made by European multinational corporations that are not typically made by U.S. firms. Some disclosures have a longer tradition and are better developed in Europe than in the United States. This is one area where U.S. accountants can learn from their European cousins. Indeed, a recent survey of annual reports from around the world concludes that U.S. companies have not kept up with a worldwide trend toward providing informative and innovative disclosures to the public.[1]

What, how much, and how a company discloses supplemental information varies depending on (1) the requirements of generally accepted accounting principles, (2) the needs of users, (3) the influence of users, and (4) the philosophy of management. This chapter specifically looks at

1. Geographic area and product line disclosures.
2. Financial forecast disclosures.
3. Information about shares and shareholders.
4. The value added statement.
5. Employee disclosures.
6. Environmental disclosures.

---

[1]*World Survey of Published Accounts* (London: Lafferty Publications, 1989).

Geographic Area and Product Line Disclosures

Consolidated financial statements combine the separate financial statements of a parent company and its subsidiaries so that a single set of financial statements is issued for the entire economic entity. This subject is discussed in Chapter 6, where the argument is made that for a multinational corporation operating in a number of different countries and perhaps having several different product lines, consolidated financial statements may in fact hide some important information. If a company's continued profitability depends heavily on a certain region of the world or on a particular product, knowledge of that may be useful to investors, creditors, employees, and other financial statement users. After all, not all areas of the world have equally risky business environments or present equal business opportunities. Products vary in terms of risks and returns as well. Thus, in addition to consolidated financial statements, perhaps companies should provide, supplementally, more details about where and how total profits are derived.

The purpose of *disaggregated* geographic and product line disclosure is to aid the financial statement user to identify a company's *dependency* on a country, area of the world, or product line. Accounting researchers have determined that investors can improve their predictions about a company's future prospects when they are given financial information disaggregated by geographic region and "line of business" in addition to consolidated financial information.

Large U.S. multinationals are required to observe *FASB Statement 14,* "Financial Reporting for Segments of a Business Enterprise." This standard gives guidance for disclosures by both geographic area and product line, but the guidelines are fairly vague. Exhibit 5–1 (pp. 79–80) shows how Coca-Cola Company complies with this standard. Note that Coca-Cola defines two product line segments—soft drinks and foods. The company also defines six geographic areas—the United States, Africa, European Community, Latin America, Northeast Europe and Middle East, and Pacific and Canada. Coca-Cola separately discloses the following by line of business and by geographic area: net operating revenues, operating income, identifiable operating assets, capital expenditures, and depreciation and amortization. The soft drinks information is further split between United States and international. In addition, Coca-Cola includes a more detailed discussion (not reproduced here) of its operations by geographic area.

Certain disaggregated disclosures by the British firm Cadbury Schweppes are reproduced in Exhibit 5–2 (p. 81). Cadbury Schweppes uses a matrix format to disclose sales, operating profit, and operating assets by product line and geographic area. The company defines two product lines—confectionery (candies) and beverages. It also defines five geographic regions—the United Kingdom, (Continental) Europe, the Americas, the Pacific Rim, and Africa & Other. Cadbury Schweppes also provides an in-depth analysis of its operations by product line (not reproduced here). A matrix presentation provides more detail than separate product line and geographic area disclosures. However, the approach is not very common.

EXHIBIT 5–1   Coca-Cola Company, Product Line and Geographic Area Disclosure

The Coca-Cola Company and Subsidiaries

NOTES TO CONSOLIDATED FINANCIAL STATEMENTS

20. Lines of Business

The Company operates in two major lines of business: soft drinks and foods (principally juice and juice-drink products). Information concerning operations in these businesses is as follows (in millions):

| | Soft Drinks | | | | |
	United States	International	Foods	Corporate	Consolidated
1994					
Net operating revenues	$3,506	$10,906	$1,728	$ 32	$16,172
Operating income	761	3,261	123	(437)	3,708
Identifiable operating assets	2,301	6,875	731	1,456[1]	11,363
Equity income				134	134
Investments (principally bottling companies)				2,510	2,510
Capital expenditures	214	536	39	89	878
Depreciation and amortization	92	221	38	60	411
1993					
Net operating revenues	$3,052	$ 9,205	$1,680	$ 20	$13,957
Operating income	680[2]	2,753[2]	117	(448)[2]	3,102
Identifiable operating assets	1,956	5,809	761	1,280[1]	9,806
Equity income				91[2]	91
Investments (principally bottling companies)				2,215	2,215
Capital expenditures	136	557	30	77	800
Depreciation and amortization	91	172	38	59	360
1992					
Net operating revenues	$2,813	$ 8,551	$1,675	$ 35	$13,074
Operating income	560	2,521	112	(423)	2,770
Identifiable operating assets	1,812	5,251	791	1,035[1]	8,889
Equity income				65	65
Investments (principally bottling companies)				2,163	2,163
Capital expenditures	169	736	38	140	1,083
Depreciation and amortization	87	157	35	43	322

Intercompany transfers between sectors are not material.

Certain prior year amounts related to net operating revenues and operating income have been reclassified to conform to the current year presentation.

[1]Corporate identifiable operating assets are composed principally of marketable securities, finance subsidiary receivables and fixed assets.

[2]Operating income for soft drink operations in the United States, International operations and Corporate was reduced by $13 million, $33 million and $17 million, respectively, for provisions to increase efficiencies. Equity income was reduced by $42 million related to restructuring charges recorded by Coca-Cola Beverages Ltd.

| Compound Growth Rates | Soft Drinks | | | |
Ending 1994	United States	International	Foods	Consolidated
Net operating revenues				
5 years	10%	18%	2%	13%
10 years	8%	16%	3%	12%
Operating income				
5 years	14%	17%	7%	17%
10 years	12%	19%	0%	16%

continued

EXHIBIT 5–1 *(concluded)*

The Coca-Cola Company and Subsidiaries

NOTES TO CONSOLIDATED FINANCIAL STATEMENTS

21. Operations in Geographic Areas
Information about the Company's operations by geographic area is as follows (in millions):

	United States	Africa	European Community	Latin America	Northeast Europe/ Middle East	Pacific & Canada	Corporate	Consolidated
1994								
Net operating revenues	$5,092	$522	$4,255	$1,928	$880	$3,463	$ 32	$16,172
Operating income	869	182	984	713	184	1,213	(437)	3,708
Identifiable operating assets	2,991	357	3,295	1,164	771	1,329	1,456[1]	11,363
Equity income							134	134
Investments (principally bottling companies)							2,510	2,510
Capital expenditures	252	27	201	129	149	31	89	878
Depreciation and amortization	128	6	130	36	32	19	60	411
1993								
Net operating revenues	$4,586	$255	$3,834	$1,683	$677	$2,902	$ 20	$13,957
Operating income	782[2]	152	872[2]	582	152	1,010	(448)[2]	3,102
Identifiable operating assets	2,682	153	2,777	1,220	604	1,090	1,280[1]	9,806
Equity income							91[2]	91
Investments (principally bottling companies)							2,215	2,215
Capital expenditures	165	6	239	141	129	43	77	800
Depreciation and amortization	127	3	99	33	22	17	59	360
1992								
Net operating revenues	$4,339	$242	$3,984	$1,383	$546	$2,545	$ 35	$13,074
Operating income	658	129	889	502	108	907	(423)	2,770
Identifiable operating assets	2,563	139	2,587	1,185	435	945	1,035[1]	8,889
Equity income							65	65
Investments (principally bottling companies)							2,163	2,163
Capital expenditures	204	12	386	188	120	33	140	1,083
Depreciation and amortization	121	3	99	27	14	15	43	322

Intercompany transfers between geographic areas are not material.

Certain prior year amounts related to operating income have been reclassified to conform to the current year presentation.

Identifiable liabilities of operations outside the United States amounted to approximately $2.5 billion at December 31, 1994, and $1.9 billion at December 31, 1993 and 1992.

[1]Corporate identifiable operating assets are composed principally of marketable securities, finance subsidiary receivables and fixed assets.

[2]Operating income for the United States, European Community and Corporate was reduced by $13 million, $33 million and $17 million, respectively, for provisions to increase efficiencies. Equity income was reduced by $42 million related to restructuring charges recorded by Coca-Cola Beverages Ltd.

Compound Growth Rates Ending 1994	United States	Africa	European Community	Latin America	Northeast Europe/ Middle East	Pacific & Canada		Consolidated
Net operating revenues								
5 years	7%	27%	18%	24%	27%	12%		13%
10 years	6%	6%	18%	16%	24%	14%		12%
Operating income								
5 years	13%	18%	13%	26%	23%	15%		17%
10 years	9%	7%	20%	23%	21%	19%		16%

EXHIBIT 5–2   Cadbury Schweppes, Product Line and Geographic Area Disclosure

Sales, Operating Profit, Operating Assets and Trading Margin Analysis

1994		Total £m	United Kingdom £m	Europe* £m	Americas £m	Pacific Rim £m	Africa & Others £m
Sales							
	Confectionery	1,827.3	896.2	368.9	96.5	324.5	141.2
	Beverages	2,202.3	833.1	406.2	670.5	214.5	78.0
		4,029.6	1,729.3	775.1	767.0	539.0	219.2
Operating Profit							
	Confectionery	238.1	110.9	37.4	19.4	52.3	18.1
	Beverages	282.7	120.0	14.7	113.0	14.6	20.4
		520.8	230.9	52.1	132.4	66.9	38.5
Operating Assets							
	Confectionery	863.2	356.6	191.4	41.4	197.5	76.3
	Beverages	591.1	219.0	155.4	107.7	93.6	15.4
		1,454.3	575.6	346.8	149.1	291.1	91.7
Trading Margin		%	%	%	%	%	%
	Confectionery	12.8	12.4	10.1	20.1	16.1	10.5
	Beverages	12.2	14.4	1.9	16.9	6.8	18.3
		12.5	13.4	5.8	17.3	12.4	13.3

*See Note 19 for the effect of acquisitions

1993		Total £m	United Kingdom £m	Europe £m	Americas £m	Pacific Rim £m	Africa & Others £m
Sales							
	Confectionery	1,660.1	826.9	312.3	53.0	311.5	156.4
	Beverages	2,064.7	786.8	429.2	590.6	196.5	61.6
		3,724.8	1,613.7	741.5	643.6	508.0	218.0
Operating Profit							
	Confectionery	211.3	94.2	33.3	12.3	53.9	17.6
	Beverages	238.1	100.7	16.7	89.3	14.9	16.5
		449.4	194.9	50.0	101.6	68.8	34.1
Operating Assets							
	Confectionery	743.2	332.0	129.3	30.8	174.6	76.5
	Beverages	627.7	223.1	181.5	141.5	75.1	6.5
		1,370.9	555.1	310.8	172.3	249.7	83.0
Trading Margin		%	%	%	%	%	%
	Confectionery	12.5	11.4	10.7	23.2	17.3	8.9
	Beverages	11.1	12.8	2.7	15.1	7.6	19.5
		11.7	12.1	6.0	15.8	13.5	11.9

The analysis shown above is based on geographical origin.

Presenting disaggregated data is now common among large multinational corporations. Several countries require it, the International Accounting Standards Committee has issued *Standard 14,* "Reflecting Financial Information by Segments," and both the United Nations and the Organization for Economic Cooperation and Development (discussed in Chapter 3) suggest such disclosures by multinationals. There is, however, a wide variety in the disclosure practices of multinationals. Clearly, defining product lines is easier than defining meaningful geographic segments. Countries and regions vary in terms of (1) stage of development, (2) political risk, (3) currency strength, (4) inflation levels and (5) economic stability. The risks associated with these variables somehow need to be conveyed. This represents a significant challenge for accountants.

Financial Forecast Disclosures

Given that a primary concern of investors is assessing a company's future profitability and cash flows, it is reasonable to ask whether companies provide their own internal forecasts of such financial information. Financial forecasts would seem to be relevant information for investors. In practice, few MNCs provide them. One reason is that forecasts can be unreliable because they incorporate (often highly) subjective estimates of uncertain future events. In addition, there can be legal repercussions for managements if the forecasts are not met. In litigious countries such as the United States, the potential for lawsuits is a major deterrent to providing financial forecasts.

Though unusual by international norms, some forecast disclosures can be observed, notably by some larger Swedish MNCs. For example, the 1994 annual report of SCA, the Swedish packaging, paper, and hygiene products company, forecasts the following for 1995:

> Earnings after financial net are expected to amount to SEK 4.5–5.0 billion, corresponding to approximately SEK 15 per share after tax. Net sales is estimated to amount to approximately SEK 63 billion.

Information about Shares and Shareholders

A number of continental European companies have recently begun disclosing rather extensive information about their shares and shareholders. Exhibit 5–3 (pp. 83–84) is an example of such a disclosure provided by the Swedish telecommunications company Ericsson in its annual report. Share information disclosed by Ericsson includes the following: (1) a description of Ericsson's class A and B shares, (2) the stock exchanges where Ericsson's shares are traded and the approximate percentage of total trading on the exchanges, (3) information about Ericsson's shareholders, and (4) selected other data, such as the year-end price and the yearly high and low price per share for five years. Ericsson also discloses the overall distribution of its shares and the identity and number of shares owned by its 14 largest shareholders.

EXHIBIT 5–3   Ericsson, Information about Shares and Shareholders

Ericsson Share Data

The share capital
The share capital of the Parent Company, Telefonaktiebolaget LM Ericsson, amounted at December 31, 1994, to SEK 2,172,291,180, represented by 217,229,118 shares, each with a par value of SEK 10. Of the total number of shares outstanding, 18,642,575 were A shares, each carrying one vote, and 198,586,543 B shares, carrying one thousandth of a vote.

During 1993 a subordinated convertible debenture loan was issued with a par value of SEK 2,171,719,760 and with a term of seven years. Ericsson's shareholders had preferential right to subscribe for the convertibles. During 1994 debentures have been converted into 59,220 B shares. At the end of the year 1994 debentures had been converted to a total of 72,395 B shares. Should all remaining debentures be converted, the number of B shares would increase further with 7,166,352. All shares may be owned by foreign citizens.

During 1994 the number of shares increased by 66,308 through conversion of debentures. During the period between January 1 and February 15, 1995, additional debentures were converted to 643 B shares, increasing to 217,229,761 the total number of shares entitled to dividends as of the record date.

Employee ownership of Ericsson shares
Ericsson's General Savings Fund was started in 1984. The General Savings Fund, which has 1,267

participants, has invested in Ericsson shares. At year-end 1994, the holding in this fund amounted to 190,000 shares.

Stock exchange trading
Ericsson A and B shares are listed on the Stockholm Stock Exchange. The B shares are also listed on the exchanges in Basel, Düsseldorf, Frankfurt am Main, Geneva, Hamburg, London, Paris and Zurich and are traded in the U.S. in the form of ADRs (American Depositary Receipts) via the NASDAQ electronic quotation system.

Each ADR represents one B share. The most active trading occurs in Stockholm, New York and London.

At NASDAQ, ADDs (American Depositary Debentures) are also being traded.

Approximately 470 million shares were traded during 1994. The turnover was distributed as follows (approximate percentages): 39 percent on the Stockholm Stock Exchange, 38 percent via NASDAQ, 22 percent on the London Stock Exchange and 1 percent on other exchanges.

Shareholders
Approximately 84 percent of Ericsson's shares are owned by Swedish and international institutional investors. At year-end 1994, about 47 percent of the shares were held by shareholders outside Sweden.

Trading on the Stockholm Stock Exchange

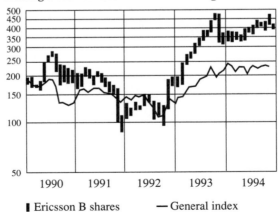

| Ericsson B shares   — General index

continued

EXHIBIT 5–3   (concluded)

Share data	1994	1993	1992	1991	1990*
Exports of shares from Sweden (SEK m.)	**24,656**	21,352	4,245	2,310	777
Imports of shares to Sweden (SEK m.)	**22,360**	13,572	3,333	1,218	1,873
Net imports (–)/exports of shares to Sweden	**2,296**	7,780	912	1,092	–1,096
P/E ratio, "B" shares[1]	**22.6**	25.8	79.7	25.1	12.4
Share prices, December 31, Stockholm Stock Exchange (SEK)					
—"A"	**420**	410	195	145	245
—"B"	**410**	341	185	108	184
—"B" High for year	**461.5**	469	189	225	280
—"B" Low for year	**334**	172	97.5	88.5	175

[1]) P/E ratio = Price per share at December 31, divided by profit per share after taxes.
*After 5-for-1 stock split

Changes in capital stock		Number of shares	Capital stock
1982	January 1	21,788,498	1,089,424,900
	1-for-2 stock dividend	10,894,248	544,712,400
1983	Special new issue, USD 62.5	4,000,000	200,000,000
	Conversions	181,677	9,083,850
1984	Conversions	39,049	1,952,450
1985	Conversions	47,789	2,389,450
1986	Conversions	1,211,121	60,556,050
1988	Conversions	52,242	2,612,100
1989	Conversions	2,760,310	138,015,500
1990	Conversions	854,413	8,544,130
1990	5-for-1 stock split	163,899,736	—
1991	Conversions	257,372	2,573,720
1992	Conversions	203,024	2,030,240
1993	Conversions	10,973,331	109,733,310
1994	Conversions	66,308	663,080
1994	December 31	217,229,118	2,172,291,180

Distribution of shares, year-end 1994 Shareholders' holding	Shareholders Number	%	Number of shares	%	Number of shares per shareholder
1– 500	80,167	84.33	11,330,468	5.22	141
501– 5,000	13,740	14.45	17,271,953	7.95	1,257
5,001–20,000	736	0.77	7,115,746	3.27	9,668
20,001–	423	0.45	181,510,951	83.56	429,104
	95,066	100.00	217,229,118	100.00	2,285

The largest shareholders, ranked by voting rights, were as follows at December 31, 1994:	Number of shares	Voting rights percent
AB Industrivärden	4,984,035	26.5
Investor AB	4,855,000	22.2
Knut och Alice Wallenbergs stiftelse	2,651,480	14.1
Svenska Handelsbankens Pensionsstiftelse	1,210,000	5.6
Livförsäkrings AB Skandia	3,663,490	5.0
Pensionskassan SHB Försäkringsförening	900,000	4.8
EB-stiftelsen, S-E-Bankens Pensionsstiftelse	460,000	2.4
Wallanders och Hedelius' stiftelse	450,000	2.4
Wallenbergs stiftelse, Marianne och Marcus	450,000	2.4
Oktogonen, Stiftelsen	500,000	1.6
Svenska Handelsbankens personalstiftelse	280,000	1.5
Trygg-Hansa	4,181,875	1.3
Fjärde AP-fonden	9,174,693	1.1
Svenska Handelsbankens aktiefonder	2,253,174	0.4

What is the value of such information? It is aimed primarily at current and prospective shareholders. Past trend data can be useful in predicting future patterns, and it is also useful when making comparisons with the trends of other companies. Shares are more marketable when they are traded on several exchanges and when the volume of trading is high. Widely scattered ownership tends to provide ready sales opportunities when present shareholders wish to dispose of some or all of their share holdings. Ownership concentration also indicates the locus of corporate control. On the one hand, dispersed ownership normally means that the company is controlled by shareholders and their agents, the company's management team. On the other hand, a concentrated ownership suggests that power is exerted by a more narrowly defined group. Management may be constrained if a large block of shares is owned by relatively few individuals or groups, and other shareholders may have relatively less influence in such situations. For example, notice that Ericsson's three largest shareholders control nearly two-thirds of Ericsson's shares on a combined basis (26.5 + 22.2 + 14.1 percent = 62.8 percent). The identities of the largest shareholders might also be of interest to current and potential shareholders for the same reason.

Information such as that in Exhibit 5–3 is provided voluntarily. There are no standards, such as from the organizations discussed in Chapter 3, that require companies to provide information about shares and shareholders. Although the practice seems to be growing, it is still not very widespread.

The Value Added Statement

The value added statement originated in Europe and is now occasionally provided by companies from outside Europe (for example, Australia and South Africa). To our knowledge, no country's GAAP require value added statements. Thus, they are provided on a completely voluntary basis.

The statement produced by the British firm Imperial Chemical Industries is reproduced in Exhibit 5–4. This statement shows that, net of materials and services used in producing its chemical products, ICI added £2,692 million to the world economy in 1994. This contribution went to the following groups:

1. Employees, in the form of salaries, pensions, etc.

2. Governments, in the form of taxes.

3. Providers of capital, in the form of interest to creditors and dividends to shareholders.

4. ICI itself—amounts reinvested in the business.

The value added statement presents the view that a corporation is a provider of wealth to society—that its presence is a positive force. Because the corporation exists, people are employed, governments receive more taxes, and investors and creditors are rewarded for risking their funds in the business. The value added statement reflects the philosophy that a business enterprise should, and actually

EXHIBIT 5–4   Imperial Chemical Industries, Value Added Statement

Sources and Disposal of Value Added
for the year ended 31 December 1994

	1994			1993†		
	Continuing operations	*Discontinued operations*	*Total*	*Continuing operations*	*Discontinued operations*	*Total*
	£m	*£m*	*£m*	*£m*	*£m*	*£m*
SOURCES OF INCOME						
Sales turnover	**9,189**	**—**	**9,189**	8,430	2,202	10,632
Royalties and other trading income	**82**	**—**	**82**	113	32	145
Less materials and services	**(6,556)**	**—**	**(6,556)**	(6,111)	(1,351)	(7,462)
Value added by manufacturing and trading activities	**2,715**	**—**	**2,715**	2,432	883	3,315
Share of profit less losses of associated undertakings	**14**	**—**	**14**	45	2	47
Value added related to exceptional items taken below trading profit	**(37)**	**—**	**(37)**	(52)	(47)	(99)
Total value added	**2,692**	**—**	**2,692**	2,425	838	3,263
DISPOSAL OF TOTAL VALUE ADDED						
Employees						
Employee costs charged in arriving at profit before tax	**1,791**	**—**	**1,791**	1,742	514	2,256
Governments						
Corporate taxes	**164**	**—**	**164**	119	70	189
Less grants	**(8)**	**—**	**(8)**	(10)	(1)	(11)
	156	**—**	**156**	109	69	178
Providers of capital						
Interest cost of net borrowings	**88**	**—**	**88**	90	63	153
Dividends to shareholders						
Cash	**199**	**—**	**199**	199	—	199
Demerger				363	—	363
Minority shareholders in subsidiary undertakings	**56**	**—**	**56**	42	—	42
	343	**—**	**343**	694	63	757
Re-investment in the business						
Depreciation	**413**	**—**	**413**	417	88	505
(Loss) profit retained	**(11)**	**—**	**(11)**	(537)	104	(433)
	402	**—**	**402**	(120)	192	72
Total disposal	**2,692**	**—**	**2,692**	2,425	838	3,263

†Restated (Note 2 to the Annual Accounts)

This table is based on the audited accounts; it shows the total value added to the cost of materials and services purchased from outside the Group and indicates the ways in which this increase in value has been disposed.

does, do more than just make a profit. It is consistent with the notion that creating employment and making other contributions to society at large are also legitimate objectives of business. This is not the prevailing attitude in the United States, but it is in most other countries of the world. One can see that the environmental variables discussed in Chapter 1 affect not only measurement practices but also disclosure practices.

Employee Disclosures

Exhibit 5–5 (pp. 88–93) is reproduced from the annual report of the French drinks company Pernod Ricard. Notice that Exhibit 5–5 shows information about age, salaries, training, and absenteeism. Employee disclosures reflect the viewpoint that a company's continued success depends in part on its employees, or human resources. Exhibit 5–5 also demonstrates the influence of organized labor in Europe, where it is relatively more powerful than in the United States.

This type of disclosure developed in Europe and is now finding its way into the annual reports of U.S. companies. For example, Exhibit 5–6 is the employee disclosure of Ford Motor Company. It includes information about the number of employees by geographic area and the number of minority group members and women employed.

Environmental Disclosures

The annual report of the German firm VEBA illustrates environmental disclosures. VEBA is an electricity generation and chemicals and oil company. The following quote begins the discussion about the environmental protection measures VEBA has taken:

> Environmental protection is crucial as a prerequisite of long-term social and economic survival; today's environmental shortcomings impair tomorrow's living standards and production conditions. VEBA remains committed to participate actively in the conservation of the environment and our natural resources.

Later in the discussion, VEBA says the following:

> Environmental protection at VEBA is built on three tenets: technology, organization and employee commitment. Environmental control is being given even more priority in all corporate decisions, at all levels and areas within the Group. The debate concerning the ecological audit concept put forward by the European Union is giving rise to fresh ideas about how to protect the environment.

The two items reproduced in Exhibit 5–7 (p. 95) are also included in VEBA's environmental disclosure. They show the five-year pattern of VEBA's expenses for environmental protection.

Such disclosures can be found in the annual reports of large continental European companies, particularly those from Germany, Switzerland, and

EXHIBIT 5–5   Pernod Ricard, Employee Disclosure

Human resources

●●●●●●●●●●●●●●●●●

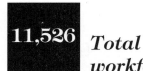

Total workforce

On 31st December 1994 the Group employed a total number of 11,526 people (marking a 19.3% increase over 1993).

This considerable increase can be explained by the aquisition of J&J Haslett (Northern Ireland) with 1,132 employees. Beijing Wineries (China) with 424 employees and the

setting up of Pernod Ricard Rouss (Russia), Perithai (Thailand), Polacek (Austria), Alvita (Czech Republic), Peribas (Hungary) and DeliFood (Poland). On a like-for-like basis, the Group's workforce would have remained stable.

Of the workforce now abroad

The percentage of employees outside of France increases to 59% of the total Group workforce, confirming

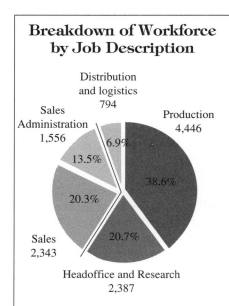

Breakdown of Workforce by Job Description

Distribution and logistics 794

Sales Administration 1,556

Sales 2,343

Production 4,446

Headoffice and Research 2,387

6.9%
13.5%
20.3%
38.6%
20.7%

Breakdown of Workforce by Category

34.9%
28.6%
13.7%
10.6%
12.2%

4,023 Workers
1,579 Line Supervisors
3,304 Employees
1,220 Sales personnel
1,410 Management

EXHIBIT 5–5   *(continued)*

the trend recorded in 1993. The workforces of several foreign subsidiaries grew (for example, Orlando was + 12%, SIAS-Food + 6%, Austin Nichols + 4% etc...), while the number of employees in France fell by 2.5%, due to the regrouping of Pernod / Cusenier and of CSR / Pampryl.

On the structural level, it is worth noting the growth in sales administration staff following the acquisition of J&J Haslett.

 1,096   *New employment*

This year the Group took on 1,096 new people of whom more than 200 were in France. 41% went into sales, 36% into production (principally with SIAS and Orlando. At the same time, 279 people were transfered within the Group.

 +4.60%   *Average salary in France*

The following figures relate only to French companies. Economic and social disparities between the different countries in which the Group operates would make worldwide analysis impossible.

In 1994, the average salary increased by 4.6%. This increase can be explained

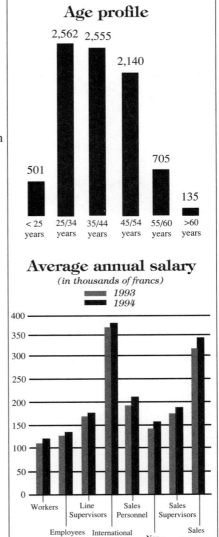

Age profile

Age group	Number
< 25 years	501
25/34 years	2,562
35/44 years	2,555
45/54 years	2,140
55/60 years	705
>60 years	135

Average annual salary
(in thousands of francs)
1993
1994

EXHIBIT 5–5   *(continued)*

---

by the impact on 1994 salaries of the healthy profits realised in 1993. A particular effort has been made with lower salaries.

 Average age

The following figures only relate to people with permanent employment within the Group.

The average age fell slightly to 38 years 7 months from 39 years 5 months the preceding year. This can be explained largely by the introduction into the Group's structure of new companies, either acquired or created, with younger personnel.

Less pronounced is a fall in the average age of people employed in companies which were already part of the Group in 1993.

For the same reasons, the average length of service went from 11 years 3 months in 1993 to 10 years 6 months in 1994.

 Training *(* of the total payroll)*

Training remains an essential thrust to the Group's strategy. Difficult economic circumstances however led to a fall in investment. As a result training expenditure represents 2.1% of the total payroll in 1994 as opposed to 2.5% in 1993 (in France alone the figure fell from 3.4% to 3%).

This decrease in training expenditure does not however mark a backing down from the Group's commitment to the subject but rather a concern to get the most from projects already underway. On the quantitive level, the

Training		Total Group	France
	1993	1994	1994
Number of hours worked	16,650,781	17,574,883	9,253,800
% of work time	0.66	0.63	0.80
Number of trainees	3,573	4,177	2,478
% of total employees	39.4	36.1	52.3
Number of hours per trainee (%)	30.53	26.03	30.06
Cost (in thousands of francs)	34,068	33,755	27,191
% of payroll	2.5	2.1	3.0

EXHIBIT 5–5 *(continued)*

number of people who benefitted from training sessions actually increased (4177 in 1994 as opposed to 3573 in 1993).

It is worth highlighting the training received by workers at Irish Distillers in the prevention of accidents, and also the courses taken by senior managers in French and overseas subsidiaries, within the international training programmes at the Pernod Ricard Training Centre.

The Group also agreed on making a marked effort to employ young people. To this ends, the Group in France took on 56 people on youth employment schemes (training, apprenticeship, adjustment).

Labour policy and working conditions

Important restructuring marked the Group's life in 1994: the affiliation of Cusenier to Pernod, the merging of CSR and Pampryl, changes to the structure of Cooymans, the closing of the Orangina factory at Rennes.....

With all of these events there was a constant concern to keep jobs. There were numerous internal transfers thanks to the synergy between Group companies, fed by a spirit of solidarity and responsibility. When internal solutions could not be found, employment agencies efficiently assisted

personnel to make the transition to employment outside of the Group.

In terms of personnel management, significant initiatives were taken:

• to begin with, attention focussed on new colleagues. In addition to the Group's existing induction sessions, certain companies, Orangina and Orlando for example, also set up initiatives to welcome new employees.

• within the same framework as the Chantiers de l'Optimisme (Optimism Workshops) instigated by Ricard, Progress Groups were set up which, in real terms, promoted a spirit of initiative amongst employees and which, in a wider sense, improved the company's efficiency.

• the Management Committees of certain companies (SIAS in particular) became totally involved in a communication project. Periodic meetings (usually monthly) brought together heads of department, research workers and management. Information exchanged was then communicated to all the employees on site or within the company. The frequent circulation of internal information in this way increased employee motivation.

In other areas, past efforts in the fields of contigency planning and retirement continued into 1994. Initiatives benefitting personnel were also brought into effect at Ricard, Irish Distillers and Lizas & Lizas.

EXHIBIT 5–5   *(continued)*

Absenteeism and accidents at work

The incidence and seriousness of accidents in the workplace are lower than those in 1993. This decrease comes as a result of efforts undertaken to improve working conditions and to avert all risks, mainly within the industrial environment. There was a clear improvement within foreign subsidiaries.

Absenteeism due to illness remains stable (2.92 in 1994).

Strengthening sales force efficiency within the Groupe.

In France

1994 was a difficult year because of the general economic situation which did little to inject any life into household spending, particularly following the increases in duties on alcohol brought into effect in 1993.

In this context, important work has been carried out to maintain the high level of sales force mobilisation.

The first step to increase motivation was reflected in a

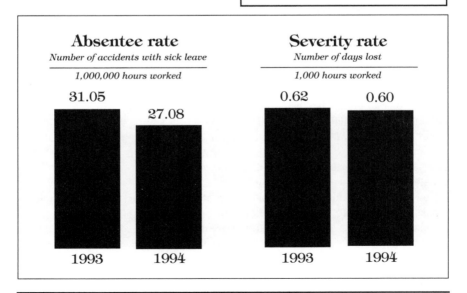

EXHIBIT 5–5   *(concluded)*

particular effort made in the field of internal communication. Conferences were organised for sales forces, support videos and company magazines were developed with the aim of stimulating them and focussing on the objectives in hand.

The second step was to equip the sales networks of certain companies (Pernod and Ricard) with modern computer systems.

Thanks to a portable P.C. each sales representative is now connected on a daily basis with his or her sales manager. This P.C. enables the representative to have at his or her disposal at any moment, information necessary for client contact. It also enables him/her to communicate effortlessly with his/her supervisor.

Finally, particular attention was paid to the methods of payment used for the Pernod sales force, taking into consideration dynamics which are only too well known.

Also worth noting is the Sales Training programme within various subsidiaries (Pernod, Ricard Orangina etc....) which continue to successfully train new sales personnel.

Abroad

In 1994, the Group continued to grow beyond the frontiers of France.

To back up the development in operations, foreign subsidiaries notably put emphasis on improved efficiency of their sales network.

Irish Distillers introduced some changes into its sales force, and now boasts a brand-led structure. Campbell Distillers mobilised its sales force in preparation for a sales conference, planned for 1995. Pracsa computerised its sales department and thus improved efficiency in billing and customer response time. Finally, Ramazzoti installed a new range of software, aimed at sales representatives' portable PCs—a more user-friendly and adaptable way of answering the needs of a sales force.

EXHIBIT 5–6   Ford Motor Company, Employee Disclosure

FORD MOTOR COMPANY AND SUBSIDIARIES

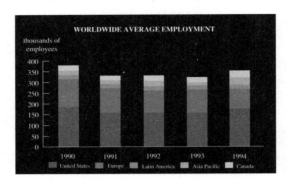

EMPLOYMENT DATA

Employment and Payrolls

In 1994, employment worldwide increased 5% to 337,778 from 321,925 in 1993. The increase resulted primarily from the inclusion of Hertz as a consolidated subsidiary beginning April 1, 1994. Worldwide payrolls were $15.8 billion in 1994, an increase of $2.1 billion from 1993.

Average employment by geographic area, compared with 1993, follows:

	1994	1993
United States	**180,460**	166,593
Canada	**16,840**	15,747
Europe	**102,738**	99,527
Latin America	**24,605**	27,321
Asia Pacific	**13,135**	12,737
Total	***337,778**	321,925

*Includes Hertz as a consolidated subsidiary.

Employment of Minority Group Personnel and Women at Year-End

	In United States*		Minorities		Women	
	1994	1993	1994	1993	1994	1993
Hourly employees	**109,500**	104,700	**24.3%**	24.1%	**14.6%**	13.4%
Salaried employees	**55,800**	54,900	**13.8**	13.3	**23.8**	23.6
Total	**165,300**	159,600	**20.8%**	20.4%	**17.7%**	16.9%

*Includes Ford U.S. and Ford Credit, Ford Electronics and Refrigeration Corp. and Ford Microelectronics, Inc. only.

Representation of Minority Group Members and Women in EEO-1 Job Categories at Year-End

Job Categories*	Blacks		Hispanics		Other Minorities**		Women	
	1994	1993	1994	1993	1994	1993	1994	1993
Officials & managers	**8.6%**	8.4%	**1.4%**	1.4%	**1.9%**	1.8%	**8.1%**	7.5%
Professionals	**7.1**	7.0	**1.9**	1.8	**5.0**	4.5	**21.9**	21.3
Technicians	**7.2**	7.3	**1.8**	1.6	**2.3**	2.3	**15.9**	16.9
Office and clerical	**16.8**	16.5	**4.1**	3.9	**1.0**	0.9	**48.0**	48.7
Craft workers (skilled)	**9.1**	9.0	**1.1**	1.0	**0.6**	0.6	**2.0**	1.8
Operatives (semiskilled)	**25.2**	25.4	**2.4**	2.3	**0.7**	0.6	**19.0**	17.7
Laborers (nonskilled)	**28.0**	28.1	**2.0**	1.8	**0.8**	0.9	**11.2**	9.9
Service workers	**26.9**	26.5	**1.6**	1.6	**0.6**	0.6	**14.7**	14.0
Percentage of workforce	**17.0%**	16.8%	**2.1%**	2.0%	**1.7%**	1.6%	**17.7%**	16.9%

*Excludes sales workers (retail), a category that is not applicable to Ford.

**Includes Asians, Pacific Islanders, American Indians or Alaskan Natives only.

EXHIBIT 5–7   VEBA, Environmental Disclosure

	1990	1991	1992	1993	1994
Capital expenditures	497	354	317	331	338
Operating costs and debt servicing	1,541	1,610	1,617	1,350	1,483

**Environmental
Protection in
DM million**

Scandinavia. In addition, one might also find extensive discussions of safety measures adopted by the company and how the company's products and services benefit the community at large.

Environmental disclosures reflect the point of view mentioned earlier: that contributing to society at large is a legitimate aim of business. We see these disclosures as an attempt to provide information to more than just the traditional financial statement users. These disclosures are directed to the consumers of the company's products and to the citizens in general who coexist with the firm. Relevant disclosures by European firms are also a reaction to environmental political parties that have some strength there.

Green accounting, as it is sometimes referred to, is just emerging, and the Europeans are leading the way. The 1990s have been dubbed the "environmental decade," and the enhanced awareness of the environment has created demands for more information on corporate environmental performance. At the present time, there is little comparability of the information provided and most of it is provided on a voluntary basis. Nevertheless, environmental disclosures are beginning to draw the attention of accounting standard setting bodies in a number of countries, including the United States. We believe that these developments bear watching.

CONCLUSION

During the 1960s and 1970s a disclosure explosion took place in most industrially developed countries, mandated by new national laws. Companies began revealing information about themselves that they had never revealed before. A major motivation for such laws seemed to be a low level of investor confidence. Beyond that, companies themselves began to realize that secrecy is self-defeating. Failure to make reasonable disclosures in response to user needs can severely limit the pool of funds available to a corporation. Potential providers of capital, when kept in the dark, will simply put their money elsewhere.

Studies by accountants have shown that firms significantly increase disclosure levels when they seek new sources of investment funds, that differences in disclosure levels among nations are rapidly narrowing, and that increased disclosure can lead to lower costs of capital for business enterprises. These findings are consistent with the arguments made in this and earlier chapters.

Disclosure is a way for the world's multinationals to reach out to investors and creditors in other countries without abandoning their own financial accounting practices. Exhibit 4–5 illustrates how the Swedish multinational Electrolux accomplishes this. Until the differences in generally accepted accounting principles observed by the world's multinationals can be reconciled and harmonized, disclosure can be a way around the transnational financial reporting problems discussed in Chapter 4.

Most accountants agree that the basic financial statements (balance sheet and income statement) have primacy over disclosures. In other words, such issues as valuing assets and determining net income—the so-called measurement issues— are, for the most part, more important than disclosure issues. Thus, disclosure issues are less controversial, and disclosure requirements tend to be easier to change than accounting measurement rules. Increased disclosure should not be a substitute for improving accounting measurements. Nevertheless, disclosure is an effective way to communicate information that does not fit what is required in financial statements by generally accepted accounting principles. Disclosures need not be constrained by financial reporting rules and are limited only by the imagination of accountants and corporate managements.

STUDY QUESTIONS

1. What is meant by the term *disclosure?* What is the difference between financial and nonfinancial disclosure? What is the difference between required and voluntary disclosure?

2. Why does the worldwide competition for investment funds seem to be propelling increased levels of disclosure by multinational corporations?

3. What is the purpose of presenting financial information disaggregated by product line and geography?

4. What is the purpose of financial forecast disclosures? Why don't more companies provide them?

5. What kinds of information about shares and shareholders can companies disclose to readers of their financial statements? What is the value of this information to the readers?

6. What is the value added statement? What is the philosophy behind it? Why don't U.S. companies prepare value added statements?

7. Why is there greater emphasis in Europe than in the United States on providing employee and environmental disclosures?

CASES

Bellhaven Ltd.

Transform the following traditional income statement of Bellhaven Ltd. into a value added statement:

BELLHAVEN LTD.
Statement of Income
For the Year Ended December 31, 1996

	£000s	
Sales	2,300	
Cost of goods sold	1,500	
Gross profit		800
Salaries and retirement benefits . . .	300	
Rent expense	45	
Outside services used	19	
Interest expense	38	402
Income before taxes		398
Provision before income taxes		160
Net income		238

NOTES:
1. All goods sold were purchased from outsiders.
2. Dividends declared and paid during 1996 amounted to £120 thousand.

Corpus Medical Equipment Company

Michael John works in the accounting department of Corpus Medical Equipment Company (CMEC), a U.S. multinational corporation. CMEC manufactures and sells medical equipment used in hospitals and doctors' offices. One of Michael's responsibilities is determining the segment disclosures that CMEC makes in its annual report to shareholders. Since CMEC is in only one product line, Michael's job is basically one of determining how to disclose CMEC's operations by geographic segment.

CMEC sells its products in the following countries, listed alphabetically: Canada, Czech Republic, France, Germany, Hong Kong, Hungary, Italy, Japan, Mexico, Netherlands, Poland, Singapore, Spain, Switzerland, Taiwan, United Kingdom, and United States. Manufacturing facilities are located in three low-wage countries, Mexico, Spain, and Taiwan, plus the United States. The facilities in these countries produce most of the products sold in their respective regions: Asia, Europe, and North America. Over 75 percent of CMEC's revenues are from four countries: Canada, Germany, Japan, and the United States. However, profit margins vary significantly, not only across regions but also across countries within regions. CMEC is just now expanding into Eastern Europe, but is well established in all other markets.

Questions

1. What criteria should Michael consider in determining the geographic segments that should be disclosed in CMEC's annual report?
2. Based on the criteria outlined in question 1, how would you disclose CMEC's operations by geographic segment? In other words, define CMEC's geographic segments. Justify your decision.

How Green Is My Balance Sheet?

When it comes to environmental accounting, many companies have yet to come clean. Those that publish green accounts usually offer a few charts (printed, of course, on recycled and unbleached paper) showing trends in their output of waste. But the gases and gunk are measured in kilos or tonnes, not pounds or dollars. Few companies convert such data into figures that can appear in financial accounts (which are usually on unrecycled, chlorine-bleached paper).[2]

The 1990s have been dubbed the "environmental decade," and the enhanced awareness of the environment has created demands for more information on corporate environmental performance. Environmental disclosures (sometimes called "green" accounting) are beginning to draw the attention of accounting standard-setting bodies in a number of countries, including the United States.

U.S. accounting standard setters are especially concerned that U.S. companies provide full disclosure of their actual and contingent liabilities for the costs of remediation and environmental cleanup. The United Nations recommends that multinational corporations provide environmental disclosures in their annual reports. Among the recommended disclosures are (1) corporate policy and programs adopted with respect to environmental protection measures, (2) emission targets and how the company is performing relative to those targets, and (3) amounts spent on environmental protection programs.

Others suggest that companies report their actual emissions of effluents into the air and water, energy consumption, and the trends of each. Compliance with environmental laws, including notices of violations received and fines paid, may also be reported.

---

[2]"How Green Is My Balance Sheet?" *The Economist*, September 3, 1994, p. 75.

Questions

1. What is the purpose of environmental disclosures in company annual reports?
2. For each of the above recommended disclosures,
   a. to whom and why is the information relevant?
   b. how reliable is the information?
3. Which if any of the above recommended disclosures do you think should be included in companies' annual reports? Why?

ADDITIONAL READINGS

Ahadiat, N., and B. R. Stewart. "International Geographic Segment Reporting Standards: A Case of the Harmonization of Accounting Reporting Practices." *International Journal of Accounting* 27, no. 1 (1992), pp. 45–56.

Emmanuel, C., and N. Garrod. "Segmental Reporting in the UK: How Does SSAP 25 Stand Up to International Comparison?" *European Accounting Review* 3, no. 3, 1994, pp. 547–62.

Fédération des Experts Comptables Européens. *FEE 1994 Investigation of Emerging Accounting Areas.* London, England: Routledge, 1995. Chapter 4, "Environmental Issues."

Gamble, G. O., K. Hsu, D. Kite, and R. R. Radtke. "Environmental Disclosures in Annual Reports and 10Ks: An Examination." *Accounting Horizons* (September 1995), pp. 34–54.

Gray, S. J., L. H. Radebaugh, and C. B. Roberts. "International Perceptions of Cost Constraints on Voluntary Information Disclosures: A Comparative Study of U.K. and U.S. Multinationals." *Journal of International Business Studies* (Fourth Quarter 1990), pp. 597–622.

Hawkshaw, A. "Accounting and the Environment: Status Quo Vadis?" *CA Magazine* (March 1991), pp. 22–27.

Meek, G. K., C. B. Roberts, and S. J. Gray. "Factors Influencing Voluntary Annual Report Disclosures by U.S., U.K., and Continental European Multinational Corporations." *Journal of International Business Studies* (Third Quarter 1995), pp. 555–72.

C　H　A　P　T　E　R

6

MULTINATIONAL CONSOLIDATIONS AND FOREIGN CURRENCY TRANSLATION

LEARNING OBJECTIVES

1. Discuss consolidations from an international perspective, including the reasons why consolidated financial statements are or are not prepared.
2. Know why exchange rates change.
3. Compare the current rate and temporal methods of foreign currency translation.
4. Understand the basic U.S. requirements for foreign currency translation under *FASB Statement No. 52.*
5. Be familiar with foreign currency translation practices in countries outside the United States.

This chapter deals with the preparation of consolidated (group) financial statements by multinational corporations. We first cover consolidation practices around the world and then examine a related issue unique to multinational corporations—foreign currency translation. These topics are complicated and advanced, so our coverage necessarily touches only the basic ideas. Nevertheless, we feel that some knowledge of these topics is important to an initial exposure to international accounting.

THE BASIC IDEA

Consolidated financial statements combine the separate financial statements of two or more companies to yield a single set of financial statements *as if* the individual companies were really one. What is the rationale for preparing consolidated financial statements? Often, a business finds it advantageous to organize itself as a set of separate (legal) corporate entities rather than as one large corporate entity. For example, tax savings sometimes occur because of the way corporate income tax rates are structured. Or a company may separately incorporate the components of its business to limit legal liability. Multinationals are often required by the countries in which they do business to set up a separate corporation in each country. The point is that a *legal* entity is not necessarily the same as an *economic* entity. From an economic point of view, the activities of these various legal entities are centrally administered from corporate headquarters. Thus, the intent of consolidated financial statements is to provide financial accounting information about the group of companies from an overall perspective.

Transactions among the members of a corporate family are not included on consolidated financial statements; only assets, liabilities, revenues, and expenses with external third parties are shown. By law, however, the separate corporate entities are required to keep their own accounting records and to prepare individual financial statements. This means that transactions with other members of the group must be identified so they can be *excluded* when the consolidated statements are prepared. The situation is analogous to preparing combined financial statements for a family. Even though a child may owe a parent some money, from the perspective of the family entity, the liability on the child's personal balance sheet and the receivable on the parent's offset one another. When the child is given his or her weekly allowance, there is a transfer of funds on an individual basis. However, the family unit is no better or worse off as a result. The family's wealth is affected only when that money is given to someone outside the family. Thus, transactions that are all in the family affect individual members but not the family as a whole. The same holds true for corporate "families."

The process of preparing consolidated financial statements involves adding up the individual assets, liabilities, revenues, and expenses reported on the separate financial statements and then *eliminating* the intracompany ones. One company—the *parent*—normally dominates the other *subsidiary* companies. Taking a simple example, assume the following selected items from the individual financial statements of the parent and one subsidiary company:

	Parent	Subsidiary
Cash	$ 100	$ 75
Receivables	360*	280
Payables	90	100*
Revenues	2,000†	2,300
Expenses	1,600	1,900†

*Subsidiary owes Parent $50.

†Subsidiary rented some machinery from Parent for $400.

The $50 receivable that Parent includes on its financial statements and the $50 payable included on Subsidiary's statements represent an intracompany item. Since the purpose of consolidated financial statements is to treat the separate entities as if they were one, it would be incorrect to include this item on the consolidated financial statements. After all, the company cannot owe itself. Similarly, from a consolidated perspective, revenues and expenses would each be overstated by $400 if the rental transaction were included on the consolidated financial statements. Accountants handle these kinds of things by preparing a *consolidation worksheet,* as illustrated by the following:

			Eliminations		
	Parent	Subsidiary	Debit	Credit	Consolidated
Cash	$100	$75			$175
Receivables	360	280		50*	590
Payables	90	100	50*		140
Revenues	2,000	2,300	400†		3,900
Expenses	1,600	1,900		400†	3,100

*Intracompany receivable/payable.

†Intracompany revenue/expense.

Thus, on a consolidated basis, receivables are $590; payables are $140; revenues are $3,900; and expenses total $3,100.

To reiterate, the purpose of consolidated financial statements is to present information from an overall perspective about a group of companies under common control and operating as an economic unit.

AN INTERNATIONAL PERSPECTIVE ON CONSOLIDATED FINANCIAL STATEMENTS

Consolidated financial statements first appeared around the turn of the 20th century in the United States. This was a time of great economic expansion during which a number of corporations grew into giants. The era witnessed a wave of corporate mergers. It is said that J. P. Morgan was so proud of his U.S. Steel Company (the first billion-dollar company in the world) that he insisted on preparing and disseminating consolidated financial statements since the company's inception in 1901. Since *holding companies* first became important in the United States, it is not surprising that U.S. accountants were the first to experiment with consolidated financial statements. These statements are now a part of U.S. generally accepted accounting principles.

Holding companies became important in Great Britain and the Netherlands in the 1920s, so consolidated financial statements appeared there somewhat later than in the United States. Today, they are required in both countries. The practice moved much more slowly in the other European countries: German law began requiring consolidations in the 1960s, although for domestic German subsidiaries only. The requirement was extended to all subsidiaries—German and non-German—effective 1990. French law requiring consolidated financial statements was enacted in the late 1980s. In Italy, only companies whose shares are listed on the stock exchange must prepare consolidated statements. In Switzerland large companies and those listed on the stock exchange must prepare them. Japan's requirement dates from 1977.

The observance or nonobservance of consolidated financial statements in a country can be related to several of the variables shaping accounting development discussed in Chapter 1.

1. The Legalistic/Nonlegalistic Orientation of Accounting.   Countries with a legalistic approach to accounting tend to focus on the legal entity as the object to be accounted for. In nonlegalistic countries, accounting emphasizes the economic entity. Therefore, consolidated financial statements are less common in legalistic countries, but are the norm in nonlegalistic countries. Nevertheless, the effect of this factor in legalistic countries is becoming less important because of the two factors discussed next.

2. The Relationship between Business and Capital Providers.   Group financial statements were first accepted in the Netherlands, Great Britain, and the United States—countries where financial accounting is oriented toward the decision needs of a diverse set of investors and creditors for whom the annual report is an important source of information about the company. Consolidated financial statements are also often used by multinational corporations—regardless of home country—that have global financing strategies. When a company secures funds on a worldwide basis, it probably prepares consolidated financial statements. Thus, the worldwide competition for funds seems to be propelling this practice (a point that is discussed in relation to disclosure issues in Chapter 5).

3. Political and Economic Ties.   Finally, political and economic ties affect this practice. Accounting technology is imported and exported, which is why consolidations are customary in Mexico and the Philippines, countries heavily influenced by the United States. As a result of U.K. influence, such statements are also widespread among British Commonwealth countries such as Australia, Malaysia, and South Africa. One of the most dramatic examples today is occurring within the European Union (EU). The *Seventh Company Law Directive* requiring consolidated accounts was adopted in 1983, and is now in force throughout the EU. It has had a considerable impact on consolidation practices in EU member countries. Indeed the effect of EU *Directives* extends to other European countries as well. Some companies from non-EU countries voluntarily comply with EU *Directives* in anticipation of their countries joining the EU.

Preparing consolidated financial statements is becoming the norm for the world's multinational corporations. Investors realize that without consolidated financial statements, companies can conceal losses in unconsolidated subsidiaries and thus hide the economic status of the entire group. To illustrate, consider the consolidations example discussed earlier. Suppose that the parent company is operating at below-normal profits. It could increase its reported profits by increasing the rental charge to the subsidiary above the current $400 amount. From a consolidated perspective, raising the rent has no effect on group profits since the rent is intracompany and gets eliminated in the consolidation process. But as far as the parent's own financial statements are concerned, an increased rental charge to the subsidiary "drops right down into income." The parent could accomplish the same result by shifting some of its employees to the subsidiary's payroll. Again, this would not affect consolidated profits, but it directly increases the parent's profits by reducing expenses. A third possibility is to sell some inventory to the subsidiary at inflated prices.

Firms that do not publish consolidated statements typically publish parent-only financial statements. Since they do not publish the subsidiaries' separate financial statements, they have an opportunity to control their profits using methods like those described above. While we are not suggesting that all multinational companies preparing parent-only statements engage in such practices, knowledge of these *possibilities* casts a long shadow over such financial statements.

The trend toward consolidated financial statements is unmistakable. *Standard 27,* "Consolidated Financial Statements and Accounting for Investments in Subsidiaries," issued by the International Accounting Standards Committee (IASC), reinforces this trend. *Standard 27* modifies (and supersedes) the earlier *Standard* issued in 1976.

Having argued in favor of consolidated financial statements, we should also point out that they have their limitations. If a company is heavily dependent on a particular product line or on a certain area of the world for its profits, consolidated financial statements can mask such dependencies without additional disclosures. Also, the existence of specific unprofitable operations may be somewhat hidden when blended with the rest of the company. And, changing product mixes are harder to detect unless the company provides additional information. For these reasons corporations are increasingly disclosing—on a supplemental basis—detailed accounting information by product line and geographic area. (This subject was explored in Chapter 5.)

FOREIGN CURRENCY TRANSLATION

The foreign subsidiaries of multinational corporations (MNCs) normally keep their accounting records and prepare their financial statements in the currency of the country in which they are located. They do this because it would be too inconvenient to transact business in anything other than the local currency and too impractical to record these transactions in accounting records using another country's currency. As a result, the individual financial statements of a multinational's foreign subsidiaries are expressed in many different currencies. For example, a U.S. multinational corporation may have separate foreign subsidiary financial statements expressed in pounds, pesos, francs, yen, marks, and lire. Yet in order for worldwide consolidated financial statements to be prepared, the subsidiaries' financial statements must all be expressed in a single currency (the U.S. dollar for U.S. multinationals). It is not possible to add up assets, liabilities, revenues, and expenses when they are expressed in different currencies. Therefore, whenever multinational corporations prepare their consolidated financial statements, the financial statements from individual foreign subsidiaries must be *translated* from the currency of the foreign country into the currency of the country where the multinational is headquartered. Foreign currency translation is accomplished using exchange rates.

Exchange Rates

The major currencies of the world are traded in many places and in many ways. An *exchange rate* is the price of one currency relative to another; that is, how much of one currency it takes to buy so much of another currency. (Those of you who have traveled outside the United States probably exchanged your U.S. dollar traveler's checks for some foreign currency. You may recall seeing quoted exchange rates in bank windows or stores.)

Exchange rates are not stable over time; they fluctuate just like the price of nearly everything else does. Exchange rates change for the following reasons:

1. *Trade balance of payments surpluses or deficits.* When a country exports more than it imports, it is said to run a trade balance of payments surplus. Surpluses cause the nation's currency to appreciate in value (i.e., to

strengthen). The opposite condition—trade deficits—causes a currency to command less of other nations' currencies.

2. *Relative rates of inflation.* Currencies of countries with higher rates of inflation depreciate relative to the currencies of countries with lower levels of inflation. Generally speaking, inflation means that one is able to buy less and less of everything (including another country's currency) for a fixed amount of one's own currency.

3. *Relative interest rates.* Whenever one nation has higher interest rates relative to other nations, its currency appreciates in value. (Foreigners purchase more of its currency in order to invest in and earn the higher interest.)

4. *Political factors and government intervention.* For international transactions, the currencies of countries considered politically stable tend to be favored over the currencies of unstable countries. Governments also buy and sell currencies when they want to change exchange rates.

Which Exchange Rate(s)?

Given that exchange rates change, a question arises as to which exchange rate should be used to translate the financial statements of a foreign subsidiary. One possibility is the exchange rate at the balance sheet date (i.e., the MNC's fiscal year-end). Accountants often refer to this as the *current,* or *year-end,* exchange rate. However, translating all financial statement items at the rate existing at the balance sheet date is incompatible with historical cost, the basis for current U.S. generally accepted accounting principles.

You can see why in the following example. Suppose a U.S. parent invests $30,000 in a foreign subsidiary and the subsidiary converts the money to its local currency when the exchange rate is 1 LC (local currency) = $1.25. The foreign subsidiary takes its LC24,000 ($30,000 ÷ 1.25) and buys land. On a historical cost basis, the land has a value of LC24,000 or $30,000. If by year-end the exchange rate changes to 1 LC = $1.50 and is used to translate the LC24,000 piece of land, it will appear on the consolidated U.S.-dollar financial statements at $36,000 [LC24,000 × (1 LC = $1.50)]. The piece of land appears to have magically increased in value!

Another possibility is to use the exchange rate when the transaction was first recorded (in this case, when the land was bought, i.e., 1 LC = $1.25). Accountants refer to this as the *historical* exchange rate. This way, the land would always appear on the consolidated balance sheet at $30,000.

Unfortunately, another problem arises when historical exchange rates are used. Since the various assets are acquired at different times, different exchange rates have to be used to translate them. When this happens, the translated balance sheet no longer balances. What to do with the difference between debits and credits is a highly controversial subject among accountants. The amount of the imbalance arises mechanically as a result of the translation process and does not fit the definition of asset, liability, or owners' equity. Yet it has to go somewhere to preserve the accounting equation.

The following example illustrates the point. Assume that on January 1, U.S. Multinational, Inc. (USMI), forms a foreign subsidiary named Foreign Sub. USMI converts $100,000 into Foreign Sub's local currency (LC) at a time when the exchange rate is 1 LC = $1.25. The initial investment, therefore, is LC80,000. Foreign Sub's opening balance sheet (in local currency and dollars) looks like this:

FOREIGN SUB
Balance Sheet
January 1

Cash	LC 80,000 × (1 LC = $1.25) = $100,000
Owners' equity	LC 80,000 × (1 LC = $1.25) = $100,000

Now, assume that on February 1, when the exchange rate is 1 LC = $1.30, Foreign Sub buys LC40,000 worth of inventory. On February 28, when the exchange rate is 1 LC = $1.40, Foreign Sub buys a fixed asset for LC40,000. The March 1 balance sheet will look like this:

FOREIGN SUB
Balance Sheet
March 1

Inventory	LC 40,000 × (1 LC = $1.30) =	$ 52,000
Fixed asset	LC 40,000 × (1 LC = $1.40) =	$ 56,000
	LC 80,000	$108,000
Owners' equity	LC 80,000 × (1 LC = $1.25) =	$100,000
	LC 80,000	$100,000

While the balance sheet before translation (in local currency) balances, it does not balance after translation into U.S. dollars. In the translated balance sheet, debits exceed credits by $8,000. What to do with the nonexistent credit is a good question, and accountants disagree on the answer.

A conclusion may be apparent to you. Preserving the historical cost basis of accounting by translating foreign financial statements at different historical exchange rates introduces a dangling debit or credit whose nature is difficult to

---

EXHIBIT 6–1   Illustration of Temporal Method

Assume that the following trial balance, expressed in local currency (LC), is received from a foreign subsidiary. The year-end exchange rate is 1 LC = $1.40, and the average exchange rate for the year is 1 LC = $1.20. Under the temporal method, the trial balance is translated as follows:

1. Inventory and cost of goods sold, at the exchange rate when the inventory was purchased. Assume this is 1 LC = $1.25.
2. Fixed assets and depreciation expense, at the exchange rate when the fixed assets were purchased. Assume this is 1 LC = $0.90.
3. Other balance sheet items, the year-end exchange rate (1 LC = $1.40).
4. Revenues and expenses that are incurred evenly throughout the year (sales and other expenses) at the average exchange rate (1 LC = $1.20).
5. Beginning owners' equity in dollars equals last year's ending owners' equity (translated) in dollars. Assume this is $81,000.
6. A "translation" gain or loss is created to balance the dollar-denominated trial balance.

Thus, the temporal method translation looks like this:

| | Local Currency | | Exchange | U.S. Dollars | |
	Debit	Credit	Rate	Debit	Credit
Cash	LC 15,000		(1 LC = $1.40)	$ 21,000	
Inventory	70,000		(1 LC = $1.25)	87,500	
Fixed assets	35,000		(1 LC = $0.90)	31,500	
Payables		LC 30,000	(1 LC = $1.40)		$ 42,000
Owners' equity					
(beginning)		70,000	—		81,000
Sales		200,000	(1 LC = $1.20)		240,000
Cost of goods sold	120,000		(1 LC = $1.25)	150,000	
Depreciation expense	5,000		(1 LC = $0.90)	4,500	
Other expenses	55,000		(1 LC = $1.20)	66,000	
Translation loss				2,500	
	LC300,000	LC300,000		$363,000	$363,000

---

define. That problem can be solved by translating financial statements using a single exchange rate, but the procedure is inconsistent with the historical cost basis of accounting. Either choice involves some undesirable side effects.

Translation Methods Used

U.S. multinational corporations must follow the requirements of *Statement 52,* "Foreign Currency Translation," issued by the Financial Accounting Standards Board (FASB) in 1981. Its provisions will be discussed in a moment. Prior to *Statement 52,* however, U.S. multinational corporations translated the financial statements of their foreign subsidiaries under the terms of *Statement 8,* issued by the FASB in 1975. *Statement 8* required the use of what is called the *temporal method* of foreign currency translation. Exhibit 6–1 illustrates the temporal method in detail. In general, a mixture of different historical exchange rates and the current exchange rate are used to translate the items on the subsidiary's balance sheet and income statement. The resulting "dangling debit or credit" is treated as a loss or gain on the consolidated income statement. Notice, for example, in Exhibit 6–1 that a $2,500 translation loss is included in the company's consolidated income.

During the years that *Statement 8* was in effect, exchange rates were highly volatile, and because the translation imbalance was required to increase or decrease reported income or loss, corporations experienced more volatility in their reported earnings than managements desired. A volatile earnings pattern normally indicates riskiness, yet managements alleged that translation gains and losses were on paper only—that they had little or no direct effect on actual cash flows. A large number of accountants cried "foul!" and it is fair to say that *Statement 8* was probably the most unpopular Statement ever issued by the FASB. For this reason *Statement 8* was replaced by *Statement 52.*

Under the provisions of *Statement 52,* a foreign subsidiary is classified as either (1) self-sustaining and autonomous or (2) integral to the activities of the parent company. A *self-sustaining, autonomous* subsidiary is one that operates relatively independently from the parent company. Revenues and expenses respond mostly to local conditions, few of the subsidiary's cash flows impact the parent's cash flows, and there are few intracompany transactions with the parent. The local (foreign) currency is said to be its "functional" currency. The balance sheet for a self-sustaining subsidiary is translated at the year-end exchange rate and the income statement at the average-for-the-year exchange rate. There is no effect on reported consolidated earnings from translating the financial statements of autonomous foreign subsidiaries. This so-called *modified current rate method* preserves the balance sheet and income statement financial ratios in U.S. dollars as in the local currency. Exhibit 6–2 illustrates this method.

On the other hand, an *integral* foreign subsidiary operates as an extension of and is dependent on the parent. Revenues and expenses are largely influenced by the parent, the subsidiary's cash flows directly impact the parent's cash flows, and there are frequent intracompany transactions with the parent. For this type of subsidiary, the U.S. dollar is said to be its "functional" currency. The financial statements of such subsidiaries are translated using the temporal method, illustrated in Exhibit 6–1. (This method has the effect of translating subsidiaries' financial statements as if their transactions originally occurred in U.S. dollars.) In other words, the same temporal method used under *Statement 8* continues to be used under *Statement 52* for integral subsidiaries. However, because the financial statements of fewer foreign subsidiaries are now translated using the temporal method, the overall impact of fluctuating exchange rates on reported earnings of U.S. multinational corporations is less.

The Australian, British, and Canadian standards on foreign currency translation basically recommend treatment similar to *Statement 52,* as does *International*

EXHIBIT 6–2   Illustration of Modified Current Rate Method

Translating the trial balance from Exhibit 6–1 into U.S. dollars would be performed as shown below. (Note that when employing the modified rate method, owners' equity stated in U.S. dollars is a "balancing" amount.)

	Local Currency		Exchange	U.S. Dollars	
	Debit	Credit	Rate	Debit	Credit
Cash	LC 15,000		(1 LC = $1.40)	$ 21,000	
Inventory	70,000		"	98,000	
Fixed assets	35,000		"	49,000	
Payables		LC 30,000	"		$ 42,000
Owners' equity		70,000	to balance		102,000
(beginning)					
Sales		200,000	(1 LC = $1.20)		240,000
Cost of goods sold	120,000		"	144,000	
Depreciation expense	5,000		"	6,000	
Other expense	55,000		"	66,000	
	LC300,000	LC300,000		$384,000	$384,000

Accounting Standard 21, "Accounting for the Effects of Foreign Exchange Rates." The requirements for foreign currency translation are generally flexible in most other nations. For example, many Japanese MNCs use the year-end exchange rate to translate current assets and liabilities, historical rates for noncurrent assets and liabilities, and defer any resulting imbalance as an asset or liability. The EU *Seventh Company Directive* (on consolidations), referred to earlier, does not specify how to translate the financial statements of foreign subsidiaries. However, nonbinding recommendations were published in 1995 by the EU Accounting Advisory Forum (see Chapter 3). Still, foreign currency translation is an unresolved issue in the European Union. Overall, it is an area with significant diversity of practice and little hope for a quick resolution. International comparability is likely to be a problem for some time to come.

In Chapter 1 we argued that inflation can strain the historical cost model of accounting. Inflation is related to foreign currency translation, since exchange rates change in response to different levels of inflation among countries. The fact that the problems of inflation and fluctuating exchange rates are related suggests that accounting solutions are also related. Hence, the use of the current rate method is another source of stress on historical cost accounting.

CONCLUSION

Consolidated financial statements are intended to present an overall look at a company's operations and financial position. Unfortunately, for multinational corporations, existing accounting tools are not always up to the task. Measuring accounting earnings is an imperfect process anyway, but when fluctuating foreign exchange rates are introduced into that process, it gets even more jumbled. In our opinion, foreign currency translation is one of the most conceptually difficult tasks facing accountants today, and potential solutions do not fit neatly into the traditional accounting framework.

When examining the financial statements of companies from different countries, special care should be taken to understand the companies' consolidation policies and how they translate the financial statements of their foreign operations. The variety of possible methods makes comparing the statements very difficult.

STUDY QUESTIONS

1. What is the purpose of preparing consolidated financial statements? Why are transactions among the members of a corporate family not included in the consolidated financial statements?

2. How do the following factors influence the practice of preparing consolidated financial statements?
   a. The legalistic/nonlegalistic orientation of accounting.
   b. The worldwide competition for funds.
   c. Political and economic ties.

3. Why is preparing consolidated financial statements becoming the norm for the world's multinational corporations?

4. What is an exchange rate and why do exchange rates change over time?

5. What does it mean to translate the financial statements of a foreign subsidiary? Why is it necessary to do this before a multinational corporation's consolidated financial statements can be prepared?

6. What does it mean to translate a financial statement item at the historical exchange rate? What does it mean to translate an item at the current exchange rate?

7. Describe the essential features of *FASB Statement 52,* "Foreign Currency Translation."

CASES

Parent and Subsidiary

The following selected amounts are from the separate financial statements of Parent Company (unconsolidated) and Subsidiary Company:

	Parent	Subsidiary
Cash	$ 180	$ 75
Receivables	385	195
Accounts payable	245	110
Retained earnings	790	680
Revenues	4,980	3,520
Rent income	0	210
Dividend income	300	0
Expenses	4,260	2,940

Additional information:

a. Parent owes Subsidiary $65.

b. Parent owns 100 percent of Subsidiary. During the year, Subsidiary paid Parent a dividend of $300.

c. Subsidiary owns the building that Parent rents for $210.

d. During the year, Parent sold some inventory to Subsidiary for $2,100. It had cost Parent $1,500. Subsidiary, in turn, sold the inventory to an unrelated party for $3,000.

Questions

1. What is Parent's (unconsolidated) net income?
2. What is Subsidiary's net income?
3. What is the consolidated profit on the inventory that Parent originally sold to Subsidiary?
4. What are the amounts of the following, on a consolidated basis?
   a. Cash.
   b. Receivables.
   c. Accounts payable.
   d. Revenues.
   e. Expenses.
   f. Dividend income.
   g. Rent income.
   h. Retained earnings.

5. If, instead of consolidated financial statements, Parent presented only its own unconsolidated statements, what kinds of transactions could it engage in with Subsidiary to improve the appearance of its own profitability?

Égalité S.A. (A)

Huge Multinational, Inc., received the following trial balance from its French subsidiary, Égalité S.A. It is expressed in French francs (FF).

	Debit	Credit
Cash	3,000	
Inventory	78,0000	
Fixed assets (net)	48,000	
Payables		2,000
Capital stock		40,000
Retained earnings (beginning)		60,000
Sales		305,000
Cost of goods sold	227,000	
Salaries	25,000	
Depreciation expense	6,000	
Other expenses	20,000	
	407,000	407,000

Notes: 1. When Égalité was formed, the exchange rate was 1 FF = $0.25. The fixed asset was purchased by Égalité immediately after formation.

   2. At year-end the exchange rate was 1 FF = $0.19. The average-for-the-year exchange rate was 1 FF = $0.21.

Questions

1. Assume that Égalité is an autonomous subsidiary. Translate Égalité's trial balance into U.S. dollars using the modified current rate method required by *FASB Statement 52*.
2. What is Égalité's net income expressed in French francs?
3. What is Égalité's net income expressed in U.S. dollars?

Égalité S.A. (B)

Assume the same information as in Égalité S.A. (A), except that the year-end exchange rate is 1 FF = $0.19, and the average-for-the-year exchange rate is 1 FF = $0.16.

Questions

1. Translate Égalité's trial balance into U.S. dollars using the modified current rate method required by *FASB Statement 52*.
2. What is Égalité's net income expressed in French francs? How does this compare to the answer you determined in (A)?
3. What is Égalité's net income expressed in U.S. dollars? How does this compare to the answer you determined in (A)?

Égalité S.A. (C)

Refer to the information provided in Égalité S.A. (A). If Égalité is deemed an integral subsidiary, Huge Multinational translates Égalité's trial balance according to the temporal method, as follows:

a. Cash and payables at the year-end exchange rate.

b. Sales, salaries, and other expenses at the average exchange rate.

c. Fixed assets and depreciation expense at the rate in effect when the fixed asset was purchased.

d. Inventory at the rate in effect when purchased. Cost of goods sold at a weighted average rate based on beginning and ending inventory and purchases.

e. Capital stock at the rate in effect when Égalité was formed.

f. Beginning retained earnings is the translated (U.S.-dollar) balance of the prior year's ending retained earnings.

g. A translation gain (loss) is credited (debited) to bring the dollar-denominated trial balance into balance.

Questions

1. Translate Égalité's trial balance according to the technique described above. Assume that the relevant exchange rates for inventory and cost of goods sold are 1 FF = $0.20 and 1 FF = $0.22, respectively. (Other exchange rates are given in Égalité S.A. (A).) Assume that the translated U.S.-dollar balance of beginning retained earnings is $7,700.
2. What is Égalité's net income expressed in French francs?
3. What is Égalité's net income expressed in U.S. dollars?

ADDITIONAL READINGS

"Accounting for Groups." Chapter 7 in Samuels, J. M., R. E. Brayshaw, and J. M. Craner, *Financial Statement Analysis in Europe*. London: Chapman & Hall, 1995.

"Consolidation." Chapter 15 in Nobes, C., and R. Parker, *Comparative International Accounting*. Hemel-Hempstead: Prentice Hall International (*UK*), 1995.

Diggle, G., and C. Nobes. "European Rule-Making in Accounting: The Seventh Directive as a Case Study." *Accounting and Business Research* (Autumn 1994), pp. 319–33.

Gray, S. J., A. G. Coenenberg, and P. D. Gordon. *International Group Accounting: Issues in European Harmonization,* 2nd ed. New York: Routledge, 1993.

Kirsch, R. J. and D. Becker-Dermer. "Proposed Revisions of International Accounting Standard No. 21 and their Implications for Translation Accounting in Selected English-Speaking Countries." *International Journal of Accounting* 31, no. 1, 1995, pp. 1–24.

Kirsch, R. J. and T. G. Evans. "The Implementation of SFAS 52: Did the Functional Currency Approach Prevail?" *International Journal of Accounting* 29, no. 1, 1994, pp. 20–33.

Lowe, H. D. "Shortcomings of Japanese Consolidated Financial Statements." *Accounting Horizons* (September 1990), pp. 1–9.

7

INTERNATIONAL FINANCIAL STATEMENT ANALYSIS

LEARNING OBJECTIVES

1. Understand how cultural values may influence a country's accounting values.
2. Identify the accounting values that influence a country's accounting system and measurement and disclosure practices.
3. Be aware that when analyzing foreign financial statements, differences exist in language, terminology, and format.
4. Recognize that interpreting return, risk, and liquidity ratios requires an understanding of the country's business practices.
5. Apply the financial analysis framework presented in this chapter to the financial statements of Sumitomo Electric Corporation and interpret the results.

Suppose you have just been recently hired as a financial analyst for a major U.S. multinational corporation. Your boss is extremely interested in expanding operations in the Pacific Rim. She has given you a set of financial statements from a Japanese corporation, one with a solid reputation for sustained growth and profitability, which comes highly recommended as an investment opportunity. You sharpen your pencils, get out your calculator, and proceed to apply the ratio analysis techniques you learned as a student. As the company comes so highly recommended, you assume it will be a routine exercise to generate the supporting numbers to back up the purchase decision.

Imagine your surprise when you finish your analysis and discover that the Japanese company is a financial disaster, apparently on the verge of bankruptcy. Its debt-to-asset ratio is nearly twice as large as that of U.S. firms. Contributing to your worries is short-term debt nearly double that of U.S. firms. The equity base is approximately half of what U.S. firms usually have. You are wondering who in the world would recommend this company as an acquisition prospect.

This chapter explores what is wrong with this picture. A *framework* is developed that uses the information from the previous chapters to analyze a foreign-based corporation's financial position in light of the environment in which it operates.

FINANCIAL ACCOUNTING REFLECTS THE ENVIRONMENT IT SERVES

One of the biggest problems in the Japanese scenario described above is the analyst's assumption that U.S. ratio analysis expectations can be "'exported" for analyzing foreign financial statements. This is effective only if the foreign financial accounting system and the operating environment closely parallel that of the United States. Chapters 1 through 6 showed that this is rarely the case. Each country's national financial accounting system evolved to serve the needs of its domestic environment and, in particular, the needs of the users of accounting information in that country. Therefore, each country's national financial accounting and reporting requirements are different. The best way to properly analyze financial statements from another country is to understand the domestic accounting system and business practices in that country.

Becoming familiar with each country's accounting and business practices is a monumental task. However, we have the necessary tools. We need to develop an approach—a framework—that we can use with any country.

A FRAMEWORK FOR FINANCIAL STATEMENT ANALYSIS

Environmental Variables

Chapter 1 discussed how an accounting system is shaped by the environment in which it operates. The many variables discussed include the relationship between business and the providers of capital, political and economic ties with other countries, the legal system, levels of inflation, the size and complexity of business enterprises, sophistication of management and the financial community, and general levels of education. Exhibit 7–1 compares the U.S. and Japanese environments using these variables. It shows that the two countries differ on two critical dimensions, the providers of capital and the legal system. Our analysis begins with an awareness of these differences.

EXHIBIT 7–1   Environmental Variables

Variable	United States	Japan
Business and providers of capital	Investors	Banks
Political and economic ties with other countries	Influenced by U.K.	Influenced by Germany; later by U.S. after WWII
Legal system	Common law	Code law
Levels of inflation	Low	Low
Size and complexity of business enterprises	Large and complex	Large and complex
Sophistication of management and the financial community	High	High
General levels of education	High	High

Cultural Values

The accounting system is also influenced by culture and the values that a society shares. Knowing something about a people's values can help us understand their accounting system. Values are defined as a tendency to prefer a certain state of affairs over another. For instance, people in the United States value the concept of individualism whereas in Japan it is not the individual who is important but how the individual relates to the group. Japanese culture maintains a strong degree of interdependence among individuals, and group norms are far more important than a single individual's opinion or professional judgment.

The Japanese society accepts that there is a natural hierarchical order in which each person has a role that is not questioned. In the United States, we do not accept the notion that power is distributed unequally. In fact, we demand that people have equality.

One final cultural dimension is discussed here—how a society feels about uncertainty and ambiguity. A culture that prefers less uncertainty depends on institutions to maintain conformity, and deviating from the norm or the rule is discouraged, as in Japan. Rules make people comfortable because the rule prescribes what to do in any circumstance, thus removing the uncertainty and need for judgment. The opposite is a society that values practice more than principles and allows for the exception to the rule, as in the United States and the United Kingdom.

Cultural values can be linked to *accounting values,* which gives us some insight into a country's accounting system and its measurement and disclosure practices. Exhibit 7–2 diagrams this link. This concept is explored more fully in the following section.

EXHIBIT 7–2   Culture, Accounting Values, and Accounting Systems—A Framework for Analysis

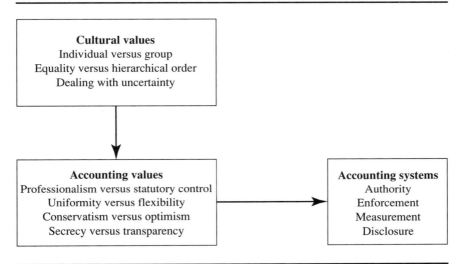

SOURCE: Adapted from S. J. Gray, "Towards a Theory of Cultural Influence on the Development of Accounting Systems Internationally," *Abacus* 24, no. 1 (1988), p. 7.

Accounting Values[1]

The following accounting values are not meant to be exhaustive, but are offered as representative of values that influence the development of national accounting systems and measurement and disclosure practices:

Professionalism versus statutory control.

Uniformity versus flexibility.

Conservatism versus optimism.

Secrecy versus transparency.

Knowing something about a country's accounting values helps us to interpret and understand the financial reports of companies operating in that environment. The goal is to be able to realistically analyze the financial reports of any multinational corporation, given the national accounting and business practices that evolved from the operating environment.

---

[1]This section is based on S. J. Gray, "Towards a Theory of Cultural Influence on the Development of Accounting Systems Internationally," *Abacus* 24, no. 1 (1988), pp. 1–15.

Accounting values include a preference for independent *professional judgment* as opposed to *statutory control.* A preference for exercising professional judgment is consistent with a preference for individualism and subjectivity, which we find in the accounting systems of countries listed in the British-American model from Chapter 1. The United Kingdom values the concept of presenting a "true and fair view" of a company's financial reports, and the auditor is given the right to use professional judgment to accomplish this goal. Statutory control, or compliance with prescriptive legal requirements, is an accounting value of both the Continental and the South American models. In Japan, France, and Germany, accountants follow legal rules and exercise much less judgment than in the United Kingdom.

A second set of accounting values that influence financial reporting systems is *uniformity versus flexibility.* A society that values uniformity shows a preference for the enforcement of uniform accounting practices, whereas a society that values flexibility takes into account the circumstances of individual companies. There is a link between this accounting value and the cultural value of dealing with uncertainty that we discussed in the prior section. Uniformity is found in the accounting practices of the code law Continental and South American models. Flexibility is exhibited by the countries in the common law British-American model. Once again, we see a difference between Japan and the United States; Japan's accounting system is influenced by uniformity, while flexibility prevails in the United States.

The accounting value of *conservatism* relates to the measurement of accounting information and manifests itself in a preference for a cautious approach to measurement as a way to cope with the uncertainty of future events. *Optimism* tolerates more uncertainty in measurement practices. To illustrate, many expenditures made by a company are expected to benefit future periods. Of course, the benefits are uncertain. Should these expenditures be expensed immediately, or should they be shown as an asset and charged to expenses in future periods? Conservatism calls for the former, while optimism would allow the latter in certain situations. The diversity of measurement practices was the topic of Chapter 2. Countries in the British-American model take a more optimistic approach to measurement than do those countries of the Continental and South American models. The difference in approach has been attributed to different providers of capital and the demands of different users as well as the influence of tax laws. For example, Japanese financial accounting is strongly influenced by the tax law, which leads to more conservative measurement practices in order to minimize taxes.

The last set of accounting values we discuss here is *secrecy* versus *transparency* in regard to disclosure practices, which was the topic of Chapter 5. The countries of the Continental and South American models show a preference for confidentiality and tend to restrict disclosure of information to management and those who provide the business financing. Secrecy and conservatism are related in that both result in a more cautious approach to reporting, as is seen in Japan. The

EXHIBIT 7–3   Accounting Models and Accounting Values

British-American	Continental	South American	Mixed Economy
Professionalism	Statutory control	Statutory control	Statutory control
Flexibility	Uniformity	Uniformity	Uniformity, flexibility
Optimism	Conservatism	Conservatism	Optimism, conservatism
Transparency	Secrecy	Secrecy	Secrecy, transparency

British-American model countries disclose more information and take a more publicly accountable approach to financial reporting, which is their response to the providers of capital being private investors. Exhibit 7–3 offers a matching of accounting values with the four accounting models discussed in Chapter 1.

ANALYSIS OF FINANCIAL INFORMATION

Language, Terminology, and Format

For English-speaking users, a barrier to usefulness exists if the report is not in English. Companies will naturally publish their reports in the national language of their country and then consider translating to second and perhaps third languages. Chapter 4 discussed convenience translations. Exhibit 7–4 provides a listing of countries whose companies provide English language translations of all or part of their annual reports. It appears that English is becoming the accepted language of business and that the language barrier is no longer an insurmountable problem.

Differences in accounting terminology also present a communication problem. Several terms in a U.K. annual report could confuse the American user. Stocks refer to inventory, receivables are called debtors, and payables are called creditors. Fixed assets refer to all assets retained for continuous use, not just property, plant, and equipment. The profit and loss account refers to the income statement and turnover means sales. Reserves usually refers to retained earnings.

The format of the British balance sheet is the opposite of a U.S. balance sheet with assets and liabilities running from lowest to highest liquidity. Fixed assets appear above current assets. The user of foreign financial statements must be observant and a little suspicious because things that appear familiar may in fact be quite different.

Convenience translations were discussed in Chapter 4. In this case, the user must be careful to notice that both the language and the monetary amounts have been translated for the user; however, the statements are still in foreign generally accepted accounting principles (GAAP) and cannot be directly compared to those of the user's home country. Chapter 4 also discussed

---

EXHIBIT 7–4   Language of Financial Statements of Leading Non-U.S.
Industrial Companies

Predominately English-Language (0–10%) of Reports Non-English)	*Considerable Percentage of Non-English (10%–50%)*	*Predominately Non-English (50% or more)*
Australia	Belgium	Austria
Canada	Brazil	France
Denmark	Italy	Mexico
Finland	Germany	South Korea
India		Spain
Ireland		
Japan		
Malaysia		
Netherlands		
Norway		
South Africa		
Sweden		
Switzerland		
United Kingdom		

Source: F.D.S. Choi and G. G. Mueller, *International Accounting* (Englewood Cliffs, N.J.: Prentice Hall, 1992), p. 414.

the fact that some multinationals provide limited restatements or secondary financial statements based on another set of GAAP, such as that of the International Accounting Standards Committee. Even if readers get financial statements in a language, currency unit, and based on accounting principles that they understand, they must still consider one additional point. Financial practices (as opposed to accounting practices) and business decision making differ around the world, and readers of foreign financial statements must understand how the business environment in a corporation's home country affects the firm's financial reports. This is especially critical if the user is comparing the accounting numbers of companies from different cultures. One device used to analyze financial reports is ratio analysis, which is the topic of the following section.

Ratio Analysis

Ratios of key items on the financial statements are calculated to determine such things as rate of return, riskiness, and the ability to pay debts (liquidity).

Indicators of Return.   Two popular ratios that provide the investor with information as to the rates of return on a particular investment are earnings per share and return on investment. Earnings per share gives the investor an indication of the earnings attributable to each share of stock and is calculated as follows:

$$\text{Earnings per share} = \frac{\text{Net income accruing to common stock}}{\text{Total shares of common stock outstanding}}$$

Return on investment indicates how efficiently capital has been employed by the company. Investment may be defined as total assets or as owners' equity. The asset base is used to indicate the return that the company generates on its asset commitment. Investors use return on equity when they are interested in the return that accrues to them on their contributed capital as common shareholders. The ratios are calculated as follows:

$$\text{Return on assets} = \frac{\text{Net income}}{\text{Total assets}}$$

$$\text{Return on equity} = \frac{\text{Net income}}{\text{Owners' equity}}$$

Indicators of Risk and Liquidity.   The ratios used to indicate risk and liquidity are the current ratio and the debt-to-asset ratio. The current ratio indicates the company's ability to pay its short-term creditors with its most liquid assets, the current assets. It is calculated as follows:

$$\text{Current ratio} = \frac{\text{Current assets}}{\text{Current liabilities}}$$

The debt-to-asset ratio provides the investor with another indicator of the relative risk of this investment. As the name implies, this ratio relates debt (investment provided by creditors) to the resources (assets) employed by the firm. Since liabilities must be paid off with company assets, the lower this ratio is, the greater the company's ability to pay off its debts, and therefore, the safer the company is perceived to be. Generally speaking, creditors should be more willing to lend money to, and investors should be more willing to invest money in, companies with lower debt-to-asset ratios. The reader should note that this is a very U.S. interpretation of the debt-to-asset ratio. More is said about this later. This ratio is computed as follows:

$$\text{Debt-to-asset} = \frac{\text{Total liabilities}}{\text{Total assets}}$$

EXHIBIT 7–5   Consolidated Five-Year Summary Sumitomo Electric Industries Ltd.

	Millions of Yen					Thousands of U.S. Dollars (Note 1)
	1994	1993	1992	1991	1990	1994
For the year:						
Net sales	¥1,101,533	¥1,136,711	¥1,157,239	¥1,113,720	¥1,001,037	$10,678,943
Cost of sales	902,300	946,718	963,854	919,077	828,273	8,747,455
Selling, general and administrative expenses	143,277	133,375	126,783	119,615	108,625	1,389,016
Operating income	55,956	56,618	66,602	75,028	64,139	542,472
Net income	29,532	29,060	32,065	31,604	26,631	286,301
Capital expenditures	51,836	56,197	96,092	88,494	68,317	502,530
Per share of common stock (yen and U.S. dollars):						
Net income—Primary	¥ 41.72	¥ 41.06	¥ 45.33	¥ 44.79	¥ 38.18	$ 0.404
Cash dividends	10.00	10.00	10.00	9.00	7.50	0.097
At year-end:						
Total assets	¥1,148,321	¥1,137,991	¥1,131,964	¥1,045,481	¥ 925,568	$11,132,535
Working capital	229,862	222,749	176,177	178,285	196,083	2,228,425
Total shareholders' equity	402,120	383,054	361,597	337,024	307,708	3,898,401
Weighted average number of shares outstanding (in thousands)	707,939	707,733	707,390	705,547	697,481	
Number of employees	39,355	34,972	33,747	32,922	28,863	

Sumitomo Electric Industries Ltd.

Let's use the consolidated five-year summary of financial statements of Sumitomo (Exhibit 7–5) to practice our financial statement analysis skills in the Japanese environment. Footnote #1 to the financial statements (Exhibit 7–6) alerts us to the fact that the statements have been translated to English and to U.S. dollars, but the GAAP remain Japanese. Our first step is to calculate the ratios, and then we interpret them. (While the ratios are calculated in U.S. dollars below, they would be the same in Japanese yen.) Earnings per share is taken directly from Exhibit 7–5 Sumitomo's consolidated five-year summary and is reported to be $0.404.

$$\text{Return on assets} = \frac{\$286{,}301}{\$11{,}132{,}535} = 2.57\%$$

$$\text{Return on equity} = \frac{\$286{,}301}{\$3{,}898{,}401} = 7.34\%$$

$$\text{Current ratio} = \frac{\$5{,}958{,}352}{\$3{,}729{,}927} = 1.60$$

EXHIBIT 7–6   Notes to Consolidated Financial Statements

---

1. Basis of Presenting Financial Statements

The accompanying consolidated financial statements are basically an English version of those which have been prepared in accordance with accounting principles generally accepted in Japan and filed with the Minister of Finance of Japan and stock exchanges in Japan. Accounting policies used for the original statements remain unchanged in this English version. The information disclosed and the manner of disclosure, however, have been modified to assist readers outside Japan to understand such information and the consolidated statements of shareholders' equity and changes in financial position have been added.

The translations of Japanese yen amounts into United States dollar amounts are included solely for the convenience of readers outside Japan and have been made at the rate of ¥103.15=US$1, the approximate rate of exchange prevailing on March 31, 1994.

Total current assets and total current liabilities are reported on the consolidated balance sheet of Sumitomo which is not reproduced here. Total debt is calculated by subtracting shareholders' equity from total assets ($11,132,535 − $3,898,401 = $7,234,134) as given on the consolidated five-year summary.

$$\text{Debt to asset} = \frac{\$7,234,134}{\$11,132,535} = 65.00\%$$

Indicators of return or profitability for Japanese companies are often lower, as they are for Sumitomo, than for U.S. companies because Japanese managers do not focus on short-term profit. Exhibit 7–7 shows us that Japanese companies appear less profitable over time than U.S. companies when comparing return on equity for Japanese and U.S. publicly listed companies. Japanese GAAP results in more conservative (lower) net income figures than U.S. GAAP. Japanese managers have more job security because stockholders are more focused on building long-term strength and less on the infamous "bottom line."

The current ratio is lower than what a U.S. investor in a U.S. company would hope to see (about 1.9 to 1 in the United States). However, a Japanese investor would not find it low at all because in Japan short-term borrowing is actually preferred to long-term debt. This allows for a more frequent adjustment of interest rates on the debt and a lower interest expense as short-term rates are usually lower than long-term. The short-term debt is continuously renewed and so serves the purpose of long-term debt and substitutes for longer-term borrowing.

The debt-to-asset ratio is high for average U.S. manufacturing companies (47 percent in the United States), but it is a sign of good health in Japan. In Japan this ratio is an indication of how much confidence the banks have in a company. Companies have low debt-to-asset ratios because they are unable to get any more credit from the banks. Rather than demonstrating a risky company, in Japan, the reverse is true—companies with high debt-to-asset ratios are generally safer.

Putting It All Together

Our analysis shows us that significant differences exist between the United States and Japanese economic environments, cultural values, and accounting values. As financial analysts we cannot simply compare U.S. and Japanese company

EXHIBIT 7–7   Average ROE for Japanese and U.S. Publicly Listed Companies

	Listed Japanese Manufacturers*	Standard & Poor's Composite 500 U.S. Stocks†
1984	9.4%	13.1%
1985	8.5	11.0
1986	5.7	10.4
1987	6.5	11.8
1988	8.1	14.8
1989	8.3	13.5
1990	7.7	12.1
1991	5.6	8.6
1992	3.1	9.1‡
1993	2.5	10.3‡

*Financial Times, September 30, 1993.
†Standard & Poors Analyst's Handbook, 1993.
‡Fortune Industrials 500 median.

Source: M. E. Haskins, K. R. Ferris, and T. I Selling, *International Financial Reporting and Analysis* (Burr Ridge, IL.: Richard D. Irwin, 1996), p. 572.

financial statements. From Chapter 2 we know that a great deal of diversity in generally accepted accounting principles exists between the United States and Japan. We know that Japanese business practices are influenced by the cultural values embraced by the Japanese people. We must study the Japanese business environment in order to interpret the financial information that we see on Sumitomo's financial statements. We know that the differences we see in return (profitability), riskiness, and liquidity ratios are the result of the way the Japanese conduct their business affairs (e.g., reporting lower net income for tax purposes, long-term focus on the "bottom line," and use of short-term debt for financing assets), and not necessarily indicators of financial weakness.

CONCLUSION

This chapter develops a *framework* for international financial statement analysis that can be used to analyze the financial reports of foreign multinational corporations. Once again, the analysis begins with a review of the environmental variables that shape a country's accounting system. Then the analysis includes attention to culture and the specific societal values that influence accounting values and, ultimately, accounting systems and measurement and disclosure practices. Analysts must pay attention to the language, terminology, and format of foreign financial reports. In addition, they must always be wary of the fact that the foreign statements probably represent foreign GAAP. When analysts interpret the financial ratios, they must keep in mind that business practices are culturally based and can have a significant impact on a company's financial statements.

STUDY QUESTIONS

1. Exhibit 7–1 compares the U.S. and Japanese environments along several environmental variables. Add a column for Germany and then compare all three countries. (Hint: You might try looking in the encyclopedia for environmental information on any country that you are analyzing.)

2. How do the cultural values discussed in the chapter affect the accountant's role as a provider of useful information?

3. How do the accounting values of statutory control and uniformity influence the accountant's role as a provider of useful information?

4. How do the accounting values of conservatism and secrecy affect the information that you expect to find in the annual reports of foreign corporations?

5. As a prospective investor, you write to Toyota, a Japanese automaker, and ask for a copy of its most recent annual report. You receive a beautiful and thorough report in English and in U.S. dollars. You are delighted that Toyota makes its report so investor friendly. Why must you be careful as you proceed with your analysis?

6. As a prospective investor, you write to British Airways of the United Kingdom for a copy of its most recent annual report. In what ways would you expect the financial statements to be similar to those of United Airlines? What differences would you expect to find?

7. Return to the financial information of Sumitomo in Exhibit 7–5. As a prospective investor, which items on the financial statements would you like to explore more fully? Why?

CASES

Whitbread

Whitbread is incorporated in the United Kingdom and is in the business of food, drinks, and leisure. Among the beers that Whitbread produces, you will find Boddingtons Draft, Stella Artois, Heineken Export, and Heineken Lager Beer (not the same as Heineken from the Netherlands). Ninety-three percent of group sales are made inside the United Kingdom. We will use the consolidated profit and loss account and the consolidated balance sheet of Whitbread to help us, as prospective investors, interpret and understand Whitbread's financial results.

Questions

1. Comment on the differences in terminology and format between British- and American-style balance sheets and income statements.

2. Prepare a balance sheet for Whitbread that follows the American-style format.

3. Select some financial ratios that are of interest to you in your analysis. Why have you selected these particular ratios? What do the results of your ratio analysis tell you about the financial health of Whitbread?

4. What will you need to do if you want to compare your results for Whitbread to those of Budweiser?

Whitbread Group profit and loss account

		1994/95			1993/94		
Year ended 25 February 1995	Notes	*Before exceptional items* *£m*	*Exceptional items* *£m*	*Total* *£m*	*Before exceptional items* *£m*	*Exceptional items* *£m*	*Total* *£m*
Turnover from continuing operations	2	**2,471.8**	—	**2,471.8**	2,360.4	—	2,360.4
Cost of sales		**(1,915.4)**	—	**(1,915.4)**	(1,840.2)	—	(1,840.2)
Gross profit		**556.4**	—	**556.4**	520.2	—	520.2
Net operating expenses		**(291.8)**	—	**(291.8)**	(262.3)	—	(262.3)
Operating profit from continuing operations	3	**264.6**	—	**264.6**	257.9	—	257.9
Nonoperating items							
Net profit on disposal of fixed assets in continuing operations		—	**40.3**	**40.3**	—	2.3	2.3
Provision for loss on the disposal of a business		—	**(20.0)**	**(20.0)**	—	—	—
Profit before interest		**264.6**	**20.3**	**284.9**	257.9	2.3	260.2
Interest	7	**(9.5)**	—	**(9.5)**	(26.2)	—	(26.2)
Profit before taxation		**255.1**	**20.3**	**275.4**	231.7	2.3	234.0
Taxation	8	**(70.0)**	—	**(70.0)**	(64.6)	—	(64.6)
Profit after taxation		**185.1**	**20.3**	**205.4**	167.1	2.3	169.4
Equity minority interests		**(0.3)**	—	**(0.3)**	(3.6)	—	(3.6)
Preference dividends		**(0.4)**	—	**(0.4)**	(0.4)	—	(0.4)
Profit earned for ordinary shareholders	9	**184.4**	**20.3**	**204.7**	163.1	2.3	165.4
Ordinary dividends	10	**(96.9)**	—	**(96.9)**	(89.9)	—	(89.9)
Retained profit for the year	24	**87.5**	20.3	**107.8**	73.2	2.3	75.5
Earnings per share (pence)							
Basic	11			**42.76**			34.88
Adjusted basic	11	**38.52**			34.39		

Whitbread Balance sheets

25 February 1995	Notes	Group 1995 £m	Group 1994 £m	Company 1995 £m	Company 1994 £m
Fixed assets					
Tangible assets	12	**2,464.6**	2,356.2	**2,272.0**	1,747.9
Investments	13	**165.0**	348.7	**432.2**	1,177.2
		2,629.6	2,704.9	**2,704.2**	2,925.1
Current assets and liabilities					
Stocks	18	**125.4**	113.3	**118.3**	88.7
Debtors	19	**183.2**	165.2	**171.5**	155.0
Cash at bank and in hand		**314.3**	157.1	**281.5**	131.5
		622.9	435.6	**571.3**	375.2
Creditors—amounts falling due within one year	20	**(605.9)**	(577.2)	**(554.6)**	(555.5)
Net current assets/(liabilities)		**17.0**	(141.6)	**16.7**	(180.3)
Total assets less current liabilities		**2,646.6**	2,563.3	**2,720.9**	2,744.8
Creditors—amounts falling due after more than one year					
Loan capital	21	**(338.0)**	(347.8)	**(324.4)**	(341.7)
Provisions for liabilities and charges	22	**(30.1)**	(10.5)	**(5.2)**	(3.0)
		2,278.5	2,205.0	**2,391.3**	2,400.1
Capital and reserves					
Called up share capital	23	**129.7**	129.3	**129.7**	129.3
Share premium account	23	**114.0**	108.4	**114.0**	108.4
Revaluation reserve	24	**654.5**	706.1	**686.8**	531.5
Other reserves—nondistributable	24	**184.0**	219.6	**314.0**	313.4
Profit and loss account	24	**1,191.4**	1,037.3	**1,146.8**	1,317.5
Shareholders' funds	25	**2,273.6**	2,200.7	**2,391.3**	2,400.1
Equity minority interests		**4.9**	4.3	**—**	—
		2,278.5	2,205.0	**2,391.3**	2,400.1

Whitbread or Sumitomo?

You have some extra money to invest in the stock market and are trying to decide between buying stock in Whitbread or Sumitomo Electric. You just recently visited the United Kingdom and some of its pubs. However, you plan to go on an exchange program to Japan and admire the way the Japanese conduct business.

Questions

1. Outline the steps that you would follow to compare the financial results of Whitbread to Sumitomo.

2. How will you analyze the operating environment of each company?

3. Compare the rates of return, riskiness, and liquidity of the two companies.

4. Which company will you invest in? You must choose one or the other.

Parlez-vous Français?

Let's turn our attention to France, the home of Peugeot, Renault, L'Oreal, and Pernod Ricard. Go to your library and find a recent annual report for a French multinational. (Alternatively, you may wish to request a copy directly from the company.) Prepare an analysis of the report and the French operating environment. Remember that France is an important player in the world economy and in the European Community.

Questions

1. Discuss the French environment (e.g., business practices, legal system, providers of capital), the cultural variables influencing business practices and financial reporting, and the accounting values of the French system.

2. Analyze the financial statements using the same framework that we used with Sumitomo.

3. Comment on the differences in terminology and format between French- and American-style balance sheets and income statements.

4. How do the French financial statements illustrate the characteristics that you described in your answer to question 1?

ADDITIONAL READINGS

Bhushan, R., and D. R. Lessard. "Coping with International Accounting Diversity: Fund Managers' Views on Disclosure, Reconciliation and Harmonization." *Journal of International Financial Management and Accounting* (Summer 1992), pp. 149–64.

Bindon, K. R., and H. Gernon. "The European Union: Regulation Moves Financial Reporting Toward Comparability." *Research in Accounting Regulation* 9 (1995), pp. 23–48.

Brown, P., V. Soybel, and C. Stickney. "Achieving Comparability of U.S. and Japanese Financial Statement Data." *Japan and the World Economy* 5 (1993), pp. 51–72.

Choi, D. S., and R. M. Levich. "Behavioral Effects of International Accounting Diversity." *Accounting Horizons* (June 1991), pp. 1–13.

Lowe, H. D. "Shortcomings of Japanese Consolidated Financial Statements." *Accounting Horizons* (September 1990), pp. 1–9.

Weetman, P., and S. J. Gray. "A Comparative International Analysis of the Impact of Accounting Principles on Profits: The USA versus the U.K., Sweden, and the Netherlands." *Accounting and Business Research* (Autumn 1991), pp. 363–79.

Zarzeski, M. T. "Spontaneous Harmonization Effects of Culture and Market Forces on Accounting Disclosure Practices." *Accounting Horizons* (March 1996), pp. 18–37.

8

ACCOUNTING INFORMATION SYSTEMS FOR MULTINATIONAL CORPORATIONS

LEARNING OBJECTIVES

1. Gain familiarity with the nature of business information systems and the functions they perform

2. Be able to explain the different forms of organization used by multinational corporations (MNCs) to coordinate worldwide activities

3. Understand how top managements of MNCs determine policies for operating in the international environment

4. Know the trade-offs between use of a single accounting information system (AIS) worldwide versus individually tailored AISs for foreign subsidiary companies

5. Appreciate various MNC characteristics that affect the development of high performance AISs

---

We live in the Information Age. The integration of the telephone, the computer, and television is producing the "information highway." Information feeds managerial decision making and control. Here is a forecast for the year 2004 by an international expert on the subject:

The primary tool for management control will be the information system. This will allow managers to understand the operation of the organization, to read the market, and to anticipate the impact of their actions. The information system will no longer be used exclusively by a controller whose purpose is to detect deviations from the plans. In 2004 systems will be accessible to all managers and will be user friendly, interactive, and updated daily. They will be the key instruments in organizational learning, the cornerstone of intelligent organization.[1]

Information systems come in many different shapes and sizes—financial/ nonfinancial; formal/informal; computerized/pen and ink; strategic/operational; future oriented/historical; etc. Professor George M. Scott observes:

Information systems . . . are created by analysts and managers to perform specific tasks that are essential to the functioning of the organization. These tasks range from simple data processing . . . to providing sophisticated managerial analyses on which the management of the organization is based.[2]

The backbone of an organization's information system is its functional information systems . . . The accounting information system is a major functional information system in virtually every organization. It is also a feeder information system: much of its information is used by other functional information systems.[3]

In many organizations, about one-third to one-half of the total transactions processed are accounting transactions, and in the typical small organization 70 percent or more of all transactions processed may be accounting transactions.[4]

In international business operations, the accounting information system provides the information that the multinational corporation (MNC) needs to plan, control, evaluate, and coordinate all of its business activities.

It is senior management's responsibility to maximize the economic well-being of the MNC as an international entity, which normally translates to maximizing long-run profits globally.

This is not as easy as it sounds. The profit strategies of Japanese managers are more long-run than those of U.S. managers. Germans often base profit goals on costs incurred, the Swiss are more oriented to "what the market will bear," and Italians usually like to negotiate. Scandinavian countries control MNCs based there rather tightly, whereas Holland does not. Thus, accounting information needs vary not only from country to country and culture to culture, but also between central management (headquarters) and individual country managements.

---

[1]Hugues Boisvert, "A View of Tomorrow: Management Accounting in 2004," *A View of Tomorrow—Management Accountancy in the Year 2004*. International Federation of Accountants, Sept. 1994, p. 18.

[2]George M. Scott, *Principles of Management Information Systems*. New York, NY: McGraw-Hill, 1986, p. 4.

[3]*Ibid.*, p. 402.

[4]*Ibid.*, p. 371.

Earlier chapters dealt with reporting information to users *external* to the MNC (stockholders, creditors, employees, and customers). Much of the information reported externally is required in the form of annual reports. Our attention now turns to the information needs of *internal* users—MNC management.

Management uses internal information to plan, control, and evaluate in both the short and long run. For example, short-run budgets are determined for the operating year and then used to determine how well managers have run their business unit, say, a subsidiary company located in another country. Long-run budgets may be developed for five years—thus the short-range annual budgeting process is turned into a long-range strategic plan for the MNC and all of its subsidiaries.

Managers at all levels in the MNC need internally developed and reported information to monitor and improve their decision making. An MNC's accounting information system must incorporate and report changes in the economic and political environments, legal constraints, cultural differences and fads, and sociological differences in each country of operation. This information is generally provided by the subsidiary managers and includes notice of anticipated changes in the exchange rates, in political ideology (for example, the downfall of Communism), or even in teenage buying habits (from heavy-metal rock groups to rappers to alternative). Such external conditions need not be considered when designing an accounting information system for a single-country situation, but they are important inputs for decision making in the MNC.

The information processed in an accounting information system comes from sources internal and external to the MNC and is used by all levels of management to make decisions that in turn affect the MNC both internally and externally. Externally, the MNC affects the operating environments of its subsidiaries; hence, the process is mutual. The accounting information system is pervasive, since all subsidiaries generate data and all managers use information. The system must be responsive to the changing needs of managers, and it must respond to changes internal and external to the subsidiaries. The quality and quantity of information received by management is critical to achieving the goals of the entire multinational organization.

Information Resource Management (IRM)

Since information systems in general, and accounting information systems in particular, have assumed key roles in MNC well-being, the management of information resources has become an MNC "hot button." In its January 1995 Exposure Draft of a Proposed Statement on International Management Accounting Practice, the Financial and Management Accounting Committee of the International Federation of Accountants urges strategic planning for IRM to help:

- quantify and interpret the effects of economic events related to the organization (e.g., changes in interest or inflation rates; foreign investment restrictions; ratification of trade agreements like NAFTA)

- evaluate data for trends and relationships that help assess the implications of events (e.g., consequences of a lawsuit lost by a competitor company; analysis of corporate legal fees over time; industry-wide spending for environmental protection)

- assure the integrity and accuracy of information concerning an organization's activities and resources (e.g., pay only for hours actually worked by hourly employees; avoid overinsurance on buildings and equipment; put money into pension funds as required by employment contracts)

- monitor and measure performance and induce corrective action where necessary (e.g. prepare current sales reports—maybe daily—for each store or sales territory; compare actual with budgeted production output; monitor telephone versus e-mail and fax charges per each customer representative of the company)

- implement a reporting system which provides people throughout the organization with timely information relevant to their responsibilities (e.g., provide price reports from different countries so that company purchases are always at "best price"; have strategic planners continuously update lists of possible merger candidates; assess and report periodically the degree of obsolescence of company computing equipment—especially in foreign locations)

- prepare financial statements and reports (e.g., file all corporate tax returns on a timely basis; send financial accounting personnel to training sessions for updates on latest accounting requirements; comply readily with a request from the Board of Directors for a special cash flow report and analysis)[5]

The foregoing list represents six critical functions a state-of-the-art management information system must perform.

MNC ORGANIZATION AFFECTS THE ACCOUNTING INFORMATION SYSTEM

An MNC has various levels of managers with varying degrees of authority and responsibility. The distribution of these management levels constitutes the MNC *organizational structure* and determines what information each level needs to plan and control its operations. The information needs define how the data are

---

[5]IFAC Financial Management Accounting Committee, *Strategic Planning for Information Resource Management* (Exposure Draft). New York, NY: International Federation of Accountants, January 1995, p. 18. Examples in parentheses *not* in original.

collected and processed within the accounting information system. Therefore, the structure of data collecting, processing, and reporting within an accounting information system ought to parallel and complement the organizational structure of the MNC.

Transnational Organizational Capability

Companies seeking success in the competitive world of the twenty-first century must be simultaneously local and global. This crossover of business emphasis has triggered much definitional confusion. The media and professional journals not only refer to companies as international, multinational, transnational, and global, but they add modifiers like multicultural, nonhierarchial, globally integrated, and borderless.

For our purposes, we use the term MNC (multinational corporation) throughout this book in a broad generic sense to cover *all* companies whose activities regularly cross national boundaries. At the same time we recognize, especially in the context of this chapter on accounting information systems, that MNC organizational structures are different from company to company, are constantly undergoing change, and have recently "flattened out" in response to information technology advances.[6]

As we explore MNC organizational aspects further, the reader should keep in mind that the classic *multinational* company has operated as a decentralized unit with the ability to respond to national and local differences and opportunities. The traditional *global* company has managed operations by tightly controlling its worldwide subsidiaries through centralization. Today's companies, as already pointed out, must be local *and* global, i.e., *transnational*. The transnational company must operate efficiently and economically through global-scale operations. It must be able to respond to both national and local differences, retaining local flexibility while achieving global integration. The innovative company that can transfer knowledge quickly and efficiently by linking operations to each other will survive. Never before has the design of the accounting information system been so critical to the success of the transnational company. Information processing and technology transfer systems between parent and subsidiary and among the subsidiaries must be flexible and shared. Companies that can develop this transnational organizational capability will have the key to long-term success.

Forms of Organization

Worldwide competitive pressures have recently forced many MNCs into structural reorganizations. Many mixed organizational formats have emerged (e.g., Sony, Lever Brothers, and Unilever), and the traditional matrix organization

---

[6]John A. Byrne and Kathleen Kerwin, with Amy Cortese and Paula Dwyer, "Borderless Management," *Business Week* (May 23, 1994), pp. 24–26.

is back in vogue. Nevertheless, we distinguish five separate MNC organizational forms in order to get a clearer picture of the information needs involved. The five basic forms of organization used by MNCs are (1) the international division or international department, (2) a grouping by product line, (3) a grouping by function, (4) a grouping by geographic area, and (5) the global matrix organization. The *international division* separates foreign operations from domestic operations. This international division is usually evaluated as an independent operation and compared with domestic divisions. Hercules, Inc., Quaker Oats, 3M Company, and Microsoft are all examples of corporations that originally used this form to organize their international operations.

Organization by product line results in the integration of domestic and foreign operations and the evaluation of product lines based on worldwide results. DuPont and Motorola have highly diverse product groups, a situation that lends itself to using product line organization.

A company grouped by specialty (such as marketing, manufacturing, or accounting) is called a *functional organization,* and management maintains centralized control over the functions. In a U.S.-based MNC, the vice president for marketing at headquarters would be responsible for the marketing function worldwide. The VP for manufacturing or production would be responsible for this function in all subsidiaries. Organizing by function is not as common as the other forms, but is popular among extractive companies (for example, oil and coal), whose products are quite homogeneous. Exxon uses this form because methods used to produce and market oil do not vary much from one country to another and are therefore easily centralized at headquarters. The Swedish pharmaceutical company Astra also is organized in functional form (Exhibit 8–1).

Geographic organization separates operations into geographic areas (North America, Europe, etc.). A company would use this form when it has substantial foreign operations that are not dominated by a particular country or area of the world. U.S. MNCs are often dominated by their U.S. domestic market and, therefore, do not use this form as often as European and Japanese MNCs do. Nestlé, the Swiss chocolate company, is an example of an MNC organized by geographic area. This structure is appropriate for Nestlé because no one geographic region dominates its operations.

The *global matrix organization* blends two or more of the forms just discussed (e.g., the general manager of a French subsidiary will report to the vice president for worldwide product lines and to the vice president for Europe). Union Carbide's international operations are organized as area companies (geographic) reporting to the highest management levels in the company (function). The area companies are viewed as separate, profit-responsible entities, not as extensions of domestic divisions. Dow Chemical uses the matrix organization to avoid the problems inherent in either integrating or separating foreign operations. Asea Brown Boveri, the Swedish/Swiss electrical engineering MNC, believes in matrix management because it ". . . provides decision makers in the organization with a richer flow of information . . ."[7] Exhibit 8–2 provides a diagram of each MNC organization form.

How do these various forms of organization affect the MNC accounting information system? The form of organization affects the direction of the information *flow*, not the information itself, that is reported by the accounting information system. In all cases information about foreign operations is collected, processed, and reported within the overall MNC system.

With the international division, information flows from subsidiaries to the VP of the international division. In MNCs organized by product line, information flows from subsidiaries to the VP of the product line. In an MNC organized by function, information flows from subsidiary to headquarters according to specialty—marketing, manufacturing, accounting, and so on. When MNCs are geographically organized, the subsidiary information is collected within a geographic area and then sent to headquarters With the matrix form, information flows in two directions; for example, from the subsidiary to the geographic location headquarters, say, Asia, and also by product line to MNC headquarters.

Attitudes, Organization, and Control

The organizational structure and control functions of the MNC differ depending on the attitude of headquarters management toward multinational business. These attitudes, which are reflected in the MNC's business policies, can be classified as (1) ethnocentric (home-country-oriented), (2) polycentric (host-country-oriented), and (3) geocentric (world-oriented).

An *ethnocentric* MNC thinks that home-country standards are superior and therefore applies them worldwide. A *polycentric* MNC assumes that host-country cultures are different and, therefore, allows local affiliates to operate quite autonomously (i.e., evaluation and control functions are determined locally). The goal of the *geocentric* approach is to focus on worldwide objectives and to consider foreign subsidiaries as part of a whole. To accomplish this goal, corporate managers try to establish standards for evaluation and control that are both universal and local. The organizational structure of this MNC must facilitate the global coordination of decisions, while at the same time being able to respond to the demands of host governments and the local consumer. Operating with a geocentric attitude is an ideal model not achieved by many MNCs.

Automakers have typically been ethnocentric. Home-country attitudes have prevailed for Fiat from Italy; for Citroen and Renault from France; for Mercedes-Benz and BMW from Germany; for Saab from Sweden; for Toyota and Nissan from Japan; and for General Motors, Ford, and Chrysler from the United States. But, as U.S. automakers try to break into the Japanese market, Japanese

---

[7]Anonymous, "Big is Back," *The Economist* (June 24, 1995), p. 18 (from section under margin bar "Thoroughly Modern Corporations Know No Borders").

EXHIBIT 8–1 Astra's Organization, March 1995

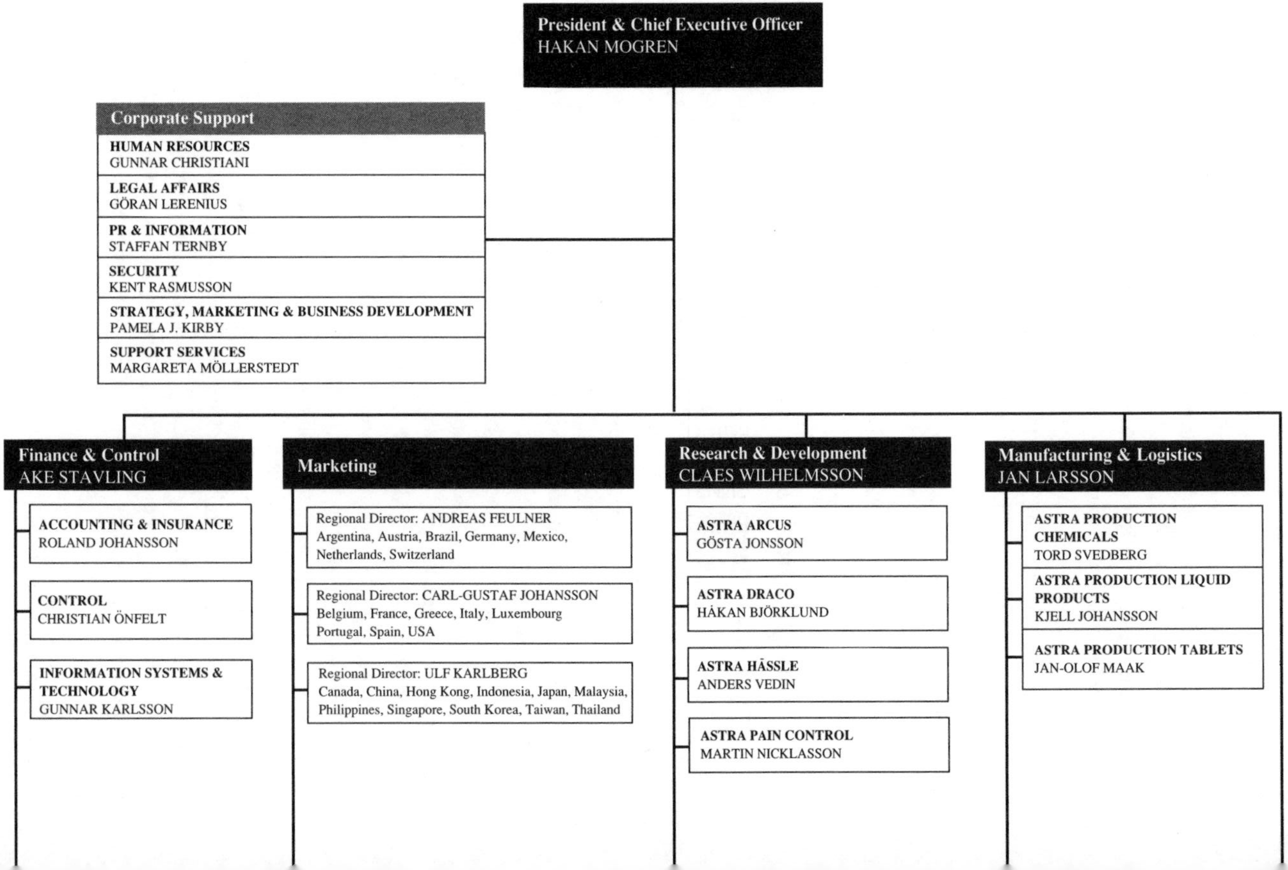

President & Chief Executive Officer
HAKAN MOGREN

Corporate Support

HUMAN RESOURCES
GUNNAR CHRISTIANI

LEGAL AFFAIRS
GÖRAN LERENIUS

PR & INFORMATION
STAFFAN TERNBY

SECURITY
KENT RASMUSSON

STRATEGY, MARKETING & BUSINESS DEVELOPMENT
PAMELA J. KIRBY

SUPPORT SERVICES
MARGARETA MÖLLERSTEDT

Finance & Control
AKE STAVLING

ACCOUNTING & INSURANCE
ROLAND JOHANSSON

CONTROL
CHRISTIAN ÖNFELT

INFORMATION SYSTEMS & TECHNOLOGY
GUNNAR KARLSSON

Marketing

Regional Director: ANDREAS FEULNER
Argentina, Austria, Brazil, Germany, Mexico,
Netherlands, Switzerland

Regional Director: CARL–GUSTAF JOHANSSON
Belgium, France, Greece, Italy, Luxembourg
Portugal, Spain, USA

Regional Director: ULF KARLBERG
Canada, China, Hong Kong, Indonesia, Japan, Malaysia,
Philippines, Singapore, South Korea, Taiwan, Thailand

Research & Development
CLAES WILHELMSSON

ASTRA ARCUS
GÖSTA JONSSON

ASTRA DRACO
HÅKAN BJÖRKLUND

ASTRA HÄSSLE
ANDERS VEDIN

ASTRA PAIN CONTROL
MARTIN NICKLASSON

Manufacturing & Logistics
JAN LARSSON

ASTRA PRODUCTION CHEMICALS
TORD SVEDBERG

ASTRA PRODUCTION LIQUID PRODUCTS
KJELL JOHANSSON

ASTRA PRODUCTION TABLETS
JAN-OLOF MAAK

M & L Support

ADMINISTRATION & TECHNICAL SERVICE
JOHN OLSSON

CONSTRUCTION & FACILITIES
STIG TALLQVIST

ENVIRONMENTAL AFFAIRS
LARS-GÖRAN BERGQUIST

INTERNATIONAL COORDINATION PURCHASING
KJELL SJÖBERG

LOGISTICS
STEN BERGLUND

QUALITY MANAGEMENT
TOMAS FLOCK

ASTRA TECH
GÖSTA WENNERSTRÖM

R & D Support

CLINICAL AFFAIRS
ANTHONY POTTAGE

PATENTS
MATS PARUP

REGULATORY AFFAIRS
COLIN REDDROP

R&D COORDINATION AND EUROPEAN AFFAIRS
KERSTIN EKBERG-ERIKSEN

SAFETY ASSESSMENT
PETER MOLDEUS

SCIENTIFIC AFFAIRS, SPECIAL VENTURES
SUNE ROSELL

SCIENTIFIC INFORMATION SYSTEMS
MATS LÖRSTAD

Regional Director: PAMELA J. KIRBY
Australia, Ireland, New Zealand, United Kingdom

Regional Director: ANDERS LÖNNER
Denmark, Finland, Iceland, Norway, Sweden

ASTRA EXPORT & TRADING
KAARE GYLLVIK

TAXES
SVEN-OLOF PRINTZ

TREASURY
PER NORDBERG

EXHIBIT 8–2   Diagrams of Various Forms of MNC Organization

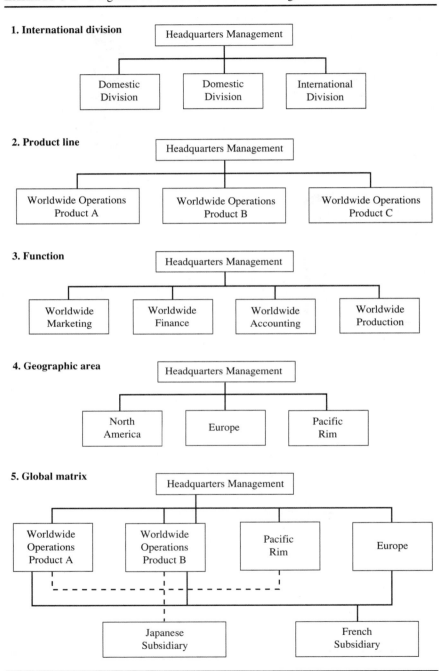

perceptions about U.S. cars have taken on an added importance and U.S. managers have taken on more of a polycentric attitude, recognizing the Japanese consumer's resistance to buying a standardized homogenized global product.

Pharmaceutical companies generally exhibit polycentric business strategies. Bayer of Germany wants all consumers from all cultures to think of its aspirin as a local product, just as Roche of Switzerland does with Valium. U.S. pharmaceuticals have established quite a successful presence in Japan and are known as "kakujitsu na kaisha," or reliable company. They have made a long-term commitment to doing business in the Japanese local economy and have built the necessary relationships between customer and supplier. At the same time, they have made an attempt to understand the culture while being open to learning from the Japanese.

Dutch/U.K. multinationals like N. V. Philips and Unilever come close to being geocentric. People of many different nationalities serve on their boards of directors and senior management teams. It is companies like these that are able to gain firm strategic control of their worldwide operations and manage them in a globally coordinated manner that will succeed in the emerging international economy.

The attitude of headquarters management also affects the location of decision making. If an MNC headquarters allows foreign subsidiaries to make important decisions, the corporation is considered *decentralized*. This attitude is currently the most prevalent among MNC managers who strive for global diversity. Many European and American multinationals have well-established networks of fairly independent and self-sufficient national subsidiaries. Foreign subsidiaries are granted a great deal of autonomy, and therefore subsidiary managers must have information to plan, control, and evaluate their own operations at the local level. These information needs must be built into each subsidiary's accounting information system. At the same time, headquarters management also needs information about the subsidiaries to plan, control, evaluate, and coordinate on a global level. This strategy, and the organizational structure that supports it, makes it difficult to design a system that is able to coordinate and control these worldwide operations, while still responding to global forces.

If decision-making authority rests with headquarters, an MNC is said to be *centralized*. MNCs generally do not make all decisions at one location but aim for a collaborative approach between headquarters and other levels. Many Japanese companies centralize operations in Japan, which allows them to respond to opportunities presented by changing global forces (e.g., movements in exchange rates). An MNC may centralize functions considered critical for success and decentralize those that are less critical. For example, IBM and Nestlé centralize their research and development activities, because headquarters feels R&D is critical to the company's long-run success and wants to maintain tight control over it. However, these companies take a more decentralized approach to their foreign operating subsidiaries, because the success of each one is not as critical to the long-run success of the MNC as a whole.

EXPORTING THE DOMESTIC ACCOUNTING INFORMATION SYSTEM

In the past U.S. companies have used basically the same accounting information system to collect and process data from foreign and domestic operations. This was true for several reasons. It is much less expensive to export an already established system than to design a new one. For control purposes, the headquarters accounting group could require all domestic and international subsidiaries to use similar reporting forms. In addition, because top management was already familiar with the domestic system, it was easier to use it internationally.

However, exported versions of the domestic control system are seldom as successful or effective internationally as they are domestically. A domestic system is designed to operate within the parent company's external environment. It incorporates political, economic, cultural, technological, and legal factors of the home country. Exporting such a system ignores the foreign subsidiary's operating environment and may result in a breakdown of communication. Obviously, communicating with a subsidiary manager who does not speak your language can present some formidable hurdles. Financial terminology often poses additional challenges. For example, in Spanish there is no equivalent for terms like leveraged buyout, short sales, or insider trading. Successful multilingual communication requires companies to be more culturally aware and sensitive to the importance of effective translation and idea processing. Exhibit 8–3 can be used to visualize the pervasiveness of the impact of environmental diversity on an MNC's system of financial control. It illustrates that the four financial control functions—measurement, communication, evaluation, and motivation—must accommodate the environmental variables and constraints of every country in which the MNC operates. The same is true for an MNC's other control systems, such as those for manufacturing and marketing.

Example.   An MNC is based in the United States, and all domestic subsidiaries operate as decentralized units with the objective of maximizing after-tax profits in U.S. dollars. The foreign subsidiaries are not allowed as much autonomy in decision making. They primarily supply partially manufactured materials to the U.S. subsidiaries. The parent needs information on changes in foreign exchange rates, export controls, import controls, tax rates in various countries, and so on, to effectively plan and control foreign operations. This information is not necessary when dealing with domestic subsidiaries.

The foreign subsidiaries of this MNC should not be evaluated on the same basis as domestic subsidiaries, because maximizing after-tax profit in U.S. dollars is not the foreign subsidiary's objective. Instead, each foreign subsidiary should be evaluated based on its service as a supplier. To make this evaluation, headquarters needs different accounting information from the foreign subsidiaries than it does from U.S. subsidiaries.

EXHIBIT 8–3   Framework for Multinational Financial Control

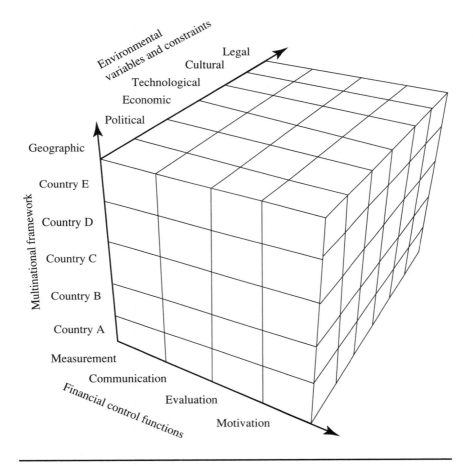

SOURCE: Frederick D. S. Choi and Gerhard G. Mueller, *International Accounting* (Englewood Cliffs, N.J.: Prentice Hall, 1992), p. 475.

THE MNC ACCOUNTING INFORMATION SYSTEM

To repeat, a major responsibility of the accounting information system is to provide the information necessary for planning, controlling, and evaluating an organization's operations. An MNC divides itself into organizational units when it selects an organizational structure. The information required by a particular unit depends on its assigned goals and functions. The designer of an MNC's accounting information system must understand the nature and purpose of the MNC, the subtleties of its organizational structure, the degree of centralization/decentralization, the levels of decision making, and the needs of each decision maker.

The size of the organization is another factor affecting informational requirements. A larger, more sophisticated MNC needs more complex information than a smaller MNC or domestic corporation.

Size also corresponds to the number of management levels. Depending on organization and management philosophy, each level may have a different responsibility and decision-making authority. Therefore, the accounting information system may have to supply various levels with information that differs in detail, timing, and scope. For example, a large MNC may be more centralized than a smaller MNC and prefer to control worldwide decision making at headquarters. A smaller, less sophisticated MNC may allow the foreign subsidiary managers more control over their operations; therefore the information used for decision making would be gathered and used at the subsidiary level.

Size may also affect the flow of information from foreign operations to headquarters. For example, a large MNC organized by international division may have all of the subsidiaries operating in Europe report to a manager for Europe, who in turn reports to the international division manager. A smaller MNC may have each European subsidiary manager report directly to the international division manager.

In summary, the designer of an accounting information system for an MNC must be aware of (1) the organization's nature and purpose, (2) the organizational structure, (3) the degree of centralization/decentralization, (4) the size of the MNC, and (5) management's basic philosophy and attitude toward foreign operations.

Each of these factors should be identified, studied, and evaluated. They should then be incorporated into the basic accounting information system design, which provides the needed framework for long-range planning, controlling, and evaluating operations. A system developed in this way theoretically ensures that expectations have been realistically determined. Only then can management expect congruence between its goals, the structure of the organization, and available information. Congruence is discussed further in Chapter 9.

CONCLUSION

In this chapter we described the nature of business information, information systems, and information resource management—all with special reference to MNCs. Also we discussed the information that managers need to plan, control, evaluate, and coordinate worldwide operations. In the following chapters, we discuss (1) planning and control, (2) performance evaluation, and (3) transfer pricing and international taxation. Managers depend on the accounting information system to provide the information they need to improve decisions about each of these topics. Without information, it is impossible to effectively plan, control, or evaluate multinational operations.

STUDY QUESTIONS

1. Identify the six critical functions a modern management information system must perform.
2. How do the objectives of domestic information systems differ from the objectives of MNC information systems?
3. What are the differences between the ethnocentric, polycentric, and geocentric attitudes toward multinational business policies?
4. MNCs headquartered in smaller countries like Singapore, Sweden, and Switzerland tend to pursue polycentric international business policies. Why?
5. Why is it necessary to consider the individual characteristics of an MNC when designing an accounting information system?
6. What is the difference between a global operating strategy versus a multinational operating strategy? Why are these operating strategies no longer effective?
7. What is transnational organizational capability? Can you think of any company that is operating transnationally?

CASES

Why Is Change a Good Thing?

Domestic, Inc., operated its 20 U.S. subsidiaries for 30 years. Over time, a very effective accounting information system was developed to accommodate decentralized decision making by subsidiary managers. The economic, political, legal, cultural, and technological characteristics of the United States have quite naturally affected the system's development.

Now that the company is International, Inc., it has to have an accounting information system to coordinate worldwide operations. An international division manager will be responsible for reporting this information from the foreign subsidiaries to headquarters management.

During the planning stages of the foreign expansion, the designated international division manager makes the following suggestion:

> It has taken us 30 years to develop an effective accounting information system that all the subsidiary managers understand and that provides what headquarters needs for decision making. Let's use the same system with all of our subsidiaries in Asia and South America. Why is change a good thing?

Questions

1. What type of attitude toward foreign operations is this manager exhibiting? Why does management have this attitude?
2. Are the manager's justifications valid? What are the dangers in exporting a domestic system to foreign operations?
3. What changes would you suggest for the accounting information system if you were the international division manager?

Leave Well Enough Alone?

Tides, Ltd., is a highly successful producer and distributor of a well-established consumer product. The company has manufacturing subsidiaries in twenty-one countries. Each subsidiary is managed autonomously at the local level by local management. As an outside consultant, you determine that, between U.S. operations and the 21 foreign manufacturing facilities, 11 different accounting information systems (AISs) are in use, 11 different computing systems are employed, plus entirely different software packages are found from location to location. Each geographic location uses the home currency unit throughout its AIS.

Questions

1. Would you recommend that Tides, Inc., "clean up its act" and establish a single AIS for all of its worldwide operations, including the U.S.? Why or why not?

2. For purposes of consolidated financial reporting in the U.S., all currency amounts have to be translated to U.S. dollar amounts. Who does the translations—U.S. headquarters or each foreign location for itself? Why?

3. Should the AIS of each non-U.S. subsidiary simultaneously run home currency as well U.S. dollar amounts? Why or why not?

Ouch! Change Hurts

World, Inc., is not a new corporation, although it has only been operating internationally for five years. Prior to entering the international marketplace, it was called U.S. World, and the 20 domestic subsidiaries were organized as decentralized profit centers reporting directly to headquarters.

The five foreign subsidiaries currently report to an international division manager, who reports directly to headquarters. Each subsidiary is labeled a decentralized profit center; however, the international division manager maintains control over each foreign subsidiary manager, and decision making is centralized at headquarters. The foreign subsidiary managers have requested more authority and decision-making responsibility.

Headquarters has decided to reorganize worldwide operations by product line. Its goal is to develop a transnational approach to controlling all subsidiaries, both domestic and foreign. You have been hired to design and implement the new system.

Questions

1. Why were the foreign subsidiaries labeled decentralized profit centers when they were not allowed to act as such? What are the potential problems with a situation like this?

2. As the consultant, what information about this MNC will you need to develop a working accounting information system?

3. Diagram the information flows that will exist for this MNC after the reorganization by product line and the move to "transnationalize."

ADDITIONAL READINGS

Abernethy, M. A., and C. H. Guthrie. "An Empirical Assessment of the "Fit" between Strategy and Management Information System Design." *Accounting and Finance* (November 1994), pp. 49–66. (This publication is the journal of the Accounting Association of Australia and New Zealand.)

Bartlett, C. A., and S. Ghoshal. "Matrix Management: Not a Structure, a Frame of Mind." *Harvard Business Review* (July–August 1990), pp. 138–45.

Egelhoff, W. G. "Information-Processing Theory and the Multinational Enterprise." *The Journal of International Business Studies* 22, no. 3 (1991), pp. 341–68.

Elliott, R. K. "The Third Wave Breaks on the Shores of Accounting." *Accounting Horizons* (June 1992), pp. 61–85.

Harrison, G. L., McKinnon, J. L., Panchapakesan, S., and M. Leung. "The Influence of Culture on Organizational Design and Planning and Control in Australia and the United States Compared with Singapore and Hong Kong." *Journal of International Financial Management and Accounting* 5, no. 3 (1994), pp. 242–261.

IFAC Financial and Management Accounting Committee. *A View of Tomorrow—Management Accountancy in the Year 2004*. New York, NY: International Federation of Accountants, 1994, 108 pp.

Karimi, J., and B. R. Konsynski. "Globalization and Information Management Strategies." *Journal of Management Information Systems* (Spring 1991), pp. 7–26.

C H A P T E R

9

STRATEGIC PLANNING AND CONTROL IN THE INTERNATIONAL ENVIRONMENT

LEARNING OBJECTIVES

1. Identify why MNCs cannot simply export national control systems and expect them to be effective in other countries.
2. Understand that a country's cultural, economic, technological, legal, and political environments impact each phase of the MNC planning and control system.
3. Apply the concept of goal congruence to each phase of the MNC planning and control system.
4. Identify communication problems that challenge the effectiveness of the MNC planning and control system.
5. Recognize the complexity of strategic planning for the transnational corporations of the next century.

Strategic planning and control are not new—domestic corporations have been doing them for years. The development of comprehensive MNC international planning and control systems with long-range strategic focus is new.

Ford Motor Company was founded in 1903. Five years later it was selling cars overseas in France, and by 1911 Henry Ford was making cars in Great

Britain. Ford has recently undertaken a massive reorganization as the huge automaker strives to retain and reinforce its status as a global company in the 1990s. With this reorganization comes the need for planning and control systems that facilitate Ford's success as it competes with global rivals.

The corporate planning process involves deciding: (1) the corporation's objectives, (2) how these objectives will change over time, (3) the resources needed to attain these objectives, and (4) the policies that govern acquisition, use, and disposition of the resources. For a multinational corporation (MNC), planning involves incorporating the economic, cultural, technological, legal, and political characteristics of each operating environment into the MNC's worldwide master (strategic) plan.

The job of the management control system is to ensure that the objectives of the strategic plan are accomplished. Thus, the control system regulates the MNC's activities so as to achieve its goals. Planning and control are the subjects of Chapter 9 and performance evaluation is discussed in Chapter 10.

COMPONENTS OF THE MNC PLANNING AND CONTROL SYSTEMS

There are six phases in the MNC planning ad control systems:

1. Environmental assessment—identifying the relevant cultural, legal, political, and economic variables.
2. Subsidiary assessment—defining each subsidiary's strengths, weaknesses, opportunities and threats (SWOT) in relation to its environment.
3. Objective setting—setting priorities for the subsidiary.
4. Formulation of standards—developing budgets or other operating standards based on expectations.
5. Operational—measuring the actual output.
6. Evaluation—providing feedback.

Environmental Assessment Phase

A corporation involved in moving goods, people, capital, and ideas across national boundaries encounters unique environmental factors. The dominant environmental factor is different national currencies. Unexpected currency depreciation or appreciation and price-level fluctuations make currency exchange rates hard to predict. Varying rates of interest, multiple systems of taxation, and the influence of cultural differences also have significant implications for those involved in the planning and control process. Headquarters must assess the political, operating, and financial risk inherent in a foreign country. Government control of imports and exports is quite common throughout the world. Government expropriation of operations, with or without compensation, and political instability certainly have an adverse effect on business. Unfamiliar operating restrictions and increased regulations can make responding to opportunities or danger more difficult. For example, take the case of Ford Motor Company. It once had an operation in Hungary that was taken over by the government, one in France that was later bombed, and one in Mexico that was given very different operating requirements from other dealers.

Assessing risk is not easy because of the variety of environments an MNC confronts, so communication from local managers is critical. MNCs can hire outside organizations to assess the risks in foreign countries. Financial institutions and CPA firms also provide helpful information.

Subsidiary Assessment Phase

In this phase, headquarters management does a SWOT analysis of each subsidiary by country—its financial, human, and product resources. Financial resources include current and future cash flows and the ability to transfer these cash flows in and out of the operating environment, the availability of capital, and a subsidiary's borrowing capacity. Assessing human resources includes evaluating the specific and general skills of the work force and how readily employees can be transferred among various units. Would-be global companies prefer to hire local nationals. Locally hired managers understand the culture, tailor products to local markets (McDonalds now serves Teriyaki burgers in Tokyo and wine in Paris), have access to local expertise, and help MNCs shed their imperialist image. Peter A. Jacobi is president of Levi Strauss International, and he puts it this way, "I may be head of international, but to think I can make decisions in the Far East is ridiculous." Investigating product resources includes determining production capacity, whether or not the product must be adapted to foreign markets, transportation considerations, and so on. Once again, effectively communicating information from the manager of the foreign subsidiary to headquarters is critically important to success.

Objective-Setting Phase

After assessing the environments and the SWOT analysis of each subsidiary, top management must then select which products to produce (product strategy) and where (geographic strategy).

The objective-setting phase involves reviewing the available alternatives and setting priorities. In this way, the strategic plan can be altered as changes occur in the subsidiary's environment or resources. An MNC needs flexibility. The long-range strategic plan developed by headquarters management should allow for future changes.

Formulation-of-Standards Phase

This phase is more complicated than what occurs in a domestic corporation. After management decides where and what to produce, budgets are formalized for each operating subsidiary. The process involves estimating costs of production and setting selling prices.

The budget for each foreign subsidiary must be developed in the local currency. The MNC must then translate each subsidiary's budget to the parent corporation's currency (e.g., U.S. dollars). Therefore, foreign exchange rates are part of the budgeting process (see Chapter 10). MNC headquarters must also consider the possibility of changes in inflation and borrowing rates within a certain country, exchange controls, productivity, political changes, and so on, when developing budgets for foreign subsidiaries.

Subsidiary managers should understand, accept, and contribute to the budget process. When managers participate in the preparation of their own budgets, they can incorporate any cultural, legal, political, and economic factors that might affect their operating performance during a budget period. The budget can reflect anticipated fluctuations in exchange rates and price levels and allow for all of the different tax rates applicable to a specific environment that either benefit or penalize operations. Employment practices and local regulations may affect operations and can be reflected in a subsidiary's budget. In fact, any of the following environmental differences may be incorporated into a budget: (1) the fluctuating exchange rates and price levels, (2) the cost and methods of borrowing money, (3) the tax system, (4) the customer payment terms, (5) the local regulations, (6) the employment practices, and (7) the accounting system. This is only a partial list.

Operational Phase

In this phase, subsidiaries are actually conducting business operations to carry out headquarters' plans. Operations must be measured. Whether an organization is a domestic corporation or an MNC, it should be careful to measure actual operations according to the same rules it used for setting budgets. (More is said about this in Chapter 10.)

Evaluation Phase

Two types of feedback are provided by the evaluation phase. One deals with past operations by comparing budgeted results to actual. The second deals with future plans; based on the information provided by the budget-to-actual comparison, management may institute corrective actions, make changes, and reevaluate priorities.

The MNC strategic planning process generally ranges from intermediate to long (i.e., from one to five years). The purpose is to define the company's current and future objectives and to formulate a way to achieve the company's overall goals. The plan is a synthesis of immediate objectives, anticipated world changes, and input from managers all over the world. It results in both long- and short-term strategies that will affect the MNC's operating results and growth.

INTEGRATION OF THE PHASES OF THE PLANNING AND CONTROL SYSTEMS

As mentioned previously, the management control system functions to ensure that the objectives of the strategic plan are accomplished. An effective management control system should (1) enhance corporate goal congruence across all domestic and foreign subsidiaries, (2) make certain that projections have been fully communicated, (3) communicate results, and (4) provide useful information to headquarters and subsidiary managers so that the plan can be implemented, evaluated, and changed.

Goal congruence is a buzzword frequently found in management and control literature. It means that everyone in an organization is "operating on the same wavelength" (i.e., individual managers accept, support, and work toward generally agreed on corporate goals, even if their personal goals for their own subsidiary differ).

The management control system and the strategic planning process should be completely integrated. The management control system ensures that headquarters resource allocation decisions are tracked and measured, and thus the system works to accomplish management's objectives.

The management control system is generally made up of several subsystems developed for use in foreign subsidiaries, domestic subsidiaries, and headquarters. Company standards have been formulated as part of the strategic planning process. Hence, the control process compares actual with budgeted performance specified in the individual subsystem for each subsidiary. Exhibit 9–1 shows how the components and phases in the MNC planning and control systems are integrated.

COMMUNICATION PROBLEMS

Differences in Measurement and Disclosure Practices

As discussed in Chapters 1 through 7, accounting measurement, disclosure, and reporting practices vary a great deal across geographic boundaries. In many countries accounting systems are not well developed, and reporting practices are not as defined as those in the United States. However, for effective control an MNC needs an internal reporting system with standardized, consistent, and uniform accounting principles and practices. Ideally, all subsidiaries should use comparable accounting practices. Assets and liabilities should be valued and reported according to a common plan. Expense recognition should be consistent from year

---

EXHIBIT 9–1   Basic Components of MNC Planning and Control Systems

```
┌─────────────────────┐                              Feedback
│  MNC Headquarters   │◄──────────────────────────────────────┐
│    (Phases 1–3)     │                                         │
│  (Phases 4 and 6)   │                                         │
└─────────────────────┘                                         │
           │                                                    │
┌──────────┼─────────────────────────────────────────────────┐ │
│          ▼                                                  │ │
│  ┌─────────────────────┐      Feedback                      │ │
│  │ Foreign subsidiaries │◄────────────────┐                 │ │
│  │     (Phase 4)       │                  │                 │ │
│  └─────────────────────┘                  │                 │ │
│          │                                │                 │ │
│          ▼                                │                 │ │
│  ┌─────────────────┐         ┌────────────────────┐         │ │
│  │ Operating process│───────►│   Performance      │         │ │
│  │    (Phase 5)    │         │   evaluation       │         │ │
│  │                 │         │    (Phase 6)       │         │ │
│  └─────────────────┘         └────────────────────┘         │ │
└─────────────────────────────────────────────────────────────┘ │
```

Source: Adapted from H. Itami, *Adaptive Behavior: Management Control and Information Analysis* (Sarasota, Fla.: American Accounting Association, 1977), p. 9.

to year (e.g., each subsidiary should use the same depreciation method from year to year). All domestic and foreign managers should understand how headquarters defines the word *profit*. All domestic and foreign subsidiaries of U.S.-based MNCs should use U.S. generally accepted accounting principles for reporting back to corporate headquarters. Consistency and uniformity are particularly important when the information is used to compare one subsidiary's performance to another's.

Differences in cultural, technological, legal, political, and economic heritage pose barriers to communicating uniform information from subsidiaries to the parent company. Simply requiring uniformity does not make these barriers disappear, and simply requiring that certain information be reported on a regular and consistent basis does not guarantee that a subsidiary manager can or will comply. For instance, cultural differences can affect control systems in several ways. Japanese managers, by nature, are far more secretive and less comfortable with disclosing information than are U.S. managers. Japanese managers and employees are quite used to the team approach and naturally use team performance evaluation measures to enhance cooperation. American workers and managers are used to being evaluated as individuals. MNCs cannot simply export control systems and expect them to work in every cultural environment. Then there is the problem of businesses in developing countries not having the technical ability to maintain extensive records or formal accounting reports. For example, it is probably more difficult to acquire standardized information from, say, a subsidiary in Indonesia than from one in Australia. While uniformity is necessary, the system must remain adaptive and flexible to the information needs of both corporate headquarters and the operating subsidiaries. Nevertheless, adaptability is an obstacle to uniformity, and vice versa.

Ease of Communication

Geographic proximity is also a consideration in terms of facilitating the flows of information back and forth between the subsidiaries and headquarters. For example, a U.S.-based MNC would probably find it easier to communicate to a subsidiary in Mexico than one in Chile, simply because the Mexican subsidiary is physically closer. In addition, the availability and quality of telecommunication equipment can affect the frequency of contact with a foreign subsidiary. Developments in electronic transmission networks are making instantaneous communication between a parent and a distant subsidiary possible, or, at least they are reducing the lag in communication. Even so, communication across borders can be difficult. For example, Ford Motor Company lacks compatible computer systems between North American and European operations. Unilever has e-mail systems in place; however, training the 31,000 employees to use the systems poses difficulties. Unilever employees can access a live tutorial session on how to use the system from anywhere in the world. Few companies have really mastered the skills of globally gathering and exploiting information. Cultural barriers sometimes prevent global teams from talking with one another. U.S. West reports that the folks running the cellular phone investment projects in Eastern Europe don't interact enough with the U.S. West teams exploring possible cellular phone investment opportunities in Spain and Latin America. All of these problems pose real costs to the global corporation as it designs and implements control systems worldwide.

Financial and Operating Information for Internal Reporting

Many firms equate volumes of reports with good financial control. However, subsidiaries' local management may complain that the volume of required reporting hampers its ability to cope with daily operating problems. In fact, local management is responsible for reporting financial data to the parent *and* operating the subsidiary successfully.

Therefore, the problem is to identify the relevant information that top management needs to maintain the strategic planning and management control systems. This is difficult to achieve. In fact, several studies have shown that MNC headquarters may require a single subsidiary to submit over 200 different financial reports annually. Even with this many reports, there is no assurance that the MNC is well managed.

Goal Congruence

Most major companies in the United States use the profit center or investment center concept for domestic control systems.[1] This approach works relatively well domestically, because profit center managers make the major decisions affecting their center's performance. Good decision making ensures good performance evaluation, and good performance evaluation ensures good decision making. The goals are congruent because authority and responsibility are delegated to the same people. Managers are evaluated based on the performance that results from their decisions. Manager performance and profit center performance are linked.

International operations do not lend themselves to management control systems based on a profit center concept. As Chapter 11 explains, foreign subsidiary profits are often somewhat manipulated to facilitate paying the smallest possible amount of income taxes on a worldwide basis. Or, by manipulating the prices at which goods are transferred into a country, an MNC can minimize the import duties paid. Each scenario affects a subsidiary's reported profit. Therefore, using the strict profit center concept is inappropriate. In addition, headquarters management must juggle many other environmental variables (e.g., fluctuating exchange rates, inflation, and government controls).

For the profit center idea to work effectively, subsidiary managers must have the authority to make all decisions affecting their profits. Yet many MNCs maintain centralized control over subsidiaries, and many decisions are made at headquarters. Foreign managers may have responsibility for operations, but they do not have the authority to make major decisions affecting their profitability. Such a situation does not enhance goal congruence. Regardless of the situation, some degree of responsibility and authority should be provided to subsidiary managers so that they remain responsive to their local environments. These issues are discussed further in Chapter 10.

CONCLUSION

Strategic plans define a company's objectives and formulate a way to achieve them. Such plans involve a management control system and a system of performance evaluation. A management control system should complement the strategic plan, so that the goals of the international managers are congruent with the overall goals of the MNC.

---

[1]For discussion see D. Morse and J. J. Zimmerman, *Management Accounting* (Burr Ridge, IL: Richard D. Irwin, 1997), Chapter 7.

STUDY QUESTIONS

1. Discuss how the strategic planning process and the management control system of a multinational corporation are integrated.

2. What communication problems would be encountered if a traditional U.S. financial control system was simply exported to a subsidiary operating in Russia? In Malaysia? In Portugal?

3. What problems develop when an MNC tries to establish a uniform system of reporting for its worldwide operations? How can these problems be solved?

4. What purpose does the environmental assessment phase of the MNC planning and control systems serve? Does this phase exist for domestic operations? If so, how do the two differ?

5. How would you monitor the risk of physical expropriation of your subsidiary's assets if the subsidiary operates in Cambodia? In Argentina? In Mexico?

6. What demands will the evolution of the transnational corporation place on the strategic planning and control systems of traditional multinational companies? (Hint: Chapter 8 holds the clue.)

7. Briefly describe the planning and control implications of the polycentric attitude toward international business; the ethnocentric attitude; the geocentric attitude. (Refer to Chapter 8.)

CASES

Building the Transnational Team

Euphoria Chocolates is a U.S.-based MNC that has successfully captured 20 percent of the U.S. chocolate market under the direction of Fanny May Farmer. Euphoria has been operating in Europe for 20 years and has had success in convincing the Europeans that Americans can make chocolate. However, top management wants Euphoria's European market share to grow and has decided to open a regional European office in Brussels, Belgium. Until now, the European managers reported directly to Roslyn Stover in New York City, as did Fanny May Farmer, because Roslyn is the president and chief executive officer of Euphoria.

Fanny May assumes that she will get this new position in Brussels. At this moment she is meeting with four other managers from the United Kingdom, France, Germany, and Spain. Roslyn Stover has asked them to select the ideal manager to take charge of the regional office.

Questions

1. Selecting managers is part of the strategic planning and control function of all companies. What makes selecting a manager for Europe different from selecting a manager for the United States?
2. Why does Fanny May assume she will get this position?
3. Would you choose Fanny May to be the manager in charge of the regional European office in Belgium?

When in Brazil

You are the financial vice president of an MNC that has 15 foreign subsidiaries operating all over the world. Your president informs you that you are going to buy a plant in Brazil, your first one in that country.

You learn that the Brazilian operation is family owned, has no accountant, has no financial reporting system in place, and is generally unreceptive to complying with any outside request for information.

Your other 15 subsidiaries report to you in U.S. dollars and use U.S. generally accepted accounting principles when compiling information for headquarters. You require the following: (1) monthly financial statements, (2) quarterly reports with appropriate footnotes, (3) annual reports, (4) annual budgets, and (5) annual review of the next five-year strategic plan. You feel that your reporting system works very effectively in controlling operations, and you intend to institute your system in Brazil.

Questions

1. What problems do you anticipate when attempting to impose your financial control system on the Brazilian subsidiary?
2. How will you solve these problems?
3. How will you gain the Brazilian subsidiary's support and cooperation?

Zannah International

Zannah International is a U.K. multinational engineering company that has made recent acquisitions in continental Europe and the United States. The company intends to continue to expand by acquiring already existing operations. Products are marketed worldwide and managed geographically by three divisions, but it is the continental Europe–U.S.A. division that is of particular interest to us. Sales of this division have tripled in the past year and account for 25 percent of the company total. The management structure is diagrammed below. The company supports decentralized control. A uniform planning and control system is applied throughout the group, and a finance team at headquarters regularly monitors progress reports. (An organization chart is shown below.)

Prior to being acquired by the company just over a year ago, the Netherlands operation was a family-owned business. Evert Slijper was annoyed when the company accounting system was imposed at the time of takeover, but he

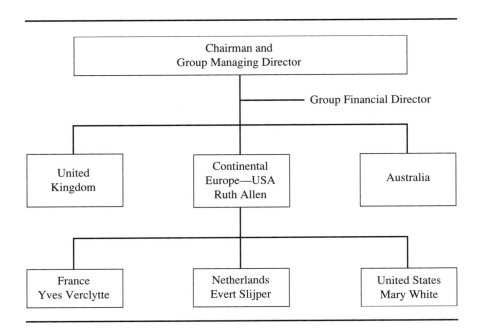

recognizes its usefulness. He has been told very little about company strategy and has had very little contact with company management. Little information about the other subsidiaries or the potential for joint actions has been given, and Evert has found himself competing for the same client's work as other group subsidiaries.

Yves Verclytte, manager of the French operation, has been on board for 18 months. Under the present arrangement, there are no opportunities for him to make presentations to headquarters management, a situation he finds unusual and frustrating. Quarterly meetings with the group finance director emphasize financial performance indicators, and discussions of strategy are confined. Yves has talked with potential target companies, not fully understanding the exact characteristics that headquarters is seeking. Interaction and cooperation with other subsidiaries, even in the same subgroup, are not encouraged.

Mary White's experience in the business spans some 20 years, although she only joined Zannah International's U.S. operation two years ago, after the takeover. Her subsidiary consistently meets the company's financial targets and therefore she has little communication with the company. She has little understanding of group strategy and cannot operate as a team player. No written feedback on performance is ever provided but Ruth Allen, the Continental Europe–USA manager, does visit once in a while and provides verbal feedback.

Questions

1. Describe the corporate strategy followed by Zannah International.

2. Critically evaluate the effectiveness of the management control system in promoting Zannah's strategy.

3. To what extent is the management style of Zannah top management creating problems or opportunities relevant to the future success of Zannah?

ADDITIONAL READINGS

Birkenshaw, J. M., and A. J. Morrison. "Configurations of Strategy and Structure in Subsidiaries of Multinational Corporations." *Journal of International Business Studies* 28, no. 4, 1995, pp. 729–53.

Chow, C., M. Shields, and Y. K. Chan. "The Effects of Management Controls and National Culture on Manufacturing Performance: An Experimental Investigation." *Accounting, Organizations and Society* 16, 1991, pp. 209–26.

Daniel, S. J., and W. D. Reitsperger. "Linking Quality Strategy with Management Control Systems: Empirical Evidence from Japanese Industry." *Accounting, Organizations and Society* 16, 1991, pp. 601–18.

Daniel, S. J., and W. D. Reitsperger. "Strategic Control Systems for Quality: An Empirical Comparison of the Japanese and U.S. Electronics Industry." *Journal of International Business Studies* 25, no. 2, 1994, pp. 275–94.

Eiteman, D. K. "Foreign Investment Analysis." In *Handbook of International Accounting,* ed. F. D. S. Choi (New York: John Wiley, 1991), pp. 27/1–19.

Macharinza, K. "Strategic Planning Systems." In *Handbook of International Accounting,* ed. F. D. S. Choi (New York: John Wiley, 1991), pp. 25/1–18.

Sambharaya, R. B., and A. Phatak. "The Effect of Transborder Data Flow Restrictions on American Multinational Corporations." *Management International Review* 3 (1990), pp. 267–89.

Ueno, S., and F. H. Wu. "Comparative Influence of Culture on Budget Control Practices in U.S. and Japan." *International Journal of Accounting* 28, no. 1, 1993, pp. 17–39.

10

PERFORMANCE EVALUATION IN MULTINATIONAL CORPORATIONS

LEARNING OBJECTIVES

1. Understand the role that the MNC performance evaluation system plays in relation to MNC strategic planning and control.
2. Know that MNCs use a variety of financial measures to evaluate their operations.
3. Consider that culture influences the selection of financial and nonfinancial measures of performance evaluation.
4. Think about why it is more difficult to evaluate the performance of foreign operations than domestic.
5. Explain why national performance evaluation systems cannot simply be exported internationally.

Performance evaluation is a critical issue in international accounting. The development of the multinational corporation (MNC) requires an accounting system that records and reports the results of worldwide operations. Now, headquarters must have information to evaluate the performance of subsidiaries all over the world.

This chapter begins with a definition of performance evaluation. We then take a look at the financial measures used by U.S., U.K., and Japanese managers to evaluate their operations. Some MNCs have begun to use nonfinancial measures to evaluate and enhance their performance. Several issues that must be considered when evaluating domestic and foreign operating environments, subsidiaries, and managers are discussed.

PERFORMANCE EVALUATION DEFINED

Performance evaluation is the periodic review of operations to ensure that the objectives of the enterprise are being accomplished. A corporation's performance evaluation system is part of its financial control system. The MNC must have accounting information to evaluate domestic and foreign operations.

FINANCIAL MEASURES USED BY MNCs TO EVALUATE DOMESTIC AND FOREIGN SUBSIDIARIES

MNCs use various measures to evaluate the results of their operations at home and abroad. For the last 20 years, U.S.-based MNCs have consistently reported using three measures more frequently than any others: profit, budgeted profit compared to actual profit, and return on investment (ROI). Exhibit 10–1 compares the results of four similar surveys that report on U.S. MNC performance evaluation measures. Although the rankings change over time, the three most frequently used measures have remained the same.

EXHIBIT 10–1   Financial Measures Used as Indicators of Subsidiary Performance Evaluation: U.S.-Based MNCs

	Rankings			
Financial Measures	*1980[a]*	*1984[b]*	*1990[c]*	*1991[d]*
Profit	1	2	1	1
Budget versus actual profit	3	1	2	2
Return on investment	2	3	3	3

[a]SOURCE: Helen Gernon Morsicato, *Currency Translation and Performance Evaluation in Multinationals* (Ann Arbor, Mich.: UMI Research Press, 1980). MNCs surveyed: 70.

[b]SOURCE: Wagdy M. Abdallah, *Internal Accountability: An International Emphasis* (Ann Arbor, Mich.: UMI Research Press, 1984). MNCs surveyed: 64.

[c]SOURCE: Ahmad Hosseini and Zabihollah Rezaee, "Impact of SFAS No. 52 on Performance Measures of Multinationals," *The International Journal of Accounting* 25, no. 1 (1990), pp. 43–52. MNCs surveyed: 109.

[d]SOURCE: Orapin Duangploy and Dahli Gray, "An Empirical Analysis of Current U.S. Practice in Evaluating and Controlling Overseas Operations," *Accounting and Business Research* 21, no. 84 (1991), pp. 299–309. MNCs surveyed: 111.

EXHIBIT 10–2   Financial Measures Used as Indicators of Subsidiary Performance
Evaluation: U.K.-Based MNCs

Financial Measures	Rankings 1988
Budget versus actual profit	1
Return on investment	2
Budget versus actual return on investment	3
Cash-flow potential from subsidiary	4
Profit	5

SOURCE: I. S. Demirag, "Assessing Foreign Subsidiary Performance: The Currency Choice of U.K. MNCs," *The Journal of International Business Studies* (Summer 1988), pp. 257–75. MNCs surveyed: 105.

A similar survey was conducted on U.K.-based MNCs and the rankings of performance measures are presented in Exhibit 10–2. The three most frequently used measures are reported to be budget compared with actual profits, return on investment, and budget compared with actual return on investment. Profit, which is reported by U.S. MNCs as the most frequently used measure, falls to fifth place when we look at the U.K. operating environment. Both return on investment and budgeted to actual return on investment are important to U.K. managers. A possible explanation for the reported differences is that U.K. managers maintain a more international focus (polycentric) as compared to the more domestic focus (ethnocentric) of U.S. managers. More will be said about these differences later in the chapter when we discuss using local currency information to assess manager performance.

Two studies have focused on Japanese performance evaluation measures. Exhibit 10–3 presents the results of asking 256 Japanese and 80 U.S. MNCs about the budget goals used for division managers. Exhibit 10–4 reports the results of a study that surveyed the performance evaluation literature in search of criteria used to evaluate Japanese and U.S. divisional managers. Both studies show how important sales measures are in Japan. Both studies also support the previous statements about U.S. managers relying on ROI and profit.

Profit and Return on Investment

We have seen that one of the frequently reported tests of profitability is the relationship of profit to invested capital. As discussed in Chapter 7 on financial statement analysis, this relationship is expressed as the rate of return on investment (ROI). This statistic retains its appeal because it presents all of the profitability components in one ratio. However, it is not the only measure of profitability and should be used only in conjunction with other performance measures.

EXHIBIT 10–3   Percentage of Time Rank in Top Three Budget Goals for
Division Managers

	Japan (%)	United States (%)
Sales volume	86.3	27.9
Net profit after corporate overhead	44.7	35.0
Controllable profit	28.2	51.8
Profit margin on sales	30.7	30.5
Sales growth	19.4	22.4
Return on investment	3.1	68.4
Production cost	40.7	12.4

SOURCE: J. C. Bailes and T. Assada, "Empirical Differences between Japanese and American Budget and Performance Evaluation Systems," *The International Journal of Accounting* 26, no. 2 (1991), p. 137.

Budgets as a Success Indicator

For some time, budgeting has been accepted as a management tool for controlling operations and forecasting future operations of domestic companies. One purpose of the budget is to clearly set out the objectives of the entity. A budget generally provides a forecast and a means of comparing the actual results of operations to the budget. This comparison produces variances that can be analyzed to evaluate performance and improve the efficiency of future operations.

When a budget is used for a foreign subsidiary, the budget should be developed by that subsidiary. The experience of the local manager is extremely important, in that it produces a very deep knowledge of the specific business situation. A budget developed on this level will help control the operations and make achievement of goals possible. This budget can be used by the local manager on a daily basis.

Budgeting gives local managers the opportunity to set their own performance standards. In international operations top management is not as familiar with what the standards should be. Headquarters must rely to a greater extent on good local or regional budgets, which help facilitate the strategic planning process.

Preparation of the budget at the local level is not always an easy task. Local managers have different degrees of budgeting expertise. Local customs and norms may affect the budgeting process and are likely to affect the degree of its acceptance and usefulness. Implementation of a system is also difficult due to a lack of familiarity with the technique on the part of local employees of foreign subsidiaries. Budgeting may be a more critical performance evaluation tool for international operations than for domestic ones.

Headquarters uses each foreign subsidiary's budget to develop a worldwide, companywide forecast. Headquarters analyses are based upon a wide spectrum of knowledge, including knowledge of possible environmental, objective, and

EXHIBIT 10–4   Important Performance Criteria Used for Evaluating
Divisional Managers

	Japan	United States
	A (%)	A (%)
Sales	69	19
Sales growth	28	28
Market share	12	19
Asset turnover	7	13
Return-on-sales	30	26
ROI	7	75
Controllable profit	28	49
Residual income	20	13
Profit minus corporate costs	44	38
Manufacturing costs	28	13
Other	8	17

SOURCE: M. Shields, C. W. Chow, Y. Kato, and Y. Nakagawa, "Management Accounting Practices in the U.S. and Japan: Comparative Survey Findings and Research Implications," *Journal of International Financial Management and Accounting* 3, no. 1 (Spring 1991), p. 68.

strategy changes at the international level. At this headquarters level, profit and return on investment provide the information necessary to assess worldwide profitability and its success or failure. Budgeted information is used more frequently to assess the individual subsidiaries' performances rather than the overall performance of the MNC.

The subsidiaries' budgets are approved at the parent-company level and often require the endorsement of the president and/or the board of directors. Presumably, headquarters uses the budget to consider the circumstances peculiar to each subsidiary. However, as noted above, executives repeatedly return to the ROI statistic. They may use the budget for *supplementary* information on subsidiary performance; but, they still select ROI as a key success indicator.

NONFINANCIAL MEASURES USED TO EVALUATE AND ENHANCE MNC PERFORMANCE

A 1995 research report issued by The Conference Board reported that a growing number of major international corporations are using the nonfinancial measures listed in Exhibit 10–5 to capture their firms' potential for future performance. These key measures help transnational companies identify, value, and communicate certain "intangible" assets that do not lend themselves to traditional measurement techniques. The "intangibles" are used internally in a systematic and continuous process for performance measurement and improvement. These companies found traditional financial measures to (1) be too historical,

---

EXHIBIT 10–5   Nonfinancial Measures Used to Evaluate and Enhance
MNC Performance

Quality of output
Customer satisfaction/retention
Employee training
Research and development
Investment and productivity
New product development
Market growth/success
Environmental competitiveness

Source: "Challenging Traditional Measures of Performance," *Deloitte & Touche Review* (August 7, 1995), pp. 1–2.

---

(2) lack predictive behavior, (3) reward the wrong behavior, (4) focus on inputs, not outputs, (5) reflect functions, not cross-functional processes, and (6) give inadequate consideration to hard-to-quantify resources such as intellectual capital. The nonfinancial measures are not meant to replace, but to enhance, the more traditional financial measures discussed previously. The participants expect that using the kind of nonfinancial measures listed in Exhibit 10–5 will lead to increased profitability.

ISSUES TO CONSIDER WHEN DEVELOPING MNC EVALUATION SYSTEMS

Separating Manager Performance from Subsidiary Performance

Many managerial accountants advocate making a distinction between the performance of the subsidiary manager and that of the subsidiary itself. In practice, MNCs report that they do not make a distinction between the evaluation of the manager and the subsidiary. Exhibit 10–6 reveals that in two surveys, U.S. MNCs reported using the same financial measures to evaluate the performance of the manager as that of the subsidiary. The three most frequently used financial measures are profit, budget compared to actual profit, and return on investment. Keep in mind that Japanese MNCs use sales when evaluating subsidiary managers.

Responsibility reporting as an accounting system traces costs, revenues, assets, and liabilities to the individual manager who is responsible for them. It follows that a manager who has the ability to control the results of operations should be evaluated on the basis of the results over which she or he has control. This system has been widely implemented in U.S. domestic operations and has proven to be generally effective as an evaluation tool. However, the very nature of

EXHIBIT 10–6   Financial Measures Used to Evaluate Foreign Subsidiaries and
Their Managers

	Use in Performance Evaluation Ranking			
	Abdallah[a]		Hosseini/Rezaee[b]	
Financial Measures	Subsidiary	Manager	Subsidiary	Manager
Profit	2	2*	1	1
Budget versus actual profit	1	1	2	2
Return on investment	3	2*	3	3

*These are ranked equally because their scores are extremely close.

SOURCES: (a) Wagdy M. Abdallah, *Internal Accountability: An International Emphasis* (Ann Arbor, Mich.: UMI Research Press, 1984). MNCs surveyed: 64. (b) Ahmad Hosseini and Zabihollah Rezaee, "Impact of SFAS No. 52 on Performance Measures of Multinationals," *The International Journal of Accounting* 25, no. 1 (1990), pp. 43–52. MNCs surveyed: 109.

international operations does not lend itself to effectively implementing a responsibility reporting system in MNCs.

MNC headquarters manages from a worldwide perspective and allocates costs and sets transfer prices to optimize companywide profits and to facilitate worldwide cash flows. (Chapter 11 focuses on transfer prices and taxation.) Therefore, it is very naive to evaluate the operating performance of foreign subsidiary managers without first considering all the possible uncontrollable costs that could be allocated to their operations (i.e., royales, interest, taxes, and exchange gains and losses).

For these reasons, evaluating a manager's performance should be separate from judging the subsidiary as an investment. The manager's evaluation should involve a degree of subjectivity that considers the uniqueness of the subsidiary, environmental peculiarities, actions of the host government, and specific goals of the manager being evaluated. If managers are delegated responsibility for results that are beyond their control, it may lead to behavior that is not in line with headquarters' goals.

Evaluating managers in their local currency before allocation of costs over which they have no direct control is ideal, although somewhat impractical because headquarters usually prefers information translated to the parent currency. Objective measures of performance, profit, and ROI may then be used effectively by headquarters to judge the subsidiary as an investment.

Treating Foreign Subsidiaries as Profit Centers

Profit centers located internationally do not operate in a uniform environment. They operate in environments with different inflation rates and different economic, political, cultural, and technological conditions. Top management is not likely to understand all of the peculiarities of each environment; therefore, it will have trouble evaluating the managers' performance. For these reasons, the profit center concept is less useful when applied to foreign subsidiaries than when applied to domestic subsidiaries. Therefore, it is less successful as a performance indicator.

MNCs also integrate and coordinate operations globally, and it becomes difficult under these circumstances to recognize a particular subsidiary's contribution. The subsidiary manager is not directly responsible for all of the subsidiary's activities. Subsidiaries of an MNC are not independent, and although some control may be decentralized, many major decisions affecting both worldwide profit and individual subsidiary profit are made at headquarters for worldwide efficiency in operations.

Transfer pricing policy (see Chapter 11) in the MNC is not compatible with the profit center concept. A transfer price is a charge for goods exchanged between subsidiaries of the same company. Transfer prices in domestic profit centers are usually set with the objective of maintaining equity between the independent subsidiaries. Transfer prices are set *internationally* for many reasons, which do not necessarily include equity among subsidiaries. These reasons include taxes, tariffs, fluctuating currencies, inflation, economic restrictions on fund transfers, and political instabilities.

Even so, local managers and subsidiaries of MNCs are often evaluated like profit centers. Yet central coordination of the MNC makes it difficult to evaluate the local managers' performance. These managers do not make many of the important decisions affecting their operations. It is also difficult to evaluate how effectively a subsidiary is using its resources.

The responsibility reporting concept implies that the manager and the local entity should be evaluated separately. Separating the two enables each to be judged according to its contribution to global optimization.

Translation

The accounting records and financial statements of a foreign subsidiary are generally maintained in the subsidiary's local currency. The U.S. parent company must be able to translate these foreign currency financial statements to U.S.-dollar terms. Translation is necessary for any of the following reasons:

1. To communicate to foreign subsidiary managers the parent company's objectives for the foreign subsidiary in terms of U.S.-dollar results and flows.

2. To judge the foreign subsidiary's profitability.

3. To evaluate the performance of the foreign subsidiary's managers.

4. To evaluate capital budgeting decisions.

5. To evaluate the return produced by the dollar investment of the U.S. company.

6. To determine the periodic gain or loss sustained by the U.S. parent company from movements in foreign exchange rates.

7. To consolidate foreign financial statements with domestic statements and present them to top management in a currency they are familiar with (see Chapter 6).

To prepare statements in U.S.-dollar terms, the amounts expressed in foreign currency must be changed to dollars. As discussed in Chapter 6, the process of changing the amounts from foreign currency to dollars is commonly referred to as *translation*. This is a measurement conversion process—it changes only the unit of measure, not the accounting principles used to prepare the statements. Translation satisfies the need to use a single unit of measure in the consolidated financial statements of domestic and foreign operations.

Management, investors, and other users of financial information need translated statements to judge the past, present, and future profitability of the foreign operations. The results of operations are more easily compared if presented in terms of a single currency (e.g., U.S. dollars).

The key issue that arises when translating financial statements is the selection of the exchange rate (method) to translate various accounts from one currency into another.

For external reporting purposes, the Financial Accounting Standards Board has issued *Statement 52,* "Foreign Currency Translation" (see Chapter 6). Assuming that we are dealing with *autonomous* subsidiaries, we use the year-end exchange rate (current rate) to translate the balance sheet and average-for-the-year rate to translate the income statement. The result is that operating relationships and income statement ratios remain intact throughout the translation process. Users of this information can then see in dollars the same relationships that existed in the currency where the revenues were earned and expenses were incurred. Notice in Exhibit 10–7, for example, that the ratio of total debt to total assets is the same in local currency (LC 1100 ÷ LC 1500 = 73 percent) as it is in U.S. dollars ($550 ÷ $750 = 73 percent).

Studies have shown that most MNCs use the same method to translate for internal reporting purposes (managerial accounting) that they use for external reporting purposes (financial accounting). Therefore, with *FASB Statement 52* requiring use of the current rate for financial reporting, it can be assumed that information used to evaluate foreign subsidiaries and their managers is also translated at the current exchange rate in effect at the time of translation. This method provides translated financial statements that are similar to local currency financial statements.

Use of Local Currency Information

If a subsidiary operates in a country with a stable currency, an evaluation of the subsidiary's performance in either U.S. dollars or local currency should be meaningful. When the currency is unstable, a foreign subsidiary's performance is more clearly reflected by its *local* currency operating results.

EXHIBIT 10–7   Effect of Translation on Balance Sheet Accounts

	Local Currency	Current Rate	U.S. Dollars
Cash	LC300	1 LC = $0.50	$150
Inventory	400		200
Building and land	800		400
	LC1,500		$750
Current liabilities	LC300	1 LC = $0.50	$150
Long-term debt	800		400
Stockholder's equity	400		200
	LC1,500		$750

Profit and ROI in U.S. dollars can be used to judge the *subsidiary's* value to the enterprise as a whole. These financial measures are less applicable when evaluating a subsidiary *manager.* As noted earlier, such managers should be evaluated on meeting primary *goals* in local currency (e.g., annual profits and sales forecasts, meeting projected production level, managing the effects of inflation, and managing employees).

Comparisons of the past, present, and future operations of a subsidiary are far more meaningful and valid if calculated in local currency. Comparing either the U.S.-dollar or local currency results of subsidiaries operating in different environments is useless. The environmental peculiarities of each operating environment need to be isolated and weighed in order to achieve a meaningful comparison. Yet U.S. managers continue to use more U.S. dollar financial measures than local currency measures. U.K. managers report a preference for using budget compared with actual profit information in local currency. They say that the local currency provides information that relates to local environment conditions and avoids distortions that result from fluctuating exchange rates.

However, there is a problem with universally employing local currency information for evaluating foreign operations. Sometimes higher-echelon managers have difficulty interpreting subsidiary results reported in local currency. These managers also have difficulty understanding and interpreting the effect that foreign exchange gains and losses have on the overall enterprise results. Decision making by boards of directors and management headquarters is generally based on U.S.-dollar information. If one level of management bases decisions on U.S.-dollar information and another on local currency information, problems with goal congruency and optimization of resources may result. To minimize these problems, multinational corporations are requiring managers and directors to become familiar with foreign currency operating results in addition to U.S.-dollar information.

The local currency perspective recognizes that foreign subsidiaries function in different countries and economic environments and may have a different operating relationship with the parent than domestic subsidiaries. Therefore, local currency financial statements of a foreign subsidiary present a more meaningful picture of the subsidiary's activities.

CONCLUSION

Multinational corporations need flexible performance evaluation models capable of incorporating factors peculiar to an MNC for the separate evaluation of subsidiary and manager. This chapter has identified the financial measures currently being used in MNC performance evaluation systems. Explanations of why these measures are inappropriate in a multinational environment have led the authors to suggest more effective techniques. Because performance evaluation systems used by MNCs have international economic impact, these systems should be under constant examination, and improvements should be made continuously.

STUDY QUESTIONS

1. What role does the MNC performance evaluation system play in relation to strategic planning and control? (Review Chapter 9.)
2. Why should financial comparisons of subsidiaries operating in different countries be made cautiously?
3. Budgeting is thought to be a more useful and critical tool for evaluating foreign subsidiary managers than domestic managers. Describe a "good" budgeting process and explain why it works in the international environment.
4. Why do Japanese managers use sales figures when evaluating subsidiary managers, while U.S. and U.K. managers prefer ROI and profit?
5. What are the alternatives to using translated information when judging foreign subsidiaries?
6. Why are MNCs beginning to use nonfinancial measures as indicators of performance? What is it about the nonfinancial measures listed in Exhibit 10–5 that makes them difficult to quantify?
7. You are the CFO (chief financial officer) of an MNC headquartered in the United Kingdom. You are thinking about how convoluted the issues are that influence the internal performance evaluation of your subsidiaries and their managers. Make a list off the issues and be ready to discuss them.

CASES

Ciba-Geigy

Ciba-Geigy is a large diversified Swiss MNC that uses the matrix form of organization in order to pay attention to products and geographic areas. Headquarters management is responsible for the development and implementation of management principles and business policies, setting strategic targets for subsidiaries and the company as a whole, allocation of resources (money, people, and facilities), and organizational structure. Other responsibilities are delegated to the subsidiaries in a highly decentralized fashion. ROI is considered the most important financial indicator of success. The calculation of ROI is dependent upon the accounting rules used in the computation. Ciba-Geigy is able to choose its own set of accounting rules because Swiss MNCs are not required to publish consolidated financial statements, although the company has voluntarily done so since 1972. Ciba-Geigy uses current values for fixed assets and an operating income concept (i.e., the only revenues and expenses appearing on the income statement of a subsidiary are those resulting from the direct operations of that unit). In general, the subsidiary managers are very happy with the performance evaluation system.

Questions

1. Can you identify any advantages to the Ciba-Geigy information and control system? Do you notice any disadvantages?
2. What influence has the Swiss operating environment had on the development of the information and control system?
3. Do you think it possible for a large U.S. MNC to adopt the Ciba-Geigy information and control system? Why or why not?

Global Enterprises, Inc.

Global Enterprises, Inc., is a large diversified U.S. MNC with operations all over the world. Headquarters takes a centralized approach to control and exhibits an ethnocentric attitude toward international business. Consequently, top management is rather suspicious of foreign nationals and attempts to use U.S. personnel throughout its foreign subsidiaries. The established control system holds managers accountable for exchange rate fluctuations, and this is incorporated in the budgeting process. Global requires that all budgets be prepared in U.S. dollars and that the actual rate at the beginning of the period be used to set the budget. The actual rate at the end of the period is then used to track results.

Questions

1. What effects might this approach have on the operating manager of a subsidiary?
2. Suggest an alternative approach that would not hold the local manager accountable for exchange rate fluctuations.
3. If you wanted to turn Global into a multicultural transnational MNC, what changes would you have to make to the strategic planning and control processes?

Innovative International

Innovative International is a U.S. transnational corporation with manufacturing subsidiaries in Asia, Europe, and North and South America. Traditionally, Innovative has used a variety of financial measures to evaluate the performance of these manufacturing subsidiaries and their managers. The Asian managers have asked for a change because they feel that the financial measures do not capture how effectively they operate their manufacturing facilities. Innovative's top management group has always had an open door policy when it comes to managing, and they are carefully listening to the managers from China, South Korea, Japan, and Taiwan. These managers want alternatives to ROI.

Questions

1. Can you effectively separate the performance evaluation of the manufacturing subsidiary from the evaluation of its manager? Discuss.
2. Are there any nonfinancial measures that Innovative can use?
3. What problems might develop in trying to quantify nonfinancial measures of performance evaluation?

ADDITIONAL READINGS

Bailes, J. C., and T. Assada. "Empirical Differences between Japanese and American Budget and Performance Evaluation Systems." *The International Journal of Accounting* 26, no. 2 (1991), pp. 131–42.

Duangploy, D., and D. Gray. "An Empirical Analysis of Current U.S. Practice in Evaluating and Controlling Overseas Operations." *Accounting and Business Research* 21, no. 84 (1991), pp. 299–309.

Haka, S. F., B. A. Lamberton, and H. M. Sollenberger. "The Ameripill Company: Developing a Financial Performance Measurement System for an MNE Which Provides Incentives and Assists in Decision Making." *Issues in Accounting Education* 9, no. 1 (Spring 1994), pp. 168–90.

Hassel, L. G. "Performance Evaluation in a Multinational Environment." *Journal of International Financial Management and Accounting* 3, no. 2 (1991), pp. 17–38.

Hosseini, A., and Z. Rezaee. "Impact of SFAS No. 52 on Performance Measures of Multinationals." *The International Journal of Accounting* 25, no. 1 (1990), pp. 43–52.

Shields, M., C. W. Chow, Y. Kato, and Y. Nakagawa. "Management Accounting Practices in the U.S. and Japan: Comparative Survey Findings and Research Implications." *Journal of International Financial Management and Accounting* 3, no. 1 (Spring 1991), pp. 61–77.

Susumu, U., and U. Sekaran. "The Influence of Culture on Budget Control Practices in the USA and Japan: An Empirical Study." *The Journal of International Business Studies* 23, no. 4 (1992), pp. 659–74.

11

MULTINATIONAL TRANSFER PRICING AND INTERNATIONAL TAXATION

LEARNING OBJECTIVES

1. List the various intracompany transactions that require a transfer price.
2. Be familiar with the conflicting objectives of international transfer pricing.
3. Understand the relationship between setting a transfer price and evaluating the performance of foreign subsidiaries and managers.
4. Know why transfer pricing is the leading international tax issue.
5. Be able to define tax credit, tax treaty, tax haven, tax exemption, and the deferral principle.

We have established that the purpose of a management control system is to accomplish the objectives of the strategic plan. The control system is designed to communicate information that enhances goal congruence and that provides the basis for decision making throughout all levels of the multinational corporation (MNC).

The MNC must deal with two additional complicating variables that do not affect domestic corporations. The first is setting transfer prices for goods and services in a worldwide arena. The second is dealing with international taxation and its pervasive influence on all aspects of MNC operations. This chapter discusses the objectives of MNC transfer pricing and then turns to a discussion of how MNCs attempt to minimize taxes on an international scale. As we shall see, the transfer price selected for transferring goods and services across national boundaries has a significant impact on the MNC's international tax liability, and vice versa.

OBJECTIVES OF TRANSFER PRICING

The need for determining a transfer price arises when goods or services are exchanged between organizational units of the same company (e.g., charges for administrative and managerial services, royalties for intangible rights, transfers of finished goods for resale, and charges for technical services). A transfer price is a substitute for a market price. It is used when one subsidiary of a corporation sells to another. The transfer pricing system places a monetary value on intracompany exchanges that occur between operating units. This price is recorded by the seller as revenue and by the buyer as cost.

Example 1.   Subsidiary A sells 1,000 units of product X to subsidiary B for $7 per unit. The $7 selling price is the *transfer price.*

It is generally agreed that the transfer pricing system for a *domestic* corporation should accomplish certain objectives including (1) the communication of information resulting in desirable decision making by managers, (2) providing a report of divisional profits that reasonably measures the economic performance of the division, and (3) enhancing goal congruence.

Achieving these objectives may be difficult. If a manager makes a decision that increases the profit of his/her particular profit center, it may affect the profits of a competing profit center negatively. An example of such a decision is charging an inflated transfer price for goods transferred to a division. The first profit center will show increased sales and a higher profit; however, the second profit center will show increased cost of purchases and a lower profit.

Example 2.   Subsidiary A sells 1,000 units of product X to subsidiary B for $8 per unit. The normal market price is $6 per unit. Subsidiary A shows increased sales of $2 per unit and a higher profit. Subsidiary B shows that cost of goods sold has increased by $2 per unit and therefore has a lower profit.

Those who develop domestic internal transfer pricing systems are aware of this potential dilemma and attempt to create a system that motivates managers not to make undesirable decisions. Ideally, a manager acts in the best interests of the company as a whole, even at the expense of the reported profits of his/her own division. To effect this ideal behavior, the system of performance evaluation must reward a manager who chooses companywide goal congruence over divisional performance.

OBJECTIVES OF INTERNATIONAL TRANSFER PRICING

Developing an MNC transfer pricing system is far more complex than developing a domestic system. As with the *domestic* corporation, an MNC pricing system should result in managers making desirable decisions that enhance goal congruence. Proving a reasonable measure of a subsidiary's economic performance is often an irrelevant transfer pricing objective when dealing with an MNC. An MNC pricing system must attempt to meet the objectives of the strategic plan, the management control system, and the system of performance evaluation. (See Chapters 9 and 10 for a discussion of these objectives.) The international transfer pricing system must also attempt to accomplish objectives that are irrelevant in a purely domestic operation. These objectives include (1) worldwide income tax minimization, (2) minimization of worldwide import duties, (3) avoidance of financial restrictions, (4) managing currency fluctuations, and (5) winning host-country government approval.

MNCs are not able to accomplish all of these objectives with a single worldwide transfer pricing strategy. In fact, strategies employed may vary depending upon the host country of operation. MNCs report several environmental variables as having an influence on setting transfer prices: market conditions and competition in the foreign country; reasonable profit for the foreign affiliate; import restrictions, tariffs, and exchange controls; income tax liabilities to host and parent country; and economic conditions in the foreign country are only a few of the variables that make the process so complicated.

Worldwide Income Tax Minimization

The transfer pricing system can be used to shift taxable profits from a country with a high tax rate to a country with a lower tax rate; the result is that after taxes the MNC retains more profits. Exhibit 11–1 reports the corporation income tax rates for a variety of countries throughout the world. The Cayman Islands have long been considered a tax haven for corporations due to the zero corporate income tax rate. As you can see, corporate rates vary considerably. Unless the performance evaluation system is compatible with the transfer pricing system, undesirable decision making can result at the subsidiary manager level. If each subsidiary is evaluated as an independent profit center, the transfer pricing policies must be considered when evaluating the manager's performance, or else conflict between subsidiary and MNC goals may result.

Example 3.   Subsidiary X operates in Pakistan, where the tax rate is 30 percent. Subsidiary Y operates in Switzerland with a tax rate of 10 percent. X sells goods to Y at an inflated transfer price of $10 per item. The current market price is $7 per item. Subsidiary X shows a higher profit and is taxed at 30 percent. Subsidiary Y shows a higher cost of goods sold and a lower profit on future sales taxed at 10 percent. These subsidiaries are not practicing worldwide tax minimization.

EXHIBIT 11–1   Corporate Income Tax Rates

Country	Rate
Australia	39%
Brazil	35
Cayman Islands	0
China, Peoples Republic of	33
Germany	50
Italy	36
Japan	38
Korea	34
Norway	28
Pakistan	30
Singapore	27
Switzerland	10
Taiwan	25
United Kingdom	33
United States	34

Minimization of Worldwide Import Duties

Transfer prices can reduce tariffs. Import duties are normally applied to intracompany transfers as well as to sales to unaffiliated buyers. If the goods are transferred in at low prices, the resulting tariffs will be lower. This same pricing strategy may be used when a country places a ceiling on the value of goods that may be imported. By valuing at low transfer prices, a subsidiary may be able to import a larger *quantity* of goods and services. If a country had a low tariff on imports, a higher transfer price could be charged.

Tariffs interact with income taxes. Low import duties are often associated with a country with high income tax rates. The opposite may also be found—high import duties with low income tax rates. The MNC must deal with the customs officials and income tax administrators of the importing country and with the income tax administrators of the exporting country. A higher import tariff would result in a lower remaining profit for determining income taxes. The MNC has to evaluate the benefits of a lower (higher) income tax in the importing country against a higher (lower) import tariff as well as the potentially higher (lower) income tax paid by the MNC in the exporting country.

Avoidance of Financial Restrictions

When a foreign government places economic restrictions on MNC operations, transfer prices may mitigate the impact of these national controls. Suppose a country restricts the amount of cash that may leave its boundaries in the form of dividend payments. Setting a high transfer price on goods imported into the country may facilitate the desired movement of cash because the importing subsidiary must remit payment. However, cash transfers are not easily accomplished in a country that watches import and export prices closely.

Some countries allow a tax credit or subsidy based on the value of goods exported. In this case, a high transfer price on exported products is followed by a larger tax credit or higher subsidy. A tax credit of this nature reduces the corresponding tax liability to the host country dollar for dollar and more than offsets the higher taxable income. A subsidy is generally a payment from the government to the subsidiary.

Restrictions may be placed on an MNC by disallowing a foreign subsidiary to deduct certain expenses provided by the parent against taxable income. Common examples include research and development expenses, general and administrative expenses, and royalty fees. By inflating the transfer price of imports to the subsidiary, such expenses may be recovered.

If an MNC desires to show lower (higher) profitability, high (low) transfer prices on imports to subsidiaries may be used. An MNC may want to appear less profitable to discourage potential competitors from entering the market. Higher profits may case the subsidiary's employees to demand higher wages or even to request some type of profit-sharing plan. Expropriation (takeover) of highly profitable foreign-owned subsidiaries may also be avoided if they appear less profitable.

Lower transfer prices on imports should improve the subsidiary's financial position. This may be desirable when the MNC wants to finance the foreign subsidiary with funds from a local lender rather than committing its own capital. In this instance, the lender would probably require that the subsidiary have a positive financial condition. Lower transfer prices may also allow the subsidiary to enjoy a competitive edge during its initial stages of growth.

Managing Currency Fluctuations

A country suffering from balance-of-payments problems may decide to devalue its national currency. Losses from such a devaluation may be avoided by using inflated transfer prices to transfer funds from the country to the parent or to some other affiliate.

Balance-of-payments problems often result from an inflationary environment. Inflation erodes the purchasing power of the MNC's monetary assets. Using inflated transfer prices on goods imported to such an environment may offer a timely cash removal method.

Winning Host-Country Government Approval

The manipulation of transfer prices has not gone unnoticed. Generally, there is increased government concern about intracorporate pricing and its effect on reported profits. In an era when an MNC must be concerned about justifying its existence, maintaining positive relations with the host government is a good idea. Continually changing and manipulating transfer prices is not good policy.

Most governments are becoming more sophisticated and aware of the results of using high or low transfer prices. Using unfavorable prices to a country's detriment results in the loss of goodwill. It is beneficial in the long run to develop transfer pricing policies that satisfy the foreign authorities, even though it may mean sacrificing some profits.

In summary, we have discussed several transfer pricing objectives that MNCs must consider and that are not applicable to a purely domestic corporation. These objectives include worldwide income tax minimization, minimization of worldwide import duties, avoidance of financial restrictions, managing currency fluctuations, and winning host-country government approval. Exhibit 11–2 provides a summary of the conditions that make it advisable to use a particular transfer price. Unfortunately, an MNC is usually faced with conditions that appear in both columns of the exhibit.

MNCs may resort to maintaining a separate set of financial information for the foreign governments and another set for headquarters to use in the management control process and the performance evaluation system. Unfortunately, the

---

EXHIBIT 11–2 Conditions in Subsidiary's Country Inducing High and Low Transfer Prices on Flows between Affiliates and Parent

Conditions Inducing Low Transfer Prices *on Flows from Parent and* High Transfer Prices *on Flows to Parent*	*Conditions Inducing* High Transfer Prices *on Flows from Parent and* Low Transfer Prices *on Flows to Parent*
High ad valorem tariffs	Local partners
Corporate income tax rate lower than in parent's country	Pressure from workers to obtain greater share of company profit
Significant competition	Political pressure to nationalize or expropriate high-profit foreign firms
Local loans based on financial appearance of subsidiary	Restrictions on profit or dividend remittances
Export subsidy or tax credit on value of exports	Political instability
Lower inflation rate than in parent's country	Substantial tie-in sales agreements
Restrictions (ceilings) in subsidiary's country on the value of products that can be imported	Price of final product controlled by government but based on production cost
	Desire to mask profitability of subsidiary operations to keep competitors out

SOURCE: Jeffrey S. Arpan, *Intracorporate Pricing: Non-American Systems and Views* (New York: Praeger Publishers, 1972).

information provided to the foreign government is often used to evaluate the performance of a subsidiary that has been told to produce a low profit to minimize income taxes. If headquarters overlooks the fact that low profits were due to an unfavorable transfer price, hard feelings between subsidiary managers and headquarters may result. It may also cause subsidiary managers to act undesirably. In the long run, morale problems could develop and destroy the short-run effect of tax minimization.

Ideally, the objectives of the management control process should be separated from those of MNC transfer pricing. Headquarters must realize that the performance evaluation system should provide information that discriminates between subsidiary performance and worldwide corporate performance.

SELECTING A TRANSFER PRICE

A headquarters management team takes a global perspective when considering the trade-offs between the costs and benefits of setting transfer prices for their operations throughout the world. Each pricing decision affects the entire multinational corporate system. It is extremely difficult to quantify the trade-offs, because each environment is different, and the variables are constantly changing. The decision makers must consider the tax rate, tariffs, inflation, foreign exchange controls, government price controls, government stability, and a whole host of other factors operating in each country. Transfer pricing decisions also affect individual subsidiaries and the multinational corporation system simultaneously. Transfer pricing choices are discussed next.

Transfer Pricing Choices

Most transfer pricing systems in use today are based on either external market prices or internal costs. The use of market prices is consistent with the concept of operating subsidiaries as decentralized profit centers. When transfers are recorded at market prices, divisional profitability approaches the real economic contribution of the subsidiary to the total MNC. Using market prices ideally creates the sense of competition that would normally be present if the subsidiaries were independent corporations transacting business at arm's-length market prices. If the transfer price does reflect market conditions, then the subsidiary may be fairly evaluated on its own performance. Market prices also appear less arbitrary to government tax authorities who are watching for manipulation of profits and, therefore, are usually less scrutinized.

Using market prices implies that subsidiaries are autonomous profit centers and that their managers have the authority to make autonomous decisions. However, this is rarely the case in multinational corporations. It may be difficult to establish a free competitive market price if no intermediate market exists for the transferred goods. Finally, using market prices does not afford the MNC much flexibility with which to manipulate profits and cash flows to accomplish the various objectives discussed earlier.

If market prices are either unavailable or cannot be reasonably estimated, then the transfer price will probably be based on the costs of the selling subsidiary. Cost may be the full cost, a variable cost, or a marginal cost with a markup added to allow the selling subsidiary some percentage of profit. Generally, cost-based transfer prices are conveniently determined, because the information on costs is available. Using cost plus markup is acceptable when dealing with government authorities, which is another important consideration when administering transfer prices.

Cost-based systems have disadvantages just as market-based systems do. Using cost gives the selling party little incentive to control costs or to operate efficiently, since the inefficiencies may be passed along to the purchasing subsidiary. Undesirable behavior may result in the form of poor decision making.

The *Internal Revenue Code* and Transfer Pricing

All multinationals doing business in the United States must consider Section 482 of the *Internal Revenue Code* when pricing intercompany transactions (intracompany transactions from a headquarters' point of view). Section 482 gives the Internal Revenue Service (IRS) the authority to reallocate income and deductions among subsidiaries if it determines that this is necessary to prevent tax evasion, the illegal reduction of taxes, or to clearly reflect the income of the subsidiary. Intercompany sales of goods must appear to be priced at arm's-length market values. In addition, the IRS also scrutinizes the transfer of services, intangibles (such as trademarks, patents, and basic research), and R&D cost sharing arrangements among commonly controlled entities. Being required to use arm's-length transfer prices does not always allow an MNC to pursue the objective of worldwide profit maximization. According to the IRS, the arm's-length principle to be applied is whether unrelated parties with a reasonable level of experience, exercising sound business judgment would have agreed to the same contractual terms. This principle does not always support the objective of MNC transfer pricing philosophy.

An MNC pursuing tax minimization must be careful to use transfer prices that appear to reflect arm's-length sales to avoid IRS scrutiny. The *Internal Revenue Code* and related regulations allow three pricing methods considered arm's length: (1) the *comparable uncontrolled price method,* better known as market price; (2) the *resale price method,* sales price received for the property by the reseller less an appropriate markup; and (3) the *cost-plus method,* better known as cost—based transfer price. Other methods are allowed if the MNC can show that they approximate arm's length.

Even though the United States has comprehensive transfer pricing rules, it remains difficult to determine the proper pricing method, and there are many issues over which taxpayers and the IRS can, and do, disagree. A recent study conducted by the international accounting firm, Ernst & Young, the results of which are sum-

EXHIBIT 11–3   Ernst & Young Survey on Transfer Prices

Transfer pricing is the leading international tax issue	48(%)
Transfer pricing is a major international tax issue	82
Currently subject to transfer pricing inquiry	49
Have experienced transfer pricing inquiries in the past	34
Expect transfer pricing to continue to be a major issue	71
Use of APAs will grow in the future	81
My company is likely to use APAs in the future	64

Source: "Transfer Pricing Draws Scrutiny from World's Tax Agents," *Accounting Today* (August 21–September 10, 1995), p. 10.

marized in Exhibit 11–3, reports that more and more MNCs' transfer pricing practices are being investigated by national taxing authorities, adding uncertainties and risks to MNC investment and strategic planning. The study surveyed 210 companies operating in Australia, France, Germany, Japan, the Netherlands, the United Kingdom, and the United States. Half of the companies are major MNCs with subsidiaries in over 20 countries. In the midst of the current global investment boom, it is clear that transfer pricing is considered the leading international tax issue.

Many companies are considering using advanced pricing agreements (APAs) as a means of reducing this uncertainty. Exhibit 11–4 provides a listing of the advantages and disadvantages of these agreements. An APA is a binding agreement between the taxpayer and the IRS on a transfer pricing method for certain international transactions. Apple Computer, Inc., was the first company to successfully submit all the necessary documents for an APA in the United States. The IRS completed 22 APA agreements in 1995; however, only 19 were completed in the first three years of the program, 1991–1994.

MNCs have been accused, by competitors as well as national taxing authorities, of manipulating transfer prices to create high taxable income in countries that have low tax rates, and vice versa. There is concern in Washington, D.C., that foreign-controlled corporations are not paying their fair share of U.S. income taxes. The U.S. Department of Treasury recently distributed the following data (covering 1990 and 1991) showing that foreign-controlled corporations' tax liability as a percentage of total receipts is lower than U.S.-controlled foreign corporations.

	Tax Liability as % of Total Receipts	
	1990	*1991*
Foreign-controlled corporations	0.70%	0.54%
U.S.-controlled corporations	1.02%	1.00%

EXHIBIT 11–4   Advantages and Disadvantages of Advanced Pricing Agreements

---

Advantages

Gives companies the opportunity to obtain prior approval of their transfer pricing policies from the IRS and foreign tax authorities.

Agreement is binding and the company will not be subject to further inquiries.

Certainty of treatment makes long-term strategic planning easier.

Useful in cases with unusual facts or circumstances that affect the profitability of an intercompany transaction.

Useful if the company implements a method not specified in Section 482 regulations of the IRS.

Disadvantages

Forces a company to disclose sensitive (confidential) information.

Lack of flexibility in adjusting transfer pricing policies.

Requires substantial documentation and administration, and requires professional expertise.

Complex, lengthy, and costly to comply with and to implement.

Economists using Commerce Department import and export databases for 1993 analyzed the data by commodity and country. They determined that the United States lost over $33 billion in tax revenue due to artificial overpricing and underpricing of products entering and leaving the United States. They reported that Japan accounted for $5.1 billion and Canada, Germany, Taiwan, and the United Kingdom combined for over $8 billion of the $33 billion. Responding to this and prior studies, Congress has raised IRS funding for international examiners and expects to increase the number by at least 50 percent for the next several years. Managers of both U.S. and foreign corporations would be well advised to expect and be prepared for a transfer pricing examination.

INTERNATIONAL TAXATION—SELECTED TOPICS

International taxation has a pervasive effect on multinationals and, therefore, enters into most management decisions. Taxation affects where an MNC invests, how it markets its products, what form of business organization it selects, when and where to remit cash, how to finance—and of course—the choice of a transfer price.

Tax systems are used worldwide to effect economic policy, social issues, and the political scene; they are as varied as the nations developing them. International taxation is extremely complex and constantly changing. As tax treaties, agreements, laws, and regulations change, the multinational tax network must be reviewed and reworked to maintain relative worldwide advantages.

Philosophy of Taxation

A country may follow the territorial principle that income earned outside its domestic boundaries is not taxed. Other nations follow the worldwide principle that they have the right to tax income earned outside their boundaries when earned by an entity based in the country. The worldwide principle results in double taxation because the income is taxed where earned and then again to the parent company.

However, double taxation is mitigated by tax credits, tax treaties, tax havens, the "deferral principle," and tax exemption. A *tax credit* allows an entity to reduce the taxes paid to the domestic government by the amount of taxes paid to the foreign government. A credit is a direct reduction of the tax liability and reduces double taxation to a certain extent. A *tax treaty* between nations establishes what items of income will or will not be taxed by the authorities of the country where the income is earned. Exhibit 11–5 provides a listing of U.S. tax treaty countries. A *tax haven* is a country with an exceptionally low, or even no, income tax. It generally offers a company the right to earn or transfer income within its borders and pay little or no tax. Tax havens are normally used by MNCs to shift income from a country with a high tax rate to the tax haven. One way to accomplish this is by using transfer prices. The *deferral principle* works so that parent companies are not taxed on foreign source income until they actually receive a dividend. A *tax exemption* allows certain corporations to pay no tax on certain income.

Many MNCs were avoiding U.S. taxation by combining the tax deferral principle with the advantage of a tax haven and repatriating dividends to the tax haven instead of to the United States. As a result, the Controlled Foreign Corporation (CFC) rules were passed by Congress. These rules tax U.S. shareholders on CFC income when it is earned, regardless of when it is received, and thus eliminate the ability to avoid taxes in the manner described.

Congress also created the Foreign Sales Corporation (FSC) to encourage foreign sales by exporters. Part of the taxable income of the FSC is exempt from U.S. income tax. There are currently about 4,500 FSCs used by U.S. corporations. The requirements for qualifying as an FSC are extremely complex and beyond the scope of this book.

MNC Tax Avoidance

Tax avoidance is the legal reduction of one's tax liability and is accomplished by tax planning. We have already established that tax avoidance enters into most managerial decisions and, therefore, plays a role in the strategic planning process, the management control system, and performance evaluation.

EXHIBIT 11–5   U.S. Tax Treaty Countries

Argentina	Hungary	Norway
Aruba	Iceland	Pakistan
Australia	India	Philippines
Austria	Indonesia	Poland
Bangladesh	Ireland	Portugal
Barbados	Israel	Romania
Belgium	Italy	Russian Federation
Bermuda	Jamaica	Slovak Republic
Canada	Japan	South Africa
China	Korea	Spain
Cyprus	Luxembourg	Sri Lanka
Czech Republic	Malta	Sweden
Denmark	Mexico	Switzerland
Egypt	Morocco	Thailand
Finland	Netherlands	Trinidad & Tobago
France	Netherland Antilles	Tunisia
Germany	New Zealand	United Arab Republic
Greece	Nigeria	United Kingdom

Source: Jack R. Fay and Judson P. Stryker, "An Update on Foreign Taxes," *The CPA Journal* (October 1995), pp. 28–29 and 50–52.

A *tax-planning information system* that attempts to accomplish worldwide tax minimization and tax avoidance should incorporate the following procedures: (1) stating the objectives of tax planning in MNC operations, (2) delegating responsibilities for tax planning to both headquarters and subsidiaries, (3) determining what operations are affected by tax considerations and how they are affected, (4) communicating necessary information to the tax planners and decision makers, and (5) evaluating the impact tax considerations on an MNC strategic plan and management control system.

CONCLUSION

We have reviewed some of the objectives of MNC transfer pricing and international taxation. Accomplishing the objectives of transfer pricing is difficult without considering the applicable tax laws. These objectives are so important at times that they take precedence over the objectives of management control and performance evaluation. However, all are components of the strategic planning system and work toward the optimal achievement of a multinational corporation's comprehensive international plan.

STUDY QUESTIONS

1. How does the MNC's attitude toward business practices (ethnocentric, polycentric, or geocentric) affect the choice of a transfer pricing method?

2. How do corporate income taxes affect the strategic planning and control systems of MNCs?

3. Use Exhibit 11–2 to develop a list of information you would need about Taiwan to establish an effective transfer price for goods going in and out.

4. Compare and contrast the role of transfer pricing in a domestic versus a multinational corporation.

5. Identify the current choices an MNC has to set transfer prices, and discuss the advantages/disadvantages of each.

6. The Internal Revenue Service cares about the use of arm's-length transfer prices. Why? Is the United States the only country that monitors transfer prices of imports and exports?

7. Locate each U.S. tax treaty country on a current world map. List 10 countries with which the United States does not have a tax treaty. Why do you suppose that the United States does not have a tax treaty with the 10 countries you have just identified?

CASES

The Monday Morning Korean Blues

You are the manager of a Korean subsidiary of a U.S.-based MNC. Your subsidiary has been operating quite profitably during the last year, and you have excess cash to invest. You expect to use this cash to strengthen your subsidiary's position in Korea and ultimately to make your performance look exceptionally good. Your subsidiary buys raw materials from other Pacific Rim subsidiaries of the U.S.- based parent to manufacture its product. You also have had permission to buy these parts from the competition if you can get a better price. Lately, you have been buying from the competition.

This morning, you had the following conversation with headquarters:

HQ:

We need cash transferred into France, and your Korean subsidiary has excess cash at the moment. We want you to facilitate the movement of these funds by Friday.

You:

You know that today is Monday?

HQ:

Yes, we know that it is Monday.

You:

How do you propose that I accomplish your request, considering the fact that my government has just stopped all movement of excess cash out of the country?

HQ:

That could be a problem. You know your country's system. Work around it. France needs the cash by Friday.

Questions

1. How could you facilitate the flow of cash from Korea to France, given the present restrictions in Korea?
2. If you are unsuccessful in transferring funds to France, how else could the parent facilitate this flow?
3. Why is your subsidiary allowed to operate so independently (i.e., investing its own excess cash where it chooses and buying raw materials from the least expensive source)?
4. What is meant by the phrase, "You know the system"?

Ah! the Tangled Webs We Weave

Seated around a table are Rhian Emmanuel, Welsh by nationality, and president of IBT-Europe; Patricia Rodary, French, and vice president of finance; and Sarah Stevens, American, and vice president in charge of sales. IBT is a U.S.-based MNC that manufactures minicomputers. IBT-Europe is a very profitable, wholly owned subsidiary. As a result of its profitability, the president is given a great deal of autonomy from the parent company. Emmanuel manages eight geographically organized subsidiaries that are treated as profit centers when it comes to control and evaluation. Budgets are set in terms of pretax profit and local managers are largely evaluated on their ability to "beat the numbers." Transfer prices are determined at the annual budget meeting, where all subsidiary managers have input. If a complicated tax situation arises, headquarters steps in and determines prices. The following conversation takes place:

Stevens:

> I received word from Ireland that the computers are en route to France at a price of $35,000. But France does not want to clear them through customs at this price, because machines from Belgium have been arriving at $25,000 and from the U.S.A. at $27,000. France wants a revised price from Ireland of $25,000.

Rodary:

> Let's lower the price. It's only bookkeeping. We don't want the European Union investigating our transfer prices.

Emmanuel:

> We can't lower the price. The whole point is to take advantage of the favorable tax deal we struck with Ireland. We have 12 years left on our exemption from income tax on all export sales. I thought this was all settled. We are in business to earn a profit.

Questions

1. What is going on here? Identify as many issues as you can.
2. Is this a centralization/decentralization problem?
3. Is minimizing payments to foreign governments an issue?
4. Can you suggest a solution?

When in Rome

You have just completed your first year as chief financial officer (CFO) for Al Italia, an Italian subsidiary of a U.S. multinational corporation. Until this past year, you had worked at U.S. headquarters as an assistant to the worldwide CFO. At headquarters, you learned all about international tax planning and tax avoidance, or so you thought. You are well aware that tax evasion is illegal. You have noticed that in Italy, little attention is paid to the tax law and deals seem to be struck between the taxpayer and the tax collector. You are quite accustomed to paying your fair share of corporate taxes; however, you are having difficulty determining what your fair share is in the Italian tax environment.

Questions

1. When in Rome, will you do as the Romans do?
2. When in Rome, will you do as the Americans do?

ADDITIONAL READINGS

Bodner, P. M. "International Taxation." *Handbook of International Accounting*. F. D. S. Choi, ed. New York: John Wiley, 1991, pp. 30/1–21.

Bradley, F. "International Transfer Pricing." *Handbook of International Accounting*. F. D. S. Choi, ed. New York: John Wiley, 1991, pp. 29/1–29.

Business International Corporation. *International Transfer Pricing*. New York: BI, 1991.

Coopers and Lybrand. *International Transfer Pricing*. New York, NY: CCH International, 1993, 194 pp.

Khan, Z. U. "Transfer Pricing in Europe." *Journal of International Accounting, Auditing and Taxation* 1, no. 1 (1992), pp. 51–60.

Leitch, R. A., and K. S. Barrett. "Multinational Transfer Pricing: Objectives and Constraints." *Journal of Accounting Literature* 11, 1992, pp. 47–92.

O'Connor, W. F. "A Comparative Analysis of the Major Areas of Tax Controversy in Developed Countries." *Journal of International Accounting, Auditing and Taxation* 1, no. 1 (1992), pp. 61–79.

C H A P T E R

12

EMERGING ISSUES IN INTERNATIONAL ACCOUNTING

LEARNING OBJECTIVES

1. Identify and understand three key factors pushing and reinforcing attention to international accounting.
2. Grasp the significance of the unanswered questions identified in Chapters 1 through 11.
3. Recognize that international accounting is still an emerging field and therefore subject to emerging issues.
4. Become aware of the nature of emerging issues in the field of international accounting.
5. Be able to explain to others what each identified emerging issue is all about.

This chapter concludes a concise and nontechnical study tour of the subject matter of international accounting. The knowledge base created for the reader contains enough detail for general sensitivity to what the field is all about. Achievement of technical expertise in international accounting requires considerable further study and analysis. As a bridge toward potential further study, but also as a *synthesis* of the many open questions identified throughout the book, this final chapter offers an assessment of the key factors that seem to drive further emphasis on international accounting as well as a catalog of its emerging issues.

SELECTED FACTORS DRIVING INTERNATIONAL ACCOUNTING EMPHASIS

It is a truism that a computer keyboard manufacturer should consider itself part of the information technology industry rather than as a plastic materials converter. Similarly, it is critical to keep an eye on the factors pushing and reinforcing international accounting aside from the subject matter itself. For illustration purposes, a sketch of three such factors follows.

MNC Restructuring

In the preface of this book, we reported the growing shift away from self-sufficient multinational corporation (MNC) hierarchies to flexible, laterally organized *network structures*.[1] The Japanese *Keiretsu* system (i.e., mutually supportive intercompany relationships) is finding more and more advocates among MNC managers. Strategic interdependent alliances are emerging where head-on competition formerly prevailed. The emphasis is on networks—from research and development (R&D), products and markets development, and employee training to systems design, sourcing of financial capital, and total quality management utilization. Information availability plays a key role in the new MNC organizational patterns. This clearly includes accounting information.

Another restructuring factor relates to *technology*. New technology of many different types is simply outpacing people and organizational capacities. As this new technology is becoming available at an increasingly rapid rate, MNC structures must be changed to capture and use it to the best possible advantage. Cross-cultural recognition is especially significant for MNCs. Global competitiveness suffers if applicable, available, and cost-effective technology is ignored.

A third element is the factor of *speed*. Things are happening so incredibly fast today that the slow are unable "to stay in the game." Just consider how many calculations a super computer can perform in one millionth of a second! Time, in the traditional sense, has lost all meaning. Therefore, MNCs must restructure themselves to cut reaction time to the shortest possible intervals. Management decisions have to be made almost concurrently with the first appearance of new opportunities and simultaneously with receipt of new critical information. To accomplish super-quick reaction patterns requires highly effective information processing and organizational structures oriented to information technology rather than to products, geographic areas, or the traditional business functions like manufacturing, sales, or finance. It goes without saying that the MNC push for speed impacts the full spectrum of international accounting.

---

[1]Bruce McKern, "International Network Corporations in A Global Economy," *Carnegie Bosch Institute Working Paper,* April 1994, Carnegie Mellon University, 25 pp.

More Regionalism

The news is mixed on economic regionalism. Late in 1992 the exchange rate mechanism of the *European Union* (EU) broke down. Early in 1993 a major international newspaper reported Asian perceptions of a decline of Europe's economic power. Influential Asian leaders were quoted to hold "views of the European Community as a declining global player" and that such views "are expressed with increasing frequency in East Asia."[2] Even though the *North American Free Trade Agreement* (NAFTA) is fully ratified and in force, its critics abound. Many of NAFTA's lofty expectations are unfulfilled so far. Trade agreements in Eastern Europe have broken down, and there is little progress with economic integration in South America. Does this mean that regionalism has met its Waterloo?

Quite the contrary! It is a fact that some EU and NAFTA goals were over-ambitious and had to be slowed down. But these regional structures are not going to go away. While their economic fabric has unraveled somewhat, their political and regulatory grip has tightened. This is precisely the point. Bureaucracies of regionalism are gaining from Africa to the Pacific and from Scandinavia to Oceania. Regional agreements of cooperation are proliferating and with them accounting and financial reporting-related provisions. The accounting regulations of the EU are discussed in Chapter 3. The *U.S.–Canadian Free Trade Agreement* is spawning professional accounting licensing reciprocity between the two countries and has encouraged mutual recognition of each others' GAAP for financial reporting under the securities laws of the United States and the Province of Ontario. The *Association of South East Asian Nations* (ASEAN) operates an accounting standards committee, as do regional groups in East and West Africa and Scandinavia. Political and regulatory regionalization is a major driving force behind the growing emphasis on international accounting.

Globalization of All Markets

Until the end of World War II, economic systems structured themselves around corporations, other large organizations, and national governments. Product availability drove consumption, large organizations were key sources of employment and pay-level setters, and governments regulated everything from foreign exchange rates to export/import policy. This system did not always provide goods and services really wanted by consumers and did not often offer the best possible prices. Thus, from 1950 to 1990, consumer demand drove the world economy to unprecedented expansion. There was a literal buying explosion culminating in the *great worldwide shopping spree* of the 1980s.

---

[2]Michael Richardson, "East Asians See Europe's Power on the Decline," *International Herald Tribune* (Tokyo ed.), February 20–21, 1993, p. 1.

As the 1990s began, a new regime took over—globalization of all markets. In a perceptive op-ed piece, management guru Peter F. Drucker laid out where the more significant new global markets will be found.[3] These markets fall into the following four categories:

1. *A new market cluster around communication and information.* This involves telephone service in developing and former Soviet bloc countries. It also covers such items as school and office operations.

2. *The environmental market.* Here we have three separate components:

    a. The market for equipment to purify air and water.

    b. The agro-biology market for replacing chemical herbicides and pesticides with nonpolluting, mainly biological, products.

    c. The substitute energy market, which will seek to replace high-polluting energy sources with solar fuel cells and nonpolluting coalburning furnaces.

3. *The physical infrastructure market.* This market will be aimed at repairing and upgrading roads, railroads, bridges, harbors, and airports.

4. *The investment products markets.* People will need these to finance survival into old age.

It takes little imagination to translate the information needs of the new global markets into *drivers* for more emphasis on international accounting. Several of the emerging issues raised in the following section are directly related to the globalization of markets in general.

KEY EMERGING ISSUES

Throughout this book, many unresolved as well as critical emerging issues have been identified. Since the entire field of international accounting and financial reporting is still evolving, it is little wonder that quite a few issues are as yet unresolved or only partially resolved. The ten topics selected for comment below are examples only. As indicated in the earlier chapters, there are many other critical issues. The emphasis here is on emerging issues.

1. Supremacy of National GAAP

Creating well-defined national *generally accepted accounting principles* (GAAP) and making sure that full enforcement occurs throughout the national economy are the first important steps toward reducing financial accounting practice diversity. But how do we know whether any set of national GAAP is of high

---

[3]Peter F. Drucker, "Where the New Markets Are," *The Wall Street Journal,* April 9, 1992, p. A14.

quality (i.e., optimal) for the national environment being served? For the time being, the quality question is a judgment call. There is no theoretical/analytical model that tells when or if national GAAP are somehow "best." Setting financial accounting standards is basically a social policymaking process and therefore subject to political, social, and legal pressures just as much as to business and economic pressures. Is an accommodating response to all or most such pressures an indicator of quality achievement?

This issue is brought into full focus when one considers the general policy of the SEC in the United States to require non-U.S. registrants (i.e., participants in various U.S. financial capital markets) to present their financial information required by the SEC either outright in terms of U.S. GAAP or reconciled with or restated to U.S. GAAP (see Chapter 3 for a few defined exceptions to this general rule). The SEC is the guardian of the public interest regarding investors in U.S. financial capital markets. By requiring U.S. GAAP-based financial reports for these investors, there is the implication that U.S. GAAP are somehow the "best." Other countries find the SEC's position on this matter rather objectionable.

Nonetheless, several hundred companies incur the additional costs of complying with the SEC's reconciliation/restatement rule in order to gain access to the huge U.S. financial capital markets. An interesting case study on this topic is the German automobile manufacturer Daimler-Benz. Its case illustrates not only the efforts necessary for a major non-U.S. corporation to list its equity shares in the United States but also the rather significant difference between U.S. GAAP and German GAAP.[4]

2. Regionalization Marching On

European regionalization dates back centuries. When the idea was seriously rekindled in the 1950s, most said it could not be done. The initial reaction to NAFTA was similar. Today, the EU as well as the NAFTA thrusts seem irreversible. Aside from their own successes (still too incomplete, to be sure), the European and North American regionalizations have given impetus to several other regionalization proposals. On a more modest scale, there are already several regional setups like *ASEAN* (mentioned earlier). But a number of large-scale regional conglomerates appear in the making, which give the topic emerging issues status as far as accounting goes.

First, it seems useful to review those areas where real-term regional integration appears *unlikely* in the foreseeable future. This includes South America, the Middle East region, Eastern Europe, and the former Soviet Union, plus the Indochina subcontinent. Geopolitical and sociocultural forces and conditions militate against effective regionalization in the areas identified.

---

[4]Lee H. Radebaugh, Guenther Gebhardt, and Sidney J. Gray, "Foreign Stock Exchange Listings: A Case Study of Daimler-Benz," *Journal of International Financial Management and Accounting* 6, no. 2 (1995), pp. 158–92.

In contrast, the Asian Pacific area (from Oceania to Japan and from Malaysia to Guam), East Africa (Ethiopia to Malawi), and West Africa (20-plus countries from Senegal to Gabon and including Nigeria and Zaire) enjoy *good prospects* for some regional fusion. While, again, long-standing national, cultural, and language factors pose considerable obstacles, there are enough common interests within the regions identified to give full regionalization a chance. If further world separation into regions occurs, will (or should) there be corresponding regional accounting development? Will regional development take place concurrently with further national development (as demonstrated by current EU experience)? Are regional interests likely to gain dominance over international harmonization efforts (Chapter 3)? It is unclear what further regionalization has in store for the next phase of accounting and financial reporting development worldwide.[5]

3. Global Harmonization

The issue of global harmonization of accounting and financial reporting is posited in Chapter 3. Four possible policy directions exist:

1. Do nothing internationally and leave whatever harmonization efforts seem desirable to networking and adaptation among national accounting standard setting agencies.

2. Segment standard setting and reporting requirements between internationally active corporations and domestically focused companies. Through cooperative efforts between expert accounting professionals (the *International Accounting Standards Committee,* or IASC), securities markets regulators (the *International Organization of Securities Commissions,* or IOSCO), and regional political authorities (e.g., EU, NAFTA, and ASEAN), define terms of reference for "internationally active" and negotiate a set of GAAP for all corporations falling within such a definition regardless of country of incorporation or other legal corporate domicile.

3. Establish international accounting standards as globally useful benchmarks that can either be used directly on their own terms, adapted into specified regional or national GAAP, or adopted as a whole or in part as local national GAAP. This alternative is the approach currently in effect.

4. Establish international accounting standards as a comprehensive set of GAAP and use market and political pressures to achieve universal acceptance.

While the present approach to global harmonization appears to be working and, in fact, gaining additional momentum, there are still many critics who would

---

[5]Anonymous, "Heading South for the Winter (and the Spring and . . .)," *Financial Executive,* September/October 1995, p. 8 (News item on the Canada/Chile/Mexico/United States committee for synchronizing accounting standards).

prefer something else. Another open point is *synergy* between IASC and EU activities. Late in 1995 the EU Commission adopted a new policy regarding accounting harmonization. Under this policy, no new EU accounting directives would be issued, the implementation consultations from the EU *Accounting Advisory Forum* and the EU [Accounting] Contact Committee would continue, and serious efforts would be initiated to achieve full synchronization between the EU Directives and IASs. This move signals the dawn of a new era in global accounting harmonization. Its full consequences are unclear at the time of this writing.

4. Mixed Economy Model Evolution

Privatization and movement toward market economics are the high-impact slogans circulating throughout the countries of the mixed economy accounting model. The geographic area covered by this model is substantial (see Chapter 1). What happens here in accounting and financial reporting is bound to be consequential.

Traditional forces in Eastern Europe and the former Soviet Union are most comfortable with national *uniform charts of accounts* and very prescriptive practice rules. In a sense, this would be a conceptual continuation of the system they had when their economies were still centrally controlled. A Western example of national uniform accounting is found in France and most Francophile African nations.

Committed reformers advocate adoption of the *British-American model.* They think that full parallels with practices prevailing in the English-speaking countries will help with better access to world financial and credit sources, quicker linkages to major markets for consumer products and all types of technology, and easier appeal for business investments and transfers of expert-level human resources. There is also the judgment that British-American types of education and training are more readily available at reasonable costs.

Finally, the idealists want international standards to start with. They want to create an accounting profession along the lines of the *International Federation of Accountants* (IFAC) and initiate a GAAP system on the basis of IASC standards. This comes through clearly in all the *United Nations*-sponsored workshops and study groups dealing with accounting in the mixed economy situations. It is also evident from the training demands addressed to Western institutions.

What will the winds of change ultimately bring? No clear directions have emerged so far, and questions of GAAP quality (see earlier section in this chapter) are clearly a big issue. Should the British-American model win the "competition," its world influence would be materially strengthened.

5. Special Disclosure Trends

As referenced throughout this book, measurement and disclosure are the "congenital twins" of accounting and financial reporting. Have the evolution and growth of these two components of the discipline been exhausted/completed? By no means. We have characterized accounting as a response mechanism to environmental factors and conditions. *As environments change, so must accounting,* in order to keep relevant. Disclosure advances are one way toward continued relevancy.

Chapter 5 puts the disclosure topic into full focus. Most interesting is the growing practice of voluntary disclosure—which means more disclosure than is required by laws and regulations. Concerned parties welcome this trend. But are more data always better? When do we start to worry about *information overload?* The whys and hows of voluntary (add-on) disclosure amount to an emerging issue in international accounting.

General disclosure questions aside, there are further considerations involving special disclosures. Chapter 5 makes the point of European attention to *social responsibility disclosures* addressing topics like employee safety, health and welfare records, consumer interests, environmental protection (i.e., "green" accounting), job security, employee training, research expenditures, equal opportunities in the workplace, or facilities for the disabled. Are any of these special disclosures more important than others? Should the IASC begin to address specific "social" disclosures? Is it time to export some special disclosure practices from Europe to the rest of the world?

Two special disclosure items deserve separate mention. These are *value-added* notes or statements, and earnings or *business activities forecasts* prepared by management. Both have received attention internationally, and both have been subjected to limited experimentation in several countries. There are, of course, pros and cons when it comes to such targeted disclosures. The consequences involved have not been sufficiently researched. But from the evidence available so far, net benefits appear to accrue from value-added and forecast disclosures. Hence, your authors support them.

6. Pace of Accounting Technology

A number of measurement issues have been addressed chapter by chapter. In the United States, standards have been published on long future accruals. These involve employers' obligations for postretirement benefits other than pensions and postemployment benefits prior to retirement. Also in the United States, a mark-to-market requirement has been established for certain financial assets and liabilities of certain financial institutions. Most developing countries are struggling with formal recognition of the effects of changing price levels. The IASC's comparability project has, among changes for ten IASs, redefined the measurement of research and development and capitalization of goodwill.[6] Consolidation and lease accounting issues have high priority on the agenda of the *Business*

---

[6]Price Waterhouse in Europe, *Financial Reporting—An International Survey,* London, U.K.: Price Waterhouse in Europe, May 1995, 72 pp.

Accounting Deliberation Council in Japan. Accounting technology is constantly changing—it is in a constant state of flux. The real question though is the rate of change. Is accounting measurement technology keeping pace with all of the demands placed upon it?

Each accounting measurement change is costly. When a change becomes official, all companies and other preparers of financial reports must change their manuals, retrain their employees, and reprogram their computers (or change or update applicable software). Auditors must change audit programs and retrain all professional staff. Financial analysts must learn to assess the effects of the changed measurements, as must loan officers at financial institutions. Reference books have to be updated and accounting textbooks rewritten. Even the *Uniform CPA Examination* has to incorporate the changes made. Cost is therefore a crucial factor.

The pace at which accounting measurement technology changes is a key issue. Should the change be incremental and more or less continual, or substantial and limited to specified time intervals? Is there any point in coordinating change between countries? How does one determine whether any set of accounting measurement standards are as up-to-date as they ought to be? Questions of this type are likely to be asked with increased frequency.

7. Information Content of Financial Statements

Financial reports derive their relevance and usefulness from the amount of information content they have. Since financial statements (i.e., balance sheet, income statement, cash flow statement, and all related explanatory notes) are the nucleus of a financial report, the information content of financial statements is critical. Ways to analyze this information content are explored in Chapter 7. Financial ratio analysis is the most widely used means of this type of information evaluation.

Why is this an emerging issue? Because an impressive amount of research has determined that the information content of conventionally prepared financial statements is less than statement users expect. This is obviously a dilemma of major proportions. In 1994 the *American Institute of CPAs* published its *Improving Business Reporting—A Customer Focus: Meeting the Information Needs of Investors and Creditors.* Its various recommendations are presumed to enhance the information content of published financial statements.[7] In Europe, the *EU Commission* is continuously being challenged by the fact that *EU Directives* contain no requirements for cash flow or funds flow statements. The FASB has an ongoing priority project about desirable characteristics of consolidated financial statements. Form and content of financial statements receive attention on the working agendas of the IASC. These issues are all accentuated in international

---

[7]Anonymous, "The *CPA Journal* Symposium on Recommendations for Improving Business Reporting," *CPA Journal,* January 1995, pp. 18–26.

financial reporting when financial statements are translated in various ways, and even restated from one set of national GAAP to another. Clearly, change is in the air concerning information content of financial statements.

Going back to the earlier distinction between measurement and disclosure, one is tempted to attribute information content shortcomings to lack of disclosure. Chapter 5 pointed the way toward some innovative disclosure approaches likely to produce useful information for financial statement users. But that is not the full story. Maybe the entire financial accounting measurement model should be changed *from a historical cost to some current cost basis.* Maybe accruals of anticipated future events and transactions would be more relevant than present practice amortizations of past events and transactions. Maybe net income should be determined over periods shorter or longer than the presently customary 12 months. Thus, we can predict with some confidence that serious changes in the information content of financial statements are on their way in most GAAP jurisdictions. The open questions are what the nature of these changes will be and when they will arrive.

8. MNC Accounting Information Systems

The central issue faced by MNC accounting information systems developers was identified in Chapter 8. It was labeled *think globally and act locally.* This really means the simultaneous achievement of global synergy among many well-established, autonomously functioning multinational subsidiary companies and high levels of effectiveness at national levels. To quote from the Chapter 8 text:

> Today's international business environment is becoming increasingly complex and competitive. Transnational strategies, organizational structures, and attitudes that allow a company to think globally and act locally are necessary for survival. The *transnational* company of tomorrow must operate efficiently and economically through global-scale operations. It must be able to respond to both national and local differences, retaining local flexibility while achieving global integration.

Four component elements define the issue more specifically:

1. Transnational (as opposed to multinational or global—defined in Chapter 8) *organization structures* (networks) dictate transnational accounting information systems.
2. *Global synergy* does not automatically produce local efficiency and effectiveness.
3. With an increasingly complex and competitive business environment, accounting information systems must deliver decision-relevant information accurately and at *high transfer speeds.*
4. Today's *information technology* (IT) is costly and continuously changing. Using cost-effective IT and knowing when and how to change it have become key accounting systems design problems.

Aside from the operational systems design factors identified in the earlier chapter, there is the tactical issue of satisfying the foregoing four elements concurrently and as optimally as can be done. Here is where one meets the emerging issues challenge. Which of the four elements gets priority? Is higher transfer speed and low transfer accuracy better than the reverse? Is it a good policy to buy, and train employees for, the latest available technology even if that means frequent systems changes? Should global synergy get the nod over best possible local effectiveness? A new round of research, analysis, and field testing is needed before questions of this type can be answered with some confidence.

9. Currency Choice for Transnational Budgeting and Reporting

A key issue springing from the discussion in Chapter 10 is the currency choice for MNC internal budgeting and reporting. First of all, there is no corresponding domestic issue. At home, companies always use the national currency unit to denominate all of their management accounting procedures.

However, there is a choice in transnational management accounting. In Chapter 10 we take a strong stand in favor of *local currency budgeting and internal reporting:*

> Managers should be evaluated on meeting primary *goals* in local currency, such as annual profits and sales forecasts, meeting projected production levels, managing the effects of inflation, and managing employees. . . .
>
> Comparisons of the past, present, and future operations of a subsidiary are far more meaningful and valid if calculated in local currency. Comparing either the U.S.-dollar or local currency results of subsidiaries operating in different environments is useless. The environmental peculiarities of each operating environment need to be isolated and weighed in order to achieve a meaningful comparison.

So what happens in actual practice? There is no consensus.[8] Europeans report mostly preferences for local currency procedures; developing country managements often dictate use of a "hard" currency like the U.S. dollar; and most U.S. managers prefer their "own" U.S.-dollar measures over local currency measures. By now, their argument is familiar to us—namely, we invested U.S. dollars to start with, we have U.S. investors who expect U.S.-dollar dividends, we finance our operations abroad from a U.S.-dollar risk management perspective, we prepare our annual report in U.S.-dollar denominated amounts, and we report to the SEC in terms of U.S. dollars. We want all of our transnational managers "to keep their eyes" on the U.S. dollar, think in dollar terms, and *manage toward dollar results.* In Chapter 10 we pointed out that for U.S.-based MNCs:

---

[8]For further discussion and analysis, see Thomas G. Evans, Martin E. Taylor, and Oscar J. Holzmann, "Currency Considerations in Performance Evaluation" (Chapter 12), *International Accounting & Reporting* (2nd ed.), Cincinnati, OH: Southwestern, 1994, pp. 360–63.

Decision making by boards of directors and management headquarters is generally based on U.S.-dollar information. If one level of management bases decisions on U.S.-dollar information and another on local currency information, problems with goal congruency and optimization of resources may result.

This is the crux of the issue. Does it make sense to use both local currency and home currency budgeting and internal reporting in the same company at the same time and maybe even concurrently? Your authors have answered with a resounding yes. Practicing managements all over the world are not so sure. Multiple currency sensitivity is difficult, especially when dozens of different national currency units are involved in a company's transnational operations. So what is a bright MNC manager to do? The *best* he or she can do, given a company's management style and organization culture. But since the issue is unsettled, it is advisable to keep an open mind about it and expect changes.

10. Tax Aspects of MNC Transfer Pricing

Anyone with even cursory acquaintance with the 1992 U.S. presidential political campaign is aware of the controversy over the amount of income taxes paid by controlled foreign subsidiaries in host countries. Then-candidate Clinton claimed that tens of billions of federal corporate income tax dollars could be collected annually if the subsidiaries of non-U.S. corporations operating in the United States paid their "fair share." The issue, of course, is an acceptable definition of *fair share*.

Assume for the sake of illustration that Honda Motor Co., Ltd., of Japan fully owns a Canadian assembly plant company and a U.S. sales company. A given Honda automobile is market researched, designed, developed, and road tested in Japan. Fifty percent of the parts needed to produce this particular car are manufactured in Japan and shipped to Canada. In Canada, the rest of the needed parts are made and the car is fully assembled. It is then shipped to the United States, where it is sold to a local consumer. Assuming the eventual sale produced a profit, tax authorities in Japan, Canada, and the United States all want their *fair share* of taxes on the transaction. Since the tax laws differ substantially between the three countries involved, what might be "fair" in one country is most likely unfair in the next. Therefore, we have a highly emotional issue begging for a solution.

Transfer pricing is obviously the key. If the transfer price of the car involved is set so high in Canada that the U.S. sale just covers this price plus selling expenses, there is no taxable income in the United States and therefore zero tax collection. Thus, any taxes paid are paid in Canada and Japan. Is that fair? It clearly depends on whose perspective is taken as the point of departure.

To grapple with the inevitable confrontations this important issue involves, the U.S. Internal Revenue Service (IRS) has launched its *Advance Pricing Agreement* (APA)) program.[9] After comprehensive review of corporate procedures and

---

[9]Ken Kral, Jack Serota, and Carmen Johnson, "Complying with Global Transfer Pricing Rules," *Journal of Accountancy,* September 1995, pp. 28–29.

data (some of them highly confidential), the IRS and the taxpayer corporation agree *in advance* on a transfer pricing mechanism that both parties will honor. Matsushita Company in Japan is party to such an APA, as are a limited number of other MNCs. Maybe this approach represents the beginnings of a solution toward the onerous taxation aspects of MNC transfer pricing.

STUDY QUESTIONS

1. Do you agree with the view that the EU is becoming a "declining global player"? Why or why not?

2. Peter F. Drucker is of the opinion that full globalization of all markets is under way. What does this have to do with international accounting?

3. In the United States the SEC continues to require all non-U.S. registrants to reconcile their financial statements to U.S. GAAP. In contrast, the EU Commission is working on achieving synergy between its accounting requirements and those of the IASC. Which approach do you prefer. Why?

4. Quite a few observers feel that the *British-American accounting model* should be instituted in the mixed economies of Eastern Europe and the former Soviet Union. Write two paragraphs in support of this proposition.

5. Should MNC managements be required to publish their annual earnings and business activities forecasts? Who would be three winners and three losers if such a requirement were to be initiated?

6. Would you support the abandonment of *all* historical cost measurements in accounting worldwide? What do you see as the biggest problem if this were done?

7. In the *Honda* illustration at the end of the chapter, how would you divide a hypothetical $1,000 income tax payment between Japan, Canada, and the United States? Is fairness a component of your proposal?

ADDITIONAL READINGS

Brown, V. H. "Accounting Standards: Their Economic and Social Consequences." *Accounting Horizons* (September 1990), pp. 89–97.

Gernon, H., and R. S. O. Wallace. "International Accounting Research: A Review of Its Ecology, Contending Theories and Methodology." *Journal of Accounting Literature* 14 (1995), pp. 54–106.

Gyllenhammar, P. "The Global Economy: Who Will Lead Next?" *Journal of Accountancy* (January 1993), pp. 61–67.

Ijiri, Y. "Global Financial Reporting Using a Composite Currency: An Aggregation Theory Perspective." *The International Journal of Accounting* 30, no. 2 (1995), pp. 95–106.

Krugman, P. R. "A Global Economy Is Not the Wave of the Future." *Financial Executive* (March/April 1992), pp. 10–13.

Pennar, K. "Is the Nation-State Obsolete in a Global Economy?" *Business Week* (July 17, 1995), pp. 80–81.

Wallace, R. S. O., and H. Gernon. "Frameworks for International Comparative Financial Accounting." *Journal of Accounting Literature* 10 (1991), pp. 209–63.

I N D E X

A

Abdallah, W. M., 165n, 170n
Abernethy, M. A., 149n
Accounting; *see also* Multinational corporations (MNCs)
auditing standards for; *see* Accounting and auditing standards
communication problems in; *see* Planning and control systems
creating national GAAP, 197–198
currency translation; *see* Foreign currency translation
disclosure practices in; *see* Disclosure
diversity in financial; *see* Accounting, diversity in
financial reporting in; *see* Transnational financial reporting
financial statements in; *see* Financial statements
globalization and, 196–197, 199–200
introduction to emerging issues in, 194
performance evaluation and; *see* Performance evaluation
regionalism and, 196, 1–199
systems in; *see* Information systems; Planning and control systems
taxation and; *see* Taxation
technology and, 201–202
transfer pricing and; *see* Transfer pricing
variables shaping financial; *see* Accounting, development of
Accounting, development of
clusters in; *see* Accounting model(s)
conclusions concerning, 16
culture and, 10–11
factors limiting, 10
global challenges for, 3–11
inflation and, 9–10
introduction to, 1–3
legal system in, 8–9
political and economic ties in, 7–8
relationship of business and capital in, 3, 6–7

Accounting—*Continued*
review of, 16–19
Accounting, diversity in
conclusions concerning, 33
consequences of worldwide, 31–33
examples of, 24–26
harmonization and, 49, 199–200
and income smoothing, 26–31
introduction to concepts in, 20–21, 37–38
reducing, 21–22
review of, 33–36
why, exists, 23
Accounting Advisory Forum, 48, 110, 200
Accounting and auditing standards; *see also* Financial statements
harmonization scenarios for, 49
international influence on, 41–46
introduction to, 38–39
pros and cons of, 40–41
regional influences on, 46–49
review of, 50–54
U.S. influence on, 39–40
Accounting model(s); *see also* Accounting, development of
British/American, 11, 14
in Communist countries, 15–16
continental, 14
international standards, 15
mixed economy, 14–15, 200
South American, 14
Accounting Standards Committee, 82
Accounting Standards Harmonization, 46
Accounting values, 118–121
Advance pricing agreement (APA), 186, 205, 206
African Accounting Council, 48
Ahadiat, N., 99n
American Institute of Certified Public Accountants (AICPA), 39, 40, 202
Apple Computer, Inc., 186
Arpan, J. S., 183n
Arthur Andersen & Co., 36n
Asea Brown Boveri, 138
ASEAN Federation of Accountants, 48

NOTES:

NOTES:

NOTES:

NOTES:

NOTES: